T0387465

Singing the Himalayan Crossroads

Singing the Himalayan Crossroads

Traditional Songs of Ladakh

NOÉ DINNERSTEIN

Cover credit: Basgo Village Singers Sonam Wandus Zasnapa and Stanzin Namgyal Zopa. (Photo: Noé Dinnerstein)

Published by State University of New York Press, Albany

EU GPSR Authorised Representative:
Logos Europe, 9 rue Nicolas Poussin, 17000, La Rochelle, France
contact@logoseurope.eu

For information, contact State University of New York Press, Albany, NY
www.sunypress.edu

Library of Congress Cataloging-in-Publication Data

Name: Dinnerstein, Noé, author.
Title: Singing the Himalayan crossroads : traditional songs of Ladakh / Noé Dinnerstein.
Description: Albany : State University of New York Press, [2025]. | Includes bibliographical references and index.
Identifiers: LCCN 2024044575 | ISBN 9798855802566 (hardcover : alk. paper) | ISBN 9798855802573 (ebook)
Subjects: LCSH: Folk songs, Ladakhi—History and criticism. | Songs, Ladakhi—History and criticism. | Music—India—Ladākh—History and criticism. | Music—India—Ladākh—Analysis, appreciation. | Music—Social aspects—India—Ladākh. | Music—Religious aspects—India—Ladākh. | Music—Religious aspects—Buddhism. | Gesar.
Classification: LCC ML3748.7.L26 D55 2025 | DDC 780.954/67—dc23/eng/20240920
LC record available at https://lccn.loc.gov/2024044575

Contents

Illustrations

Acknowledgments

ཐ་མོ་གུརུབྷྱཿ ཐ་མོ་བུདྡྷཡ། ཐ་མོ་དྷརྨཡ། ཐ་མོ་སངྒྷཡ།

Nāmo gurubhyah. Nāmo buddhaya. Nāmo dharmaya. Nāmo sanghaya.

(I bow to the gurus. I bow to the Buddha. I bow to the Dharma. I bow to the Sangha.)

Without the guidance of my teachers, spiritual and secular, none of this would have happened. To the late Lama Lozang Jamspal, PhD, I owe an inexpressible debt for first bringing me to Ladakh and setting me to work, and for his continued instruction and support over thirty years. I am grateful to Prof. Stephen Blum and Prof. Peter Manuel who guided me when this research was in its original form for my PhD dissertation. It has evolved significantly since then based on their advice.

The support of the many Ladakhi artists, scholars, friends, and acquaintances was essential to this project, especially Tsering Anchuk Ralam, Ali Mahmud, Tsering Chorol, Yangchan Dolma, Sonam Tsering Lagachirpon, Kunzes Dolma, Dorjay Stakmo, and Angdu Khigu. Throughout the years of my research, the warm friendship of Dawa Tsering, former councilor (Ladakh Autonomous Hill Development Council), and his family has been a source of support and joy.

I would like to thank my learned colleagues Ali Mahmud and Tsering Angchuk Ralam (Figure A.1) for sitting down with me in an epic recording session on July 27, 2009, going through the book *Ladvags gyi yul glu* (Folksongs of Ladakh) and identifying as many melodies as they could. I also am grateful to Tsering Chorol Patsi for a similar session on July 20, 2012.

Last, but not least, without the encouragement of friends and family, most notably my life partner and editor, Sara Sogut, this task would have been much harder.

Figure A.1. Tsering Angchuk Ralam, Ali Mahmud, and the author, at AIR Studio, 2009. Author's photo.

Recording Acknowledgments

This volume is accompanied by a series of recordings, some full performances, some just the first verses of songs. The following are the full recordings. To access the recordings for the book, readers must email arce@aiis.org.in.

Track 02. *"skyes pa'i pha yul,"* performed in 2011 by musicians from Basgo Village.

- Tsewang Paldan Wanda Yokmap—surna
- Tsering Sonam Basgo Lagachirpon—surna
- Samstan Tashi Tia Yondakpa-daman
- Tashi Gyalpo Ngey Sralukpa-daman
- Stanzin Namgyal Basgo Zopa-vocal
- Sonam Wangdus, Basgo Zasnapa-vocal

This recording is used with the kind permission of Mr. Bernard Kleikamp of PAN Records.

The following full recordings were recorded in December 2016, produced specifically for this book by Tsering Sonam Lagachirpon.

Track 01. *Sengge zhengs pai sku mkhar*

- Padma Dorje—vocal
- Ali Mohd—surna
- Skarma and Norbu—daman

Track 03. *nyi lza dbango mo*

- Padma Dolkar—vocal
- Ali Mohd—surna
- Skarma and Norbu—daman

Track 06. *rten 'brel lnga pa*

- Padma Dorje—vocal
- Ali Mohd—surna
- Skarma and Norbu—daman

Track 07. *bsod rnams mchog skyit*

- Sonam Wangdus—vocal
- Ali Mohd—surna
- Skarma and Norbu—daman

Track 08. *bstod pa zhig 'bul*

- Sonam Wangdus—vocal
- Ali Mohd—surna
- Skarma and Norbu—daman

Track 09. *ti se'i shel dkar mcod rten*

- Padma Dorje—vocal
- Ali Mohd—surna
- Skarma and Norbu—daman

Track 10. *rgyab ri 'brag mar tse mo*

- Padma Dolkar—vocal
- Ali Mohd—surna
- Skarma and Norbu—daman

Track 11. *lha sa'i skor lam phra mo*

- Padma Dolkar—vocal
- Ali Mohd—surna
- Skarma and Norbu—daman

Track 12. *a ma'i dkar 'chol du*

- Sonam Wangdus—vocal
- Ali Mohd—surna
- Skarma and Norbu—daman

Track 13. *dri ba dri lan*

- Sonam Wangdus and Padma Dorjay—vocals
- Ali Mohd—surna
- Skarma and Norbu—daman

Track 20. *sgra snyan bkra shis dbang rgyal*

- Tsering Angchuk Yakmik—vocal
- Tsering Angchuk and Tsering Sonam—damnyan/khopong
- Achey Lhadol—daf
- Tsering Angchuk—chilchil

Track 21. *rta pho zing zing khrol khrol*

- Tsering Chorol Erad—vocal
- Tsering Angchuk and Tsering Sonam—damnyan/khopong
- Achey Lhadol-daf
- Tsering Angchuk—chilchil

Track 22. *chu zang shar gi phyogs*

- Tsering Angchuk yakmik and Tsering Chorol Erad—vocals
- Tsering Angchuk and Tsering Sonam—damnyan/khopong
- Achey Lhadol—daf
- Tsering Angchuk—chilchil

Track 26. *gat pa ser gyi bya skyibs*

- Padma Dorje—vocal
- Ali Mohd—surna
- Skarma and Norbu—daman

Track 37. *rgyal lung rgyal mo*

- Padma Dolkar—vocal
- Ali Mohd—surna
- Skarma and Norbu—daman

The following are used with permission of the artists:

Track 14. *Kalam Rasul*—Tsering Sonam Lagachirpon—vocal
Track 17. *bumay ming la Fatima*—Namgyal Angmo—vocal
Track 18. *Tan tani Tanbrok*—Haji Master Hussein Silmo—vocal
Track 19. *Marsiya Ali Asgar*—Mohammed Sasirul Mehdi Shabani—vocal
Track 27. *rten 'brel gsum pa*—Tsering Chorol Patsi—vocal and daf

The following tracks have been licensed by permission of the Ladakh Academy of Art, Culture and Languages, Leh, with special thanks to the director Tsewang Paljor Olthang. The moral support and encouragement of him and other Ladakhi scholars has been invaluable.

Track 04. *sku mkhar tsho*
Track 05. *lon chen bi ta dzo gi*
Track 15. *Ali Khan*

Track 16. *Ostad Man Mir*
Track 23. *ache nyima zangmo*
Track 24. *tsig lu*
Track 25. *kaba rinpoche*
Track 28. *shel ldan yu tsho*
Track 29. *tendel nga pa-B*
Track 30. *tendel dun pa*
Track 31. *ka ltar zhabs zung*
Track 32. *rgyab ri shel dkar chod rten*
Track 33. *spyi bo gtsug tor sgom pai bla ma*
Track 34. *sngar gyi ri bo*
Track 36. *chang padmai yul*
Track 37. *mkha spyod dag pai shing khams*

Introduction

This is an ethnography and anthology of recordings and my translations of the lyrics, placing the traditional song repertoires of the former Himalayan kingdom of Ladakh in their historical and cultural contexts, while aiming to be very light-handed in applying any analytical lenses. My motivation for this effort was to learn to sing and play Ladakhi traditional songs in the larger context of learning the language and religious philosophy of the Buddhists of the region. This places me in the ranks of other ethnomusicologists who have studied the musics of societies they were not born into but came to love through close association (cf. Baily 2001; Witzleben 1997, 2010).

I was raised bicultural (Ashkenazic Jewish and Tejano [Texas Mexican] and bilingual [Spanish and English]). Throughout my childhood I lived the experience of cultural diversity fostered by my family, which extended to music. My parents, brothers, and I all sang popular musics and folksongs in English, Spanish, and with a bit of Yiddish as well. As preteens my middle brother and I both later learned guitar and played euphonium in school bands. Being a red-diaper baby (a baby boomer child of the old left), topical folksongs such as the Spanish songs of the Lincoln Brigade were a large part of my repertoire, blending the bilingual and bimusical. From there it was an easy step to the various musics of South Asia.

I first encountered Indian music in the late 1950s, and at the age of fourteen I began the study of Hindustani classical sitar and *khayal singing*. Thus, my passion for Asian studies has long been a part of my life. My first sitar teacher, Dr. Wasantha Wana Singh, was Buddhist and taught me about the spiritual and linguistic side of South Asian culture. Ultimately, this led to my study of Tibetan Buddhism and my becoming a student of the Ladakhi Buddhist lama Lozang Jamspal, a former instructor at Columbia University. As a student of Jamspal, I studied Tibetan and Sanskrit, along with Buddhist philosophy, ritual, and meditation, subsequently becoming a member of the Tibetan Classics Translators Guild of New York.

My polyglot, polycultural, polymusical approach to the world has been extensively discussed by ethnographers and ethnomusicologists. J. Lawrence Witzleben quoting Bruno Nettl noted that "so-called 'informants" are in fact the 'principal teachers of many ethnomusicologists." (Witzleben 1997, 236). This is particularly true for myself, as I have been indoctrinated into the traditional Indo-Tibetan guru-shishya pedagogical model in music, language, and philosophy. I place myself as a supplicant, seeking knowledge, connection, and acceptance.

I first traveled to Ladakh with Lama Jamspal in 1999, overland from New Delhi to Dharamsala (the headquarters of His Holiness, the Dalai Lama), and from there passing over Taglang-la, the second highest motorable pass in the world at 17,500 feet (oh, did I suffer from altitude sickness!). I then was drafted into teaching English to the young boy-monks at Likir Monastery, where Jamspal himself was a novice before he traveled to Tibet in 1950. When asked by a nephew of his whether I needed special qualifications to teach, Jamspal said of me, "*bongbu stonpa rangtak-i sgo la*" ([He is] an unladen donkey at the water mill door, i.e., always ready for a load). This became a standing joke between us.

On visits to the regional capital, Leh, I initially heard *zhung lu* (traditional songs) on All India Radio (AIR). I was fascinated by the asymmetrical rhythms and powerful instrumental timbres. I immediately bought audio cassettes by some of the big-name performers: Morup Namgyal, Tseschu Lhamo, Tsering Stanzin, Ali Mahmud, Tsering Angchuk Kidar, and Tsering Angchuk Ralam.

As a student of Lama Jamspal, and having spent time in rural Ladakhi settings, I became aware of the complex webs of interaction and causality that are represented in Tibetan/Ladakhi Buddhism—an ontological model that has resonance in the symbolic anthropology of Geertz and Turner. The Geertzian concept of "webs of significance" (Geertz 1973) is mirrored in the worldview of traditional village society. There, natural and numinous beings are linked in a matrix reflecting the syncretic union of native Tibetan/Ladakhi religion and traditional Vajrayana teachings, described in detail by anthropologist Martin Mills (2003).

Lama Jamspal, noting my interest in the song repertoire, introduced me to a historic collection of song texts, *Ladvags gyi yul glu* (Ladakhi Folk Songs, henceforth referred to as LYL) and set me the task of translating. At the same time, being a performer first, I was eager to learn to sing and play this traditional song repertoire. Nevertheless, I feel it is my duty as a translator to follow the Latin meaning of translate (i.e., "to bring over, to carry over"), bringing the totality of the songs to the English-speaking world outside of Ladakh.

The Song Repertoire

Originating in the diverse sectors of Ladakhi society—nomadic, agrarian, and urban—specific genres have traditionally been performed on different occasions by distinct classes of people. Some genres are performed unaccompanied, while others are performed with instrumental accompaniment. Genres like the *zhabro* dance from the nomads of the Changthang plateau adjoining Tibet are accompanied by the Tibetan-style three-course lute called *damnyan* or *khopong*; less frequently by the four-string fiddle called *piwang*, along with the transverse wooden flute known as *lingbu*. In the past, these instruments were probably more widespread in the agrarian and urban populations before being superseded by the prestige ensemble of *surna* (double reed shawm) and *daman* (small kettledrums like the Indian *nakara*) that came to Ladakh from Western Asia via Baltistan in the sixteenth century.

Much of the repertoire shared in this volume came out of the old royal court in Leh and was notably performed during festivals like *Losar* (lunar new year) where the singing and instrumental renditions of the songs accompanied circle and line dance. Low-caste groups like the Mon (musicians/subsistence farmers/carpenters), the traditional exponents of *surna and daman*, and Beda (itinerant drummers and singers) partake of the accompanying liminality inherent in the contradictions of prestige function versus social stigma.

This narrative examines these repertoires in their sociohistorical contexts. This is followed by a discussion of current Ladakhi discourses on songs and cultural identity and efforts being made regarding preservation, revival, and revitalization of the repertoires. Finally, I analyze songs from the aspects of melody, rhythm, form, and text. Focusing primarily on the Buddhist population, I look at several genres including:

Tendel lu (*rten 'brel glu*)—songs of auspicious signs

Zhung lu (*gzhung glu*)—congregational songs from the old royal court in Leh

Bagston lu (*bag ston glu*)—marriage songs

Chang lu (*chang glu*)—beer songs

Zhabro (*zhabs bro*)—dance songs from the nomads of the Changthang plateau

From the Muslim population I mainly look at the *ghazal* repertoire that originates primarily from the Shia community that emigrated from Baltistan five hundred years ago. This is a broad category that consists of romantic songs, narrative ballads, and songs praising local heroes. Some reflect the role that Sunni Muslim traders played in trans-Himalayan caravans and reflect a cosmopolitan relationship with South, Central, and East Asia. A few samples of Shia devotional genres will round out the discussion.

Several questions arise. How have Buddhism and pre-Buddhist religion informed the texts and performance contexts of traditional songs? With a mixed Buddhist and Muslim population, what are the relationships between the two communities in the formation of Ladakhi culture, especially music? What are the contributions of the Muslim populations to the music culture? How has Ladakh's place as a crossroads culture manifested in music hybridity? As the region becomes more integrated into modern India, how are Ladakhis from the various communities involved with expressions of musical culture, both as producers and consumers? Through socioeconomic and sociopolitical upheaval and changes since the mid-1800s, how have the circumstances surrounding music evolved?

As has been discussed in writings since the late nineteenth century, the nonliturgical music of Ladakh differs markedly from that of Tibet in many aspects. Tibetan genres such as *zhabro, ache Lhamo, nangma/toeshey,* and *dung len,* etc., showed more of a predilection for regular, symmetrical rhythms, and a preference for *damnyan, piwang*, and *lingbu* as either solo or instrumental accompaniment and where percussion is not as important. This contrasts with the prestige *surna/daman* ensemble or the significance of the *daf* (frame drum) in Ladakhi music. There is some overlap of genres, such as marriage songs and drinking songs, but again, music style and textual content differ considerably, as seen in Tibetan folksong collections such as *Lho kha'i dmangs gzhas phyogs btus* (Collection of Folk Songs of the South) (Örgyen Dorje et al. 1997).

The crossroads hybridity of Ladakhi music is apparent in terms of rhythm, melodic structures, favored instruments, etc. Furthermore, the focus of the textual content differs in terms of focusing more on natural, supernatural, and social hierarchy and militarism. The latter reflects Ladakh's position as a geopolitical buffer state. These various aspects will be examined in subsequent chapters.

Linguistic Evolution and Identity

The Ladakhi and Balti languages are both forms of Archaic Western Tibetan, with Balti being the more archaic of the two (Zeisler 2005). Both languages are significantly different from Modern Tibetan, with which there is little mutual intelligibility. Nevertheless, all groups recognize a common cultural heritage.[1] By most linguistic standards, they would be regarded as separate languages. Noticeable differences between Modern Tibetan and Ladakhi, for instance, may be found among verb forms and usages. Written Tibetan is said to have been formalized in the eighth century, but while spellings have remained unchanged, the spoken language has continued to evolve. The result is that old Buddhist and pre-Buddhist scriptures are written using the spelling and grammar of what is called Classical Tibetan or Classical Literary Tibetan. Ladakhi may be viewed as being phonetically closer to Classical Tibetan, with more of the letters being pronounced, and Balti even more so. For example, the word for "rice" can be transliterated *'bras*, in which the apostrophe represents a neutral vowel. It has different pronunciations among the various Tibetic languages:

- Modern Central Tibetan: de, dre

- Ladakhi: dras, das

- Balti: abras

Almost all literature pertaining to Ladakhi history is monastic in origin, and this has given a Tibetan and Buddhist orientation to the Ladakhi narrative. Most educated Ladakhis with whom I am acquainted view the

Ladakhi language as most closely reflecting the original pronunciation of classical Tibetan. Indeed, as a student of Tibetan Buddhism, I am accustomed to chanting the Classical Tibetan texts with a Ladakhi pronunciation. Lama Jamspal maintained as one of his goals the preservation of the "Classical Tibetan language."

Current linguistic research, however, indicates that archaic dialects such as Ladakhi and Amdo Tibetan are not direct descendants of Classical Tibetan but are instead sprouts of its progenitor that diverged prior to the emergence of Classical Tibetan as a written language. This would indicate that Tibetan settlement in the West predates the founding of the kingdom of Ladakh by King Nyima Gon in the mid-tenth century, and that Tibetic-speaking pastoralists must have arrived some centuries earlier (Zeisler 2005).

From a linguistic point of view, it may be said that Ladakhi pronunciation of the liturgical language is close to Classical Tibetan, but it is not, strictly speaking, an exact replica. The liturgical and high-culture vocabulary is informed by Tibetan monastic usage that was brought in later, although this distinction is somewhat artificial given that the entire region is part of a larger religious and cultural continuum independent of linguistic and political borders. From a sociolinguistic point of view, the monastically informed language is an acrolect, as opposed to the village-level spoken basolect.

Until the 1970s, Ladakhi was not commonly written, but was instead a spoken vernacular. Prior to that time an educated Buddhist Ladakhi would have been triglossic, speaking Ladakhi, reading scripture in Classical Tibetan, and writing in an artificial mixture of modern Central Tibetan and Ladakhi known as Bhodi or Bhoti.

Since the 1970s the efforts of scholars, social activists, and the mass media have successfully established a distinct identity for Ladakhi. Yet given its status as a minority tongue, Ladakhi has been classified as a "vulnerable" language in modern India (UNESCO 2003). Not only is business with non-Ladakhis conducted in Hindi or in English, but the same mass media that have strengthened the Ladakhi language in the modern world have also bombarded Ladakhis with content in Hindi and English. It is a balancing act whose outcome is hard to predict.

On the Pronunciation of Ladakhi

Seeing no reason to reinvent the wheel, I have adapted notes from Trewin 1995 that I lay out in Appendix A. Following usual Tibetological practice,

Ladakh words are transliterated according to standard Tibetan spellings, when that spelling is commonly used in Ladakhi. Otherwise, simpler, phonetic Ladakhi spellings are used. Some words are that in common English usage will be written using that spelling (e.g., lama instead of "*bla ma*'). Ladakhi proper names will be represented in their phonetic form (e.g., Leh instead of "*gle*"). Some Tibetan/Ladakhi words have commonly known Sanskrit synonyms that are used in English. These are used without diacritical marks (e.g., karma and mandala, as opposed to *las* and *dkyil 'khor*).

Prior Research

To date there has not been a comprehensive study of Ladakhi vernacular music. There have been some studies of Tibetan Buddhist liturgical ritual music (*rolmo*) in Ladakh (e.g., Helffer 1978, Tsukamoto 1983), but those are part of a common practice across the Tibetan cultural continuum and have no relationship with the song repertoires that are the subject of this study. In recent decades several collections of folksongs have been published in Ladakh and Tibet of varying scope and emphasis: some focusing on the poetry of the song texts, some of songs with musical notation (cf. Rabgias 1970, Orgyen Dorje et al. 1997). Since the nineteenth century some Western ethnomusicologists or ethnographers have examined these folk musics, but again not in comprehensive studies.

The following is an outline of the literature pertaining to Ladakhi vernacular music. It should be noted that there is considerable overlap with Tibetan music, especially in the realm of liturgical music, as well as in pre-Buddhist genres like the Gesar epic. As has been common in many studies of traditional musics in South and Central Asia, much emphasis has been placed on the literary content of songs (e.g., Tucci 1966, Rabgias 1970).

Early Writings

Travel in Tibet was difficult in the late nineteenth century, as the Tibetan authorities were hostile to outsiders. The independent kingdom of Ladakh had been conquered by the Dogra rulers of Jammu in 1842, subsequently becoming a British client and thus more accessible. In both Tibet and Ladakh the terrain, altitude, and weather pose obstacles even to this day—the Leh to Srinagar highway is closed for almost half the year due to snow and landslides that accompany the spring thaw. During the mid-nineteenth and early twentieth centuries several Indian, British, and European missionaries, explorers, and ethnographers traveled in Tibet and Ladakh producing extensive works of ethnography, linguistics, and lexicography. Most give, at best, peripheral attention to folk music, except to mention it from a literary point of view.

The work of Sarat Chandra Das (1849–1917), the Indian linguist, lexicographer, ethnographer, spy, and explorer, is of monumental importance to Tibetologists even today. Traveling incognito in Tibet, he gathered geographic and ethnographic data to aid the British government in its struggles against Russian expansion in the region. His lasting achievement was his monumental Tibetan-English dictionary published in 1902, including all dialects, among them Ladakhi. He published several ethnographic studies, including a translation of one Tibetan folksong.

One of the more prodigious scholars of the era was A. H. Francke (1870–1930), a German Moravian missionary and ethnographer working in Ladakh. He published numerous books and articles on Ladakhi history and culture. These include some material on music, including ethnographies of music and musicians, looking not only at the majority *Bhoti* (Tibetan-speaking) population but at minorities like the Indo-Iranian Dards. Most of these writings contain song texts only, but according to Crossley-Holland, Francke did publish twenty-two transcriptions, twenty-one of which were included in Lavignac's 1922 *Encyclopèdie de la Musique* (Crossley-Holland 1967, 173).

Mid-Twentieth-Century Ethnographers and Musicologists

Ter Ellingson did extensive work in the Tibetan diaspora in Kathmandu and the United States starting in the mid-1970s, although his focus was primarily liturgical, looking at past and current practice in Tibetan Buddhist music (*rol mo*). A couple of his works bear on the study of Tibetan folk music. First is his study of shamanic practices as relating to Tibetan music (Ellingson 1974); second is a study of chant and melodic categories that lays out a melodic taxonomy—again, primarily in Buddhist chant—but gives some terminology that is potentially useful in research and analysis of folk music as well (Ellingson 1979).

Ladakh, occupying as it does a sensitive area between India, Pakistan, and Chinese Tibet, was off limits to tourists following the Indo-Chinese conflict in the early 1960s. Access was not opened again until 1974. Soon after, two researchers produced recordings from the area. First was Mireille Helffer's *Ladakh:Musique de monastère et de village* (Le Chant du Monde LDX 74662), recorded in 1975, and released in 1978. Second was David Lewiston's 1977 Nonesuch Explorer label recording, *Ladakh: Songs and Dances from the Highlands of Western Tibet* (Nonesuch H-72075). The notes for the Lewiston album were produced with the noted scholar Tashi Rabgias, who not only helped with the liner notes but also composed several of the neotraditional songs on the album.

Late Twentieth- and Early Twenty-First-Century Writings

Since the mid-1980s, there has been burgeoning interest in Tibetan and Ladakhi music, both vernacular and liturgical. The most notable scholarship on Ladakhi music to date has been done by British ethnomusicologist Arthur Mark Trewin. These works include his 1987 survey with Susan M. Stephens, *The Music Culture of Ladakh: Report of the City University Ladakh Expedition 1986*, his 1995 PhD dissertation on the ceremonial/processional music known as *lha nga* (drum of the gods), and articles on Ladakhi and Tibetan popular music.

A 2005 article in *The Tibet Journal* by Italian music scholar Marta Salvatori focused on the Ladakh lute known as *khopong* and the Changthang song-and-dance genre known as *zhabro*. She discusses the instruments and their similarity to others in the Tibetan cultural sphere, as well as briefly discussing playing techniques and musical characteristics of *zhabro*.

Collection and Preservation Efforts in Ladakh

The texts of *Ladvags gyi yul glu* were compiled by scholar, historian, and social activist Tashi Rabgias (1927–2020) during the 1960s and published by the Jammu and Kashmir Academy of Art, Culture and Languages in 1970. The later volumes have been compiled and edited by various scholars, including Ngawang Tsering Shakspo and the Venerable Tsering

Choesphel Hornak. Unfortunately (from a musical point of view), these collections only contain song texts, which are portrayed as presenting the literature of Ladakh. Actual music preservation recording had been going on elsewhere, through All India Radio (AIR), Doordarshan TV (DDTV), various NGOs, as well as a mixture of commercial recordings of traditional and popular musics published since the 1990s and early 2000s.

Most recently, in 2014 the Ladakh Cultural Academy, working with a committee of scholars and artists has issued a three-volume set entitled *A Collection of Ladakhi Folk Songs*. This is truly a modern publication in that most of the song texts are accompanied by CD recordings of the first verses of the songs. This is intended to allow readers to learn how to sing the songs, thus aiming to engage in more active preservation of the repertoire. As of this writing (2024), they have issued two revisions to the collections, adding several hundred songs and recordings to the collection. The most recent edition has replaced the CDs with QR codes for online downloads.

Format of this Volume

To bring this repertoire to life, I have interwoven the narrative with a series of recordings. Some of these are full performances specifically commissioned for this book, ably arranged by my friend and colleague Tsering Sonam Lagachirpon, while some of these are from my fieldwork in Ladakh. A significant number are recordings of the first verses of songs from the abovementioned Academy collection. I have the kind permission of Mr. Tsewang Paljor Olthang, director of the Academy to use these as part of our collective effort to preserve the cultural heritage of Ladakh and share it with the rest of the world. To give a fully integrated experience with the fullest appreciation of the word-music relationships, I usually include the Wylie transliteration, and translation for added visual connection with the sonic element.

Dramatis Personae

Following in the footsteps of Richard K. Wolf (Wolf 2006, 35–37), I would like to introduce the main sources on this subject I have dealt with during my research.

MONKS, SCHOLARS, AND ACADEMICS

- The late Geshe Lozang Jamspal, PhD—Ladakhi Buddhist lama, Tibetan translator, former instructor at Columbia University.

- The monks of Likir Monastery, where I taught the young student monks English for three summers in the monastery school.

- Gen (professor) Tashi Rabgias (1927–2020)—scholar, writer, poet, singer, songwriter.

- Venerable Tsering Chosphel Hornak—Buddhist monk, scholar, secretary of Likir Monastery, and former editor at the Leh Ladakh branch of the Jammu and Kashmir Academy for Art, Culture and Language.

- Tsewang Paljor Olthang—current director of the Ladakh Academy for Art, Culture and Language.

- Ngawang Tsering Shakspo—scholar, and singer, former head of the Ladakh Academy for Art, Culture and Language.

- Rebecca Norman—volunteer coordinator for the Students' Educational and Cultural Movement of Ladakh (SECMOL), linguist, lexicographer, educator.

- Geshe Tsewang Dorje—Buddhist monk and scholar, director of the Ngaris Institute for Buddhist Dialectics in Saboo Village.

NOTABLE RECORDING ARTISTS

- Dorje Stakmo—well-known singer, popular songwriter, actor, playwright, and music and film producer.

- Morup Namgyal—the first famous singer/songwriter in Ladakh, recipient of the Padma Shree award, former program head of All India Radio (AIR), Leh, playwright, actor, and social activist.

- Tsering Stanzin Nyermapa of Skurbuchan village who has performed extensively on the radio and has participated in a number of commercial cassette recordings in the 1980s and 1990s.

- Stanzin Dadul, his student, who performs on AIR, Doordarshan, as well as performing in various public and private venues.

- Kunzes Dolma, singer, daughter of the late, great singer Tseschu Lhamo.

ALL INDIA RADIO (AIR) STAFF

- The late Tsewang Rigzin—former program director of AIR.

- Tsering Angchuk Ralam—music director, producer, composer, flutist, harmonium player.

- Ali Mahmud of Spituk village—singer, daman, and surna player.

- Yangchan Drolma Kidar—singer, daman and daf player.

- Tsering Chorol Patsi—singer, player of harmonium, damnyan/khopong, and daman, daughter of Morup Namgyal.

MUSICIANS AND CULTURAL ACTIVISTS

- Tsering Sonam Lagachirpon—Basgo Village, pharmacist, and musician, who is actively involved in song preservation, instrumental education, and performance.

- Samstan Tashi Yondakpa—musician from Tia village.

- Tashi Gyalpo Sralukpa—musician from Ngey village.

- Stanzin Namgyal Zopa—musician from Basgo village.

- Sonam Wangdus, Zasnapa—musician from Basgo village.

- Tsewang Paldan Yokmapa—musician from Wanda village.

- Angdu Khigu—IT support technician for Ladakh Health Dept, instrumentalist, teacher, and music revitalization activist.

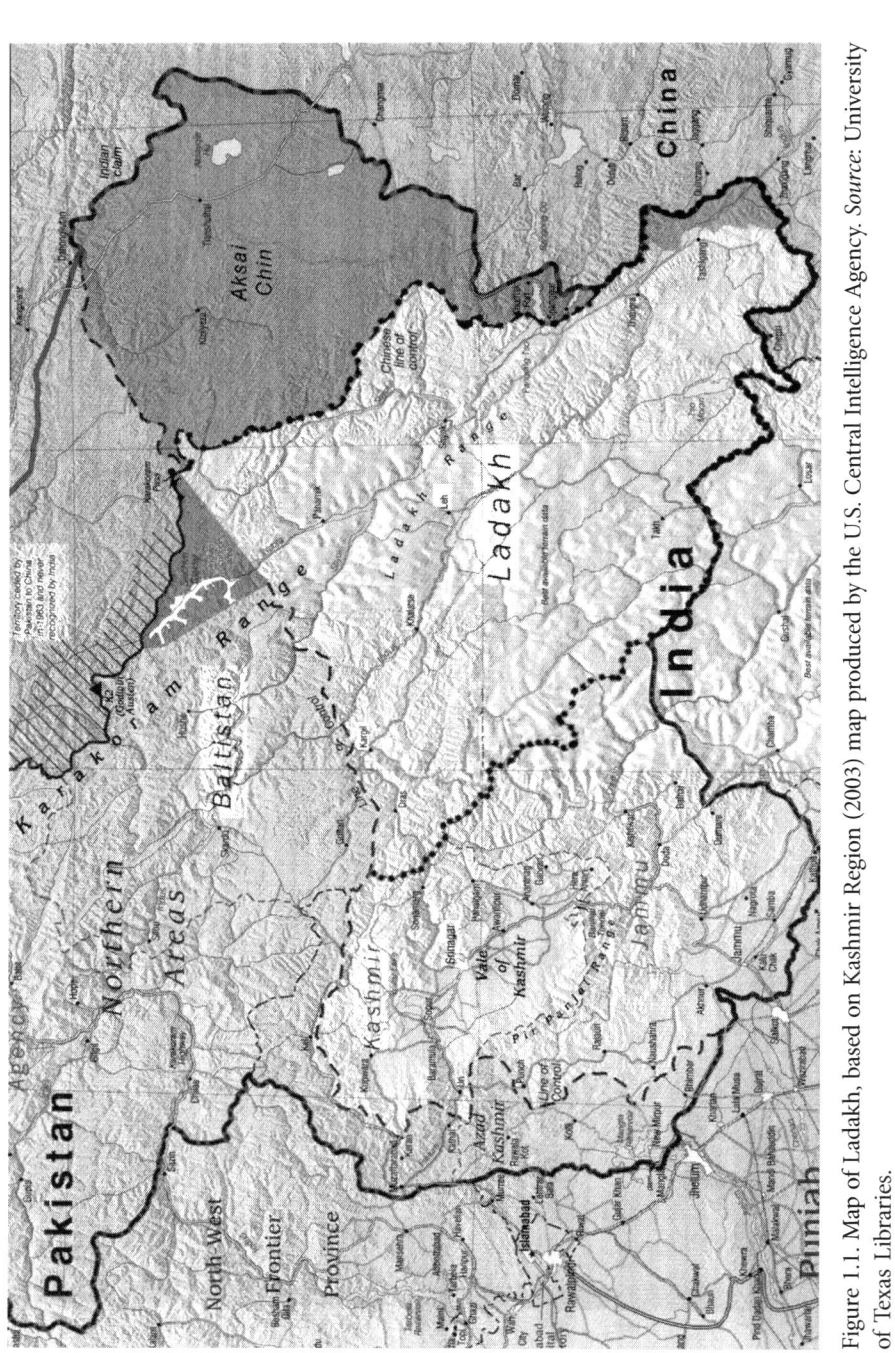

Figure 1.1. Map of Ladakh, based on Kashmir Region (2003) map produced by the U.S. Central Intelligence Agency. *Source:* University of Texas Libraries.

Chapter 1

A Cultural and Historical Overview of Ladakh

To most people, even those with some familiarity with Tibetan culture, Ladakh is a complete unknown. Because the lyrics of so many Ladakhi song genres refer to local history, religion, and geography, as well as inter-actions with both neighbors and trade routes, a discussion of Ladakh's history, geography, economy, culture, and language is a prerequisite for understanding the songs. Ladakh was a significant regional power at various points in its history and still plays a pivotal role in current geopolitics, as well as in the global luxury clothing market. Through this narrative we will examine some of the complex relationships between India/Pakistan, Tibet, and Central Asia and how they have manifested themselves in Ladakhi culture, including music. I owe much of this historical narrative to the insightful work of the British historian Janet Rizvi, whose 1998 book, *Ladakh: Crossroads of High Asia,* provided me with an overview when I first visited Ladakh in 1999.

Situated in the Karakorum and Ladakh Ranges of the Western Hima-layas (figure 1.1), Ladakh is a high, arid land, whose people have tradi-tionally survived on a combination of herding, subsistence agriculture, and trade. Even now, the fields are primarily fed by glacial runoff channeled by meticulously designed terrace farming and cooperative water management. Together with Chinese Tibet in the east and Pakistani Baltistan to the north, it is part of a Tibetan linguistic and cultural continuum, with close political, economic, and cultural interchanges across the region. Its sparse popula-tion is evenly divided between Buddhists (predominating in Leh District) and Shia Muslims (the majority in Kargil District). Leh District's land area of 45,110 sq. km. is home to only 117,000 people,[1] while Kargil District reports a population of 140,000 scattered over an area of 14,086 sq. km.[2]

This population density of 2.31 people per square kilometer (approximately six people per square mile) is about the same as that of Mongolia, which has the lowest population density on earth for a fully sovereign nation.

Origins of the Kingdom of Ladakh

Up until the closing of the borders with Pakistan and China in the late 1940s and early 1950s, Ladakh's position as a nexus of caravan trade between Kashmir, Turkestan, Tibet, China, and India gave it access to the luxuries that traversed its borders. Most notably, Ladakhi traders were and still are the middlemen in the pashmina trade, trading agricultural products for the raw goat's wool provided by the nomads on the Changthang plateau leading into Tibet, and selling it to the Kashmiris who weave it into shawls. And, as with many such crossroads areas, there were conflicts over the control of trade.

As early as the eighth century, the area was sandwiched between powerful, aggressive, and expansionist neighbors. As Rizvi observes, the area was at a contested crossroads between Tang Dynasty China, the empire of Kashmir under King Lalitaditya, and the Tibetan Empire. By the mid-eighth century a loose Tibetan suzerainty was established that lasted probably up to the collapse of the Tibetan Empire in 842 (Rizvi 1998, 55–56) (figure 1.2).

Figure 1.2. Tibetan Empire circa 700 CE. Fair use.

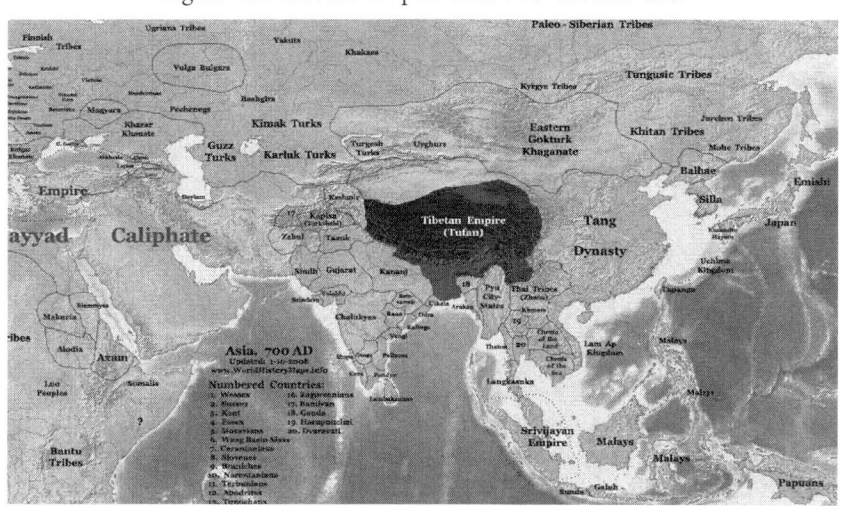

Ethnically, the area was first settled by the Indo-Iranian Dards, who are described as far back as the fifth century BCE by Herodotus (Balfour 1885, 890). The Dards are known to have adopted Indian-style Buddhism from Kashmir. A slow influx of Tibetan nomads mixed with the Dardic population prior to the founding of the Tibetan Empire in the seventh century (Rizvi 1998; Zeisler 2005). The Tibetan epic of King Gesar of Ling probably became part of the oral culture of the area during this period; it is still chanted, sung, and told by specialists, and has even been broadcast on the radio. We have no way of knowing anything about performance practices, save to note that low-caste musicians such as the Mon and Beda are mentioned in historical writings going back to the fourteenth century (Francke 1905). Extensive studies by scholars such as Francke have noted the pre-Buddhist elements in the epic that date its origins to the early days of Tibetan kingship, sometime prior to the seventh century (Francke 1923).

After the assassination of the Tibetan king Lang-dar-ma in 842, the Tibetan Empire collapsed into chaos. About 75 to 100 years after this, Lang-dar-ma's great-grandson Nyima Gon, accompanied by various Tibetan nobles, migrated westward, eventually setting up the western kingdoms of Ladakh, Guge, Zanskar, Spiti, and Kinnaur. Even at that time, we know about the influence of external elements from Ladakh's position as a trading nexus. The written records indicate that one of Prince Nyima Gon's four wives was Persian or Arab and was referred to as *sTag-gzigs-ma* (Tajik woman) (Petech 1997, 232). Such non-Tibetan influences, however, are at best only peripherally mentioned in the monastic histories such as the *Ladvags rgyal rabs* (Chronicles of the Kings of Ladakh) (Bray 2005a).

A period of Tibetanization occurred over the next two centuries, with the area remaining independent politically but subordinate to Tibet in religion and religious culture (Rizvi 1998, 57–58). During this time the western Tibetan kings continued to spread Buddhism throughout their kingdoms. Given the chaos in Tibet, the main source of Buddhist learning at the time was Kashmir. Under Nyima Gon's grandson Ye-shes-od, the great translator and teacher Rinchen Zangpo founded various monasteries throughout the area: in Kinnaur and Spiti, and in Ladakh at Tabo and Nyarma. Other monasteries, such as Alchi and Likir, date from this time but are only vaguely attributed to Rinchen.

Of less immediate—but more long-lasting—importance was the introduction of Vajrayana Buddhism by Atisha, the great Buddhist teacher from east India. Atisha founded the Kadampa monastic order, the precursor of the Gelugpa sect, and spent two years in Tholding, then the capital of

Guge. There he won over everyone, including the aging Rinchen Zangpo (Rizvi 1998, 59–60).

Expansion and Conflict

Indian and Kashmiri Buddhism soon waned under pressure from militant Hinduism and the destruction of monasteries and universities by Muslim invaders. As a result, Ladakhi Buddhism turned to Central Tibet for spiritual direction. At the same time, the western kingdoms of Kashmir and Baltistan converted to Islam. Even parts of western Ladakh (now Kargil District) embraced the new faith, although the region remained part of the kingdom. Central Ladakh, however, continued to be a bulwark against this tide, consolidating power, and incorporating most of the other small kingdoms into its expanding empire.

There is an interesting sidebar to this story. At some point during the poorly documented early thirteenth to early fifteenth centuries, the Ladakhi adventurer Gyalbu Rinchen (Prince Rinchen) became king of Kashmir. His Buddhism was acceptable to neither Muslim nor Hindu in Kashmir, and not being adoptable into any Hindu sect, he converted to Islam. The Indian and Kashmiri historical records refer to him as either Rainchan Shah or Rainchan Bhoti (Rinchen the Tibetan). Taking the name Sadr-ud-din, he is praised by the Hindu chronicle of Kashmiri kings, the *Rajatarangini*, for bringing order to the political chaos in Kashmir. There is reason to believe his conversion may have been purely a matter of political expedience since his apostasy is never mentioned in the Buddhist *Ladakhi Chronicles* (Rizvi 1998, 61–62).

It is also during this period that the various principalities of neighboring Baltistan made numerous raids into Ladakh, partly for profit, and partly in the attempt to convert the Buddhist Ladakhis. To some extent this latter effort succeeded—as mentioned, the areas around Kargil are to this day primarily Shia Muslim—but the Buddhist kings put up stiff resistance. Religious differences notwithstanding, the areas have had close relations for centuries with significant intermarriage between the ruling houses.

The early fifteenth century saw the introduction of the reform Gelugpa sect from Central Tibet into Ladakh. Under the patronage of King Takbumde (*Drags Bum Lde*), Gelugpa monasteries were founded, or existing monasteries were converted to the new sect. The kingship was divided among two fraternal lines at this time; one centered at Leh and Shey, the other at Basgo and Tingmosgang. They were united three generations later (ca. 1479) under the Basgo king, Bhagan, who adopted a new name for the dynasty: Namgyal (i.e., "Victorious," or "Complete Victory") (Francke 1907, 82).

At this point the chronology again becomes hazy. It is known that Central Asian adventurer Mirza Haidar Daughlat, who was in the employ of Sultan Saïd Khan of Kashgar, invaded Ladakh in 1532, forcing some sort of accommodation with the Ladakhi king, whoever he may have been. Haidar used Ladakh as a base to invade Tibet in 1533. He was driven back by the bitter Tibetan winter and pulled out by 1535. He had some sort of authority in Ladakh until his death in 1551 (Rizvi 1998, 64–65; Stein 1972, 83).

In the mid-sixteenth century, the Namgyal dynasty embarked upon expansionist policies. These ambitions came up short in the late 1500s, when King Jamyang Namgyal was defeated and captured by King Ali Sher Khan Anchan (aka Ali Mir) of Skardu (Baltistan). Jamyang was able to keep his throne but was obliged to marry one of Ali's daughters and disinherit all male heirs from his other wives. This was designed to convert the Ladakhi royal house to Islam, but in a well-calculated theological coup, the court lamas announced that a prophecy had revealed the queen, known as Gyal Khatun, to be an incarnation of the goddess Tara. There is also the tale that, at the time she conceived, her father dreamed that a lion jumped out of a river and entered her body. The child that was born was named Sengge (Lion) Namgyal. Born ca. 1570, Sengge became Ladakh's most renowned king and defender of the Buddhist faith, reigning from 1616 to 1642. Despite the Buddhist efforts to co-opt the public discourse about the royal marriage, Gyal Khatun remained a practicing Muslim to the end of her life.

It is important to note that part of Gyal Khatun's entourage from Baltistan included a group of palace musicians, or *khar mon,* who played the *surna* (double reed) and *daman* (kettledrum), traditional symbols of power and prestige introduced from the Muslim West. These and other Balti attendants settled in the village of Chushot outside of Leh, one of the main Shia settlements in Leh District. It is significant that this Muslim-derived ensemble is emblematic of Buddhist Ladakhi society not only at the village level but also in such high-prestige contexts as the old royal court, and in ceremonies throughout Ladakh honoring Buddhist oracles and dignitaries (Trewin 1995). Historical records going back to the reign of Takbumde in the early fifteenth century note the presence of the low-caste Mon and Beda musicians in Ladakh (Francke 1907, 79). Thus, it can be inferred that these groups, likely of foreign or pre-Tibetan origin, were performing on various instruments at both the village and palace level. The palace Mon from Baltistan were a privileged group compared to the village-level musicians, although no doubt still liminal in status.

Despite the Muslim family connection, Jamyang and Sengge were devout Buddhists and did much to promote the religion in Ladakh. Jamyang invited the famous Tibetan lama Stagtsang Raspa (Tib. the Tiger Nest Ascetic) to come to Ladakh, but it was not until Sengge's reign that he finally came. Under the tutelage of the Tiger Lama, the Lion King founded several important monasteries devoted to the Drukpa (Bhutanese) Kargyu sect, including Hanle and Hemis. Under Namgyal dynasty patronage, this sect came to rival the reform Gelugpa sect. We see Sengge portrayed as conqueror and defender of the faith in various traditional songs, which will be examined in later chapters.

Sengge's kingdom was a frontier state, functioning as a buffer between Buddhist Tibet and Muslim powers like Kashmir and Baltistan. This meant that his rule developed significant militarism associated with a strong central monarchy. This was in contrast with the theocratic feudalism, client/patron relationship that evolved between the Dalai Lamas and the Qosot Mongols, and then between the Dalai Lamas and Manchus.

Sengge Namgyal's aggressive military campaigns led to the conquest of the vassal kingdoms of Zanskar and Guge and brought the Ladakhi Empire to its greatest extent. He was eventually defeated by the combined Kashmiri and Mughal armies in 1639 and was obliged to pay tribute to the Mughals' Kashmiri proxies. Though the tribute was never paid during Sengge's lifetime, the implication of vassal status was to have repercussions later.

In a fit of pique, Sengge Namgyal cut off all trade with Kashmir, including the lucrative pashmina trade that was channeled from the Changthang plateau joining Ladakh and Tibet to the Kashmiri shawl weavers. Though intended to punish the Kashmiris, this embargo disrupted the commerce that was the lifeblood of the Ladakhi economy. Although this amounted to economic suicide, it was enforced by Sengge's successors for more than twenty years and marked the beginning of Ladakh's decline as a regional power (Rizvi 1998, 66–69).

During his lifetime, Sengge erected flamboyant displays of power and devotion, including temples and *mani walls*. His most ostentatious achievement was the royal palace in Leh (figure 1.3), whose nine stories were home to the Namgyal Dynasty until the Dogra Conquest in 1842.

Figure 1.3. Leh Palace, built by King Sengge Namgyal. *Source*: Author's photo.

Ladakhis say that this was conscious rivalry with the Dalai Lama's Potala Palace in Lhasa, but it predates the Potala, which was started in 1645 and finished in 1694. Rizvi suggests that increased Central Asian trade, brought about by regional stability under Sengge's reign, prompted him to put up this showplace at what had become a major trading nexus (Rivzi 1998, 69). His building of the palace is celebrated in the song "Sengge zhengs pa'i sku mkhar" (The Palace that Sengge Built) (track 01).

> *lte ba dang gting mo sgang du seng ges bzhengs pa'i sku mkhar 2x*
> *seng ges bzhengs pa'i sku mkhar gyi nang sengs ge rnam rgyal*
> [In the central and depths of the castle that Sengge built
> The castle which was built by Sengge Namgyal.]
>
> *ya re'i gdeng dang yongs pa'i ya rabs kyi bu*
> *ya re'i gdeng dang yongs pa'i dbon po'i dpal 'byor.*
> [Each one of the confident noble's sons has come,
> Each one of the confident noble's grandsons has come with
> glory.]
> *a zhang a ne'i sku mdun ming gcig sring gcig*
> *tshe dbang dang rab brtan gyi sku mdun na ming sring gcig.*
> [May the uncle and aunt's names be exalted for a long time.
> May Tsewang and Rabstan's names be exalted for a long time.]

ming gcig sring gcig gnyis ka la tshe la
sku bsrung mdzod cig.
ming gcig snying gcig gnyis ka la
lha yis sku bsrung mdzod cig.
[For both name and long life
May we make offerings to the guardian's image.
For both name and long life
May we make offerings to the deity's image.]

Under Sengge's grandson, Delek Namgyal, the inconclusive nature of Ladakh's tributary relationship with both Kashmir and its Mughal overlord, the emperor Aurangzeb, became untenable. In 1663, Delek was pressured into renewing his grandfather's promise of tribute and loyalty: he agreed to build a mosque, have the *khutba*—the prayer for the secular authority—recited, and have coins struck in the name of the emperor. This promise went unfulfilled until partly enforced by a show of military strength from the Kashmir border. It is from this period—ca. 1666–67—that the erection of the first mosque in Leh is dated. The pledge to encourage Islam in Ladakh was never taken seriously, however, and the tribute was paid irregularly, if at all; though it is clear from their exchanges that Aurangzeb viewed the Ladakhi king as his vassal. It is also from this time that the devastating trade embargo with Kashmir was finally lifted (Rizvi 1998, 70–71).

After matters with the Mughals were settled, Delek Namgyal embarked on a series of military campaigns whose purpose was to reassert control over the principalities of Purig, Henis, Stagtse, Chigtan, and Kartse. Campaigns into Baltistan installed puppet rulers in three principalities. Flushed with success, but doubtless chafing under the yoke of Aurangzeb, Delek precipitated a confrontation with Tibet. Ladakhi records state that the confrontation was brought about by support for the Drukpa lama, who was both temporal and spiritual leader of far-off Bhutan—part of the Tibetan cultural area. Tibet attempted, unsuccessfully, to invade Bhutan, whereupon Delek sent a provocative letter to the Fifth Dalai Lama. The "Great Fifth," in response, sent an expedition, comprising mainly Mongolian cavalry, in 1679 to engage the Ladakhis in Guge. Inconclusive skirmishes ensued, but no strategic gains were made. Finally, a large-scale invasion took place in 1681, initiating what is referred to by Ladakhis as the "Great Mongol War." The Mongols and Tibetans laid siege to Basgo Castle (figure 1.4) for three years, yet they could neither conquer it nor be driven away. Finally, Delek was obliged to call upon Kashmir for assistance.

Figure 1.4. Basgo Village with palace complex above. *Source*: Author's photo.

The Kashmiris succeeded in pushing the Tibetans back to the original Ladakhi border but in exchange for their help insisted on confirmation of Mughal suzerainty, including Delek's conversion to Islam. Apparently, Delek went through the ceremony, only to have it reversed. The Fifth Dalai Lama had died during the war, and given the Kashmiris' terms, the regent Sangye Gyatsho became deeply concerned about the safety of Buddhism in Ladakh. He asked the head of the Drukpa sect to help negotiate a treaty, and following the 1684 Treaty of Tingmosgang, Delek reconverted to Buddhism and Tibet, and Ladakh agreed to give equal protection to both Drukpa and Gelugpa. Moreover, Ladakh had to surrender territories in Western Tibet (Shakspo 1999, 288) and was obliged to send a symbolic tribute to the Dalai Lama every three years (Rizvi 1998, 74).[3]

In the popular imagination, the Great Mongol War is cast in a heroic light. Several songs from Basgo talk about the futility of the Mongolian siege. For example, the song *"Skyes pa'i pha yul"* (Fatherland of our birth), recorded by my colleague Dr. Stephen Dydo and me in Basgo in 2011, presents an interesting spin on events. The following is my translation of the text written down for us by Sonam Tsering Lagachirpon of Basgo (track 02) as recorded in August 2011 in Basgo Village :

Skyes pa'i pha yul: (Fatherland of Our Birth)

skyes pa'i pha yul gyi gyas phyogs la gzigs sang/
tshugs sa ba mgo yi phyogs la gzigs sang/
dpa' bo tham cad g.yas bral la bzhugs yod/
dpa'mo tham cad po gyon gral la bzhugs yod/
[Look to the right side of the fatherland of [our] birth.
Look to the right side of firm Basgo.
All the heroes are seated in a row to the right.
All the heroines are seated in a row to the left.]

mi chen gong gser khri ba'i steng na/
sengge rnam rgyal bo gser khri ba'i steng/
dga' ba la gzings sang sang mi chen gyi gong ma/
skyid nyams la gzings sang sengge rnam rgyal/
[When the superior great man is seated on the golden throne,
When Sengge Namgyal is seated on the golden throne,
Behold with joy the superior great man,
Behold with joy Sengge Namgyal.]

rgyal pa'i sku mkhar la dgra bo lo gsum bskor bskor song/
ba mgo lha bris can la sog po lo gsum bskor song/
dmag gi dmag sgar ma chag dbra bo rang dul la song/
dmag gi dmag sgar ma chag sog po rang dul la song/
[The enemy surrounded the royal palace for three years.
The Mongolians surrounded Basgo's defenders for three years.
The encampment of unbreakable enemy warriors itself was
    subdued.
The encampment of unbreakable Mongolian warriors itself
    was subdued.
Then high above [were] the royal mother fields.
Then high above [were] the lord's bare fields.]

rgyal po'i ma zhing po pang ka rtse steng na/
mi dbang gi sang zhing po pang ka rtse steng na/
ska snang brgyad brgyad bcu la shau gsum stong lnga brgyad/
ska snang brgyad brgyad bcu la zhau gsum stong lnga brgya/
hor ngan sog po'i rta'i rta'i cung nub bed// sog po dga' lnga
    tshe dbang gi rta'i
[High above were the king's mother fields

High above were His Majesty's bare fields
Suddenly in a hundred and ten lights there were a thousand
five hundred scars.
Suddenly in a hundred and ten lights there were a thousand
five hundred scars.
The Mongol Galdan Tshewang's horses are fortunately waning.]

In addition to celebrating the men and women who defended the citadel, a ruler is praised. This ruler is not Delek Namgyal, however, but Sengge Namgyal. The martial prowess of Sengge has been conflated with images of the Ladakhi struggle to survive, and the hapless Delek has disappeared from the narrative.

The next period of Ladakhi history, known as the Little Empire, was a time of shrinking power and territory. A diminished empire continued to flourish with kings of varying competency and/or sanity. Delek's son Nyima Namgyal (1695–1750) was a competent ruler. He was married twice. The first time was to a princess from Shey, who died young leaving a son, Deskyong Namgyal (there is a song about her called "The Princess from Shey," which laments her leaving him bereft). The second queen, the Balti Zizi Khatun, was kind to her stepson, but exerted control over him for much of his reign and was a rather ruthless Machiavellian figure.

Deskyong Namgyal married a woman named Nilza Wangmo, who was a princess of Lomanthang in Mustang (now part of Western Nepal). Nilza Wangmo gave birth to a son Saskyong Namgyal who grew up to be king from 1775 to 1780 (Francke 1907, 120). According to Lama Jamspal, Deskyong was a drunkard and beat his wife, so she made the hard decision to walk away from the palace, leaving her son behind. She returned to Mustang and from there went to Tibet where she married again and gave birth to a boy who was recognized as the Seventh Panchen Lama, Palden Tenpai Nyima (1782–1853). This song "Nyilza Wangmo'i lu (Nyilza Wangmo's song) (track 03) is in the style of a woman's lament—common in Ladakh—bowing to the various powers in her life (supernatural/spiritual and familial) and lamented her leaving her young son behind in the palace.

nyi zla bang ma'i glu—The Song of Nilza Wangmo (LYL, 109–11)

Nyi ma'i nub phyogs o rgyan gling na
yi dam padma can bzhugs 2x
no mo nga lho de la mi bskyod pa'i
byin rlabs dang dngos grub stsal

nyi lza dbang mo lho la mi bskyod pa'i
byin rlabs dang dngos grub stsal.
[To the north of the sun in the realm of Urgyan
The deity Padmasambhava resides.
May he bestow blessings and wisdom,
So that I, the girl, don't return to the south.
May he bestow blessings and wisdom,
So that Nyilza Wangmo does not return to the south.]

mang spro'i phu ru bzhugs pa
a pha rong btsan rgyal po 2x
no mo nga lho la mi bskyod pa'i
lung bstan zhig stsal
nyi zla dbang mo lho la mi bskyod pa'i
lung bstan zhig stsal.
[O King Rongstan,[4]
You who live in the upper valleys of Matho,
May you predict
That I, the girl, don't return to the south.
May you predict
That Nyilza Wangmo will not return to the south.]

g.yas phyogs kyi gser lcang ser po de
no mo nga yi yab chen yin nam bsam
gyas phyogs kyi gser lcang ser po
zhabs drung ngag dbang yin nam bsam
no mo nga yi yab chen yin nam bsams te
zhabs drung ngag dbang yin nam bsams te
nyi lza dbang mos phyag gsum 'tshal
[To the right is the yellow, golden willow tree,
That was thought to be the great father of this girl.
To the right is the golden willow tree,
That was thought to be of Zhabdrung Ngawang?[5]
Thinking that it was the girl's spiritual father,
Thinking it was Zhabdrung Ngawang,
Nyilza Wangmo made three bows.]

g.yon phyogs kyi gyu lcang sngon po de
no mo nga yi a ma yin nam bsam

gyon phyogs kyi gyu lcang sngon po de
zi zi rgyal mo yin nam bsam
no mo nga yi a ma yin nam bsams te
no mo nga yis phyag gsum phul
zi zi rgyal mo yin nam bsams te
nyi zla dbang mos phyag gsum phul.
[To the left is the blue, turquoise willow tree.
Thought to be my, the girl's, mother.
To the left is the blue, turquoise willow tree.
Thinking it to be the Queen ZiZi,
Thinking it to be my, the girl's, mother,
I, the girl, made three bows.
Nyilza Wangmo made three bows.]

gom chen phyi ru rgyab pa dang
sems pa nang du lus 2x
a ma la bltams pa yi bu chung de
sku mkhar gyi nang du bzhugs
nyi zla la bltams pa'i sa skyong de
sku mkhar gyi nang bzhugs
[While taking large steps outside
The mind stays at home.
A baby was born to the mother,
Left behind in the royal palace.
The little prince[6] born to Nyilza Wangmo
Left behind in the royal palace.]

Deskyong Namgyal remarried after Nyilza Wangmo left him, choosing another queen named Butri Wangmo. According to contemporary accounts, she was very well liked, was very cheerful and funny, beautiful, and devout. She is praised equally with her husband in the song, "sku khar tsho" (The Castle) (track 04). The castle itself is praised—it *is* impressive. However, the praise heaped on Deskyong Namgyal is in the realm of fiction or pro forma and formulaic. He is referred to as the jewel that fulfills wishes—a common type of praise, and is called "restrainer of enemies," but was not involved in military exploits. He is later called "The youth, great star of the dawn." Again, formulaic praise. The majority of the praise seems directed at the queen: she is compared to the saffron crocus, which is chief of flowers, a stupa of jewel crystal, a row of pearls, to the full moon, and walls of yellow barley, and "white sheep" barley.

sku mkhar tsho—The Castle (LYL, 61–62)

sku mkhar tsho ming du snyan byung
sku mkhar lha yi pho brang
gle chen tsho ming du snyan byung
gle chen tsho dbang rab brtan
nang na nor bu bzhugs yod
dgos 'dod yid bshin nor bu
mi dbang sde skyong rnam rgyal
dgra bo 'dul ba'i kha gnon
[The castle is famous.
The castle, abode of the gods.
Great Leh is famous,
Great, strong, steadfast Leh
The jewel is inside.
The jewel that fulfils wishes,
The lord Deskyong Namgyal,
Restrainer of enemies.]

gur kum tsho gzhung gi me tog
tshes chen bco lnga'i zla ba
gur kum tsho gzhung gi me tog
yar ngo bco lnga'i zla ba
nor bu shel gyi mchod rten
lha lcam bu 'khrid dbang mo
mu tig tshar du dngar byung.
[The saffron crocus is chief of flowers,
The full moon of the fifteenth waxing day [of the month].
The saffron crocus is chief of flowers,
The full moon, of the fifteenth day of the first half of the month
The *chorten* of jewel crystal.
The Lady, Butri Wangmo becomes a row of pearls.]

yul chung tsho thang ga legs po
bkra shis lha yi 'dun sa
khyog tog nam langs kyi skar chen
shar pa rang dang 'dra
na chung yar ngo'i bco lnga po'i
gan pa'i zla ba 'dra.
[The good plain of little villages,

The place of the auspicious god,
The youth, great star of the dawn,
Like the risen one itself,
The maiden of the fifteenth day of the first half of the month
 [full moon],
Like the full moon.]

rtsig pa tsho ma btsigs pa'i rtsig pa
ser mo nas kyi rtsig pa
rtsig pa tsho ma btsigs pa'i rtsig pa
g.yang dkar nas kyi rtsig pa
rtsig de la 'gyur bya mi 'dug
lha lcam bu 'khrid dbang mo.
[Walls do not build walls.
The wall of yellow barley
Walls do not build walls.
The wall of "white sheep" barley
The wall does not change.
The Lady, Butri Wangmo.]

Considering how powerless Deskyong seems to have been, it is not sur-prising that songs merely give him lip service. It was the women in his life that were important: the mother who died, his kind, but Machiavellian stepmother, the wife he abused, and the wife that seemed to be genuinely adored by the court.

We see a wide variety of personalities portrayed in songs about the Namgyal Dynasty. Sengge Namgyal outshines almost everyone. Some, like Delek Namgyal are discounted due to failures in battle and the diminution of the empire. Deskyong Namgyal initially gets sympathy for losing his mother as a young child but later does not fare well in the song record. His absence in Nyilza Wangmo's song speaks volumes in the light of the backstory, and he subsequently is eclipsed by his second wife in the song, "The Castle." Later kings like the insane Tsewang Namgyal II are not even mentioned in song and, as a bad example, is implicitly mentioned in a famous aphorism about the low-caste Beda woman he married. That, however, is a story for another day.

The conquest of Ladakh in 1842 by the Dogras of Jammu under Maharajah Gulab Singh, a client of the British, brought the Little Empire to an end, and the exile of the Namgyal kings to a small palace in the village of Stok outside of Leh. Now incorporated into the princely state of Jammu and Kashmir, Ladakh suffered excessive taxation, exploitation, and diminished trade. There is little reference to this period in traditional songs, except for a gentle satire directed at an Indian minister referred to as Pita (i.e., father) Jogi: (track 05)

blon chen bi ta dzo gi—The Minister Pita Jogi (LYL, 66–67)

nyi ma shar nas shar byung, grib ma tshur nas babs byung. (2x)
sprin bar chad pa'i nyi ma, bdag gi dpon po bzang po.
sprin bar chad pa'i nyi ma, blon chen bi Ta dzo gi.
[The sun rises in the east, the east, in the shadow it sets (2x)
The sun is blocked by clouds, my good lord.
The sun is blocked by clouds, Minister Pita Jogi.]

dpa' 'dum mkhar gyi khang ltag na, se ba ser po'i me tog. (2x)
se ba ser po'i me tog, bdag gi dpon po bzang po.
se ba ser po'i me tog, blon chen bi Ta dzo gi.
[On the top of Padum Castle [there is] a gold rose flower. (2x)
A gold rose flower, my good lord.
A gold rose flower, Minister Pita Jogi.]

*ya gi shed gnam stod mthong po na, bya chung rma bya zung
  gcig. (2x)*
bya chung rma bya ma yin, bdag gi dpon po bzang po.
bya chung rma bya ma yin, blon chen bi Ta dzo gi.
[Up in yon high sky [there are] a couple of small peacocks. (2x)
It will not be a small peacock, my good lord.
It will not be a small peacock, Minister Pita Jogi.]

*ya gi shed mtsho stod mthon po na, nya chung gser mig zung
  gcig. (2x)*
nya chung gser mig ma yin, bdag gi dpon po bzang po.
nya chung gser mig ma yin, blon chen bi Ta dzo gi.
[Up in yon high lake [there are] a couple of small golden-eyed fish.
It will not be a small golden-eyed fish, my good lord.
It will not be a small golden-eyed fish Minister Pita Jogi.]

Most of my informants were not able to confirm the identity of this minister, but noted singer Morup Namgyal says that he was a minister in or from Shey (personal comm., August 7, 2014). It is nonetheless clear that, whoever he might have been, he was not attended by auspicious signs, given that the sun is "blocked by clouds."

With Indian independence in 1947, the area became a battleground between India and Pakistan, with parts of Jammu and Kashmir such as Baltistan and parts of the Kashmir valley now in Pakistan. Further loss of territory occurred in 1963 when China seized part of the desolate Aksai Chin in a short border conflict. Given its strategic importance, Ladakh is now host to a huge Indian Army contingent, which has helped to transform the local economy and thus the society as well. Land reform, civil rights legislation, public education, improved roads, and food subsidies have allowed oppressed segments of the population to leave the land and pursue jobs in local public works, the military, and so on. This has included the low-caste Mon and Beda musicians, contributing in part to the loss of traditional repertoire. Meanwhile, the introduction of radio and television has in part promoted the preservation of Ladakhi language and culture, while at the same time subjecting it to pressures from Hindi-language mass media.

Religion and Identity in Ladakh

The communal violence between Hindu, Sikh, and Muslim that has plagued the Indian subcontinent since before independence has not generally afflicted Ladakh to the same extent as the rest of India. Since the Dogra conquest of Ladakh, however, there was a perception that Buddhist Ladakhis were oppressed by the Muslim majority of Jammu and Kashmir. As anthropologist Martijn van Beek notes, the communal divisions of the subcontinent into India and Pakistan were counteracted by the principles of secularism enshrined in the Indian constitution. This dynamic has been affected by the religious nationalism of the BJP government, with communal strategies becoming embedded in Ladakhi politics (van Beek 2000, 528).

Van Beek points out how Ladakhis—both Muslim and Buddhist—were initially unrepresented in the Jammu and Kashmir (J and K) government until the formation of a partially elected assembly in the early 1930s, when representatives were appointed for the Ladakh area with two Buddhist seats for Leh, and one each for Muslim Kargil and Skardu in Baltistan. This action enshrined political divisions based on religious affiliation (van Beek 2000, 532).

At the same time the Young Men's Buddhist Association (YMBA) was formed in Ladakh with the aim of aiding the growth of the Buddhist community. YMBA members identified factors that they felt contributed to the backwardness and poverty of the Buddhist community: polyandry, primogeniture in property inheritance, lack of education, and various social evils, such as the drinking of *chang*—the barley beer that forms a staple of the Ladakhi diet. As a result of such advocacy, the J and K *Praja Sabha* (assembly) passed legislation abolishing polyandry in 1941, followed by a "Ladakh Succession to Property Act" passed in 1943, which banned primogeniture. After independence and incorporation of J and K into India, reforms like abolition of excessive debt to landlords and land reform helped small landholders (van Beek 2000, 533–35).

Throughout the 1950s and 1960s, Ladakhis, both Buddhist and Muslim, complained that the J and K state government was ignoring Ladakh and neglecting its financial needs. Since most Ladakhis were subsistence-level farmers, this complaint was mainly expressed by the urban populations of Leh and Kargil. Their agitation, which involved both religious and political leaders, resulted in the creation of plays and songs intended to educate the rural populace (van Beek 2000, 537).

This was a time when traditional lifestyles were being transformed by the large Indian Army presence, increased public education, and government subsidies for various imported food staples such as rice and wheat. Youth were no longer interested in going back to the farms, but instead clamored for job opportunities. Their demands were a significant factor in pushing for separation from J and K.

At the same time, advocates such as Kushog Bakula Rinpoche pressed for classification of Ladakh's Buddhists as "backward classes," giving them protected status as Scheduled Tribes under the Indian Constitution and making them eligible for quotas in government jobs and education. Such advocacy created divisions between Buddhists and Muslims, as well as within the Buddhist community.

During the 1980s and 1990s, anti-Muslim sentiment greatly increased and was incited by the Ladakh Buddhist Association (LBA). This was paralleled by the rise of Hindu nationalist parties such as the Rashtriya Swayamsevak Sangh (RSS) and the Bharatiya Janata Party (BJP), and the forming of Buddhist alliances with the latter. This culminated in the LBA organizing a social boycott of Muslims that lasted from 1989 to 1992. Nevertheless, the general sentiment in Leh District was not excessively hostile (van Beek 2000, 541–42). As one acquaintance of mine noted, "Ladakhis remembered who they were."

As a result of the increase in violence in the Kashmir valley during the 1990s, Ladakh has become an attractive alternate mountain destination for tourists, both Indian and foreign. The dramatic increase in tourism has had a profound impact upon the local economy, most notably in the building boom throughout the region but also in the explosion of cultural activity. Yet continued friction with the Kashmir state government increased agitation, especially in the Buddhist Leh sector, to have New Delhi take over direct rule of Ladakh as a Union Territory. This finally occurred in 2019, and it was hoped that would to some extent reverse the Kashmiri/ Dogra conquest and restore Ladakhi autonomy within the Indian union. As of this writing in 2024 full Schedule 6 protections under the Indian Constitution guaranteeing protected status regarding residence, land ownership, and self-rule have not been put in place. The struggle continues.

Of interest to this study of Ladakhi music is the continued agitation of the LBA against *skugdragism,* or domination of society by the old elite, or *sku-drag.* Ladakhi society has traditionally been divided into hereditary classes (*rigs*), with *sku-drags* consisting of royalty (*rgyal-rigs*) and nobility (*rigs dan*). Most commoners were known as *mang rigs*; blacksmiths (*gara* or *gar-ba*) and musicians (*mon* and *beda*) (*rigs-ngan*) have traditionally been stigmatized socially. There have been efforts to fight this discrimination: His Holiness the Dalai Lama lectured against it during teachings in Ladakh, beating on a Mon drum, and sharing a meal with a *gara* (blacksmith) family (van Beek 2000, 545; Trewin 1995; Rather 1993). However, discrimination still lingers, particularly in rural communities.

Buddhist and Pre-Buddhist Heritage in Ladakhi Poetry and Music

The literary output of Ladakh over the ages has been fragmentary. The best-known works from the early period of Tibetan colonization are the various versions of the Gesar epic. The legendary king Gesar is a pre-Buddhist Tibetan archetype of the "heaven-sent king" (Hermanns 1965). Gesar is a supernatural / superhuman figure who singlehandedly overcomes enemies—human or otherwise—through a mixture of martial prowess, great strength, magic, and cunning. As Buddhism incorporated pre-Buddhist religion and lore, Gesar became an example of the *chos-gyal*, or Dharma king, who both upholds and is upheld by religious virtue. This is a common concept in the various religious cultures of South and East Asia: Hindu, Buddhist, and Bonpo.[7]

For almost a thousand years, bards have spread this symbol of a greater Tibetan consciousness. The epic transcends religion in Ladakh and Baltistan, with Muslim storytellers known to be some of its most renowned exponents. We have records of texts and melodies dating from the late nineteenth and early twentieth centuries, transcribed by Moravian missionaries such as Francke and Ribbach.

One of the rhetorical themes of the Gesar epic is a recitation of the hero's superhuman childhood conquests. An example is a song Francke calls "Kesar's Four Victories" (Francke 1902, 306).[8]

> *1) When I, a boy, had reached my eighth year*
> *I subdued the three Anubandhas[9] of the East.*
> *The boy has been triumphing over all of them.*
> *2) When I, a boy, had reached my twelfth year,*
> *I subdued all the great ministers of the hills.*
> *The boy has been triumphing over all of them.*
> *3) When I, a boy, had reached my sixteenth year,*
> *I subdued the devil Khyabpa Lagring[10] and his men.*
> *The boy has been triumphing over all of them.*
> *4) When I, a boy, had reached my eighteenth year,*
> *I subdued all the bad Yārkandis.[11]*
> *The boy has been triumphing over all of them*

Hermanns notes that this epic depicts a nomadic view of leadership based on personal charisma, rather than the kingship found in nation-states such as the Yarlung dynasties of Tibet (Hermanns 1965).

Emulating this model, the song "Sonam mchog skyid" (discussed in detail in chapter 2) weaves praise of Sengge Namgyal into the Gesar myth adding the Buddhist slant of identifying him with Chenrezig, looking with compassion on all sentient beings.

There is very little reference in Ladakhi traditional songs to the proto-historical Yarlung Dynasty period in Tibetan history. Some of the few exceptions are references in court songs about King Sengge Namgyal that trace his lineage back to Nyatri Tsanpo, the semi-legendary founder of the Yarlung Dynasty. In for instance, the song *Sonam mchog skyid* (Meritorious Happiness) (LYL, 70):

> *In King Nyatri Tsanpo's bloodline,*
> *The leaves of the wish-fulfilling tree are in full bloom . . .*
> or the song *Shel ldan g.yu mtsho* (The crystalline turquoise ocean) (LYL: 76):
> [The copper, white crystal,
> House of complete victory [Namgyal]
> Inside on the lion's throne [that of Senge (Lion) Namgyal]
> Nyatri Tsanpo's lineage.]

These assertions of the royal lineage, however, should not be construed as an expression of nationalist sentiment at a grassroots level. They were validations of royal authority cloaked in history and myth. The concept of Ladakhi "national" identity is, to a certain extent, a modern construct. As historian John Bray has observed of the Namgyal Dynasty period (c. 1470–1842):

> Although Ladakh had developed its own cultural tradition, which was distinct from Tibet and other neighboring regions, there was no unifying sense of Ladakhi 'national' identity. Ladakh farmers may have identified with their village, their valley or perhaps their monastery, but not with the region as a whole. Similarly, Buddhist monks and Muslim merchants also would have lacked a sense of Ladakhi identity not because they were too parochial, but because they were too international. The monks would have associated on equal terms with their counterparts in Tibet; Muslim merchants both traded and had relatives in Srinagar, Kashgar and indeed Lhasa. (Bray 1991, 118–19)

Writing about the pre-Buddhist and legendary period of Nyatri Tsanpo, R.A. Stein notes that Tibetan historians—especially those favoring Bon—described Tibet as having been "protected" (i.e., ruled) by Bonpos (priests), storytellers, and singers. There must have been some parallel functions among the Bonpos, where the storytellers (*sgrung*) passed on legends and other lore, and the singers (*lde'u*) sang riddles and—proba- bly—genealogies. For the latter, this body of lore constituted the "religion of men" (*mi chos*) and was distinct from the "religions of the gods" (*lha chos*) presided over by the Bonpos and Buddhist lamas. The few examples of *mi chos* that have come down to us, and are known as such, are wise sayings told by the old men of the clan. These are always couched in poetic language, using metaphors, clichés, and proverbial sayings (Stein 1972, 191–92).

Similarly, there are many such sayings in Ladakh, which are often couched in metaphorical language. Some are along the lines of Aesop's fables or are like proverbs with lengthy stories behind the short pithy sayings. Some are based in Ladakhi history; some comment on the Ladakhi social order (Khan 1998).

Another remnant of pre-Buddhist culture in Ladakh is the use of mythical references in the wedding song repertoire (*bag-ston lu*), for example, in what Tashi Rabgias calls the Ceremonial Arrow Song:

Behold upon that snow mountain a great lion proudly posing.
Behold upon that great lion a vast turquoise mane.
Behold under the sutra the round turquoise lake.
Behold upon the turquoise lake a female fish floating.
Behold upon the female fish, the agile wing extended.
Behold upon the agile wing the beloved solid ice.
Behold upon the solid ice the beloved earth and stone.
Behold upon the earth and stone the beloved mother fields.
Behold upon the mother fields' ripe grain. (LYL, 14)

Other songs show an awareness of local gods of the household, fields, waters, and so on. This reflects the pre-Buddhist worldview that situates people in a matrix of multiple realms: the human, the natural, and the supernatural. Throughout the Tibetan cultural sphere these pre-Buddhist elements have joined seamlessly with Buddhism, fitting into the concept of the six classes of sentient beings: gods, demigods, humans, animals, hungry ghosts, and hell-beings.

According to the anthropologist Martin A. Mills, traditional Ladakhi people view themselves as being rooted in local space and place; that is, they are not just physically connected to the landscape but also chthonically bound to the natal earth and are in a complex matrix of relations between people and various spirits, such as household gods and protectors, *nāga*, and itinerant demons. These deities are associated with features of the local geography, and they regulate and influence local agricultural and social production, so birth in one area or another signifies a relation with the deity presiding over it. The land itself is imbued with a notion of personhood and agency. Rituals are performed according to an astrologically and agriculturally influenced calendar, as well as in response to births, deaths, spirit possession, and unintentional pollution of places or household objects. These all function to maintain and/or restore proper relations with local spirit numina [*jig rten pa*].

This matrix extends to groups of household estates associated with a *p'a-llza* (*pha.lha*), or household god, shared as the locus of ritual action by a group of two to ten estates called a *p'a-spun* (*pha.spun*) or "father's kin." Within the *p'a-spun* group, one estate will have a main shrine dedicated to the p'a-lha located on the upper floors of its central house. This is composed of a vase (*bum-pa*) filled with grain and precious minerals. A central "life-wood" (*la-shing, bla.shing*) and several ritual arrows placed pointing down into the vase are wrapped in a ceremonial scarf and juniper. The shrine receives daily offerings from the household head, and every king's new year (*lo-sar, lo. gsar*) the main heir of the household cleans the shrine, replaces the juniper and scarf, and brings new arrows from the main shrine rooms of each of the *p'a-spun* estates (Mills 2000, 21). It was the Mon in their role as carpenters who make these arrows and give them to all village households. Similarly, the *gara* would give iron needles as their offerings.

Both Mills and Ribbach have described this complex of relationships in the extensive Ladakhi marriage rituals, in which the bride transfers her allegiance from her paternal household god (*pha lha*) to that of her husband. This transference is so complete that she is no longer allowed into the paternal shrine (Francke 1923; Mills 2003; Tucci 1980; Ribbach 1985).

The local matrix is part of an extended traditional cosmology, consisting of the three levels of heaven, earth, and under the earth. Additionally, the earth is envisioned as four continents with either Mount Kailash (Tib. *Tise*) in Tibet, or the mythical Mount Sumeru, in the center. The known world of India, Tibet, etc., is in the southern continent of Jambudvipa (Tib. Dzambu Ling). In unknown, mythical regions in various directions are legendary realms of righteousness. These are the heavenly, blissful abodes of buddhas and/or bodhisattvas into which one may be born for a time. This concept also appears in Bon and Taoist mythology. Notable examples are:

- Shambala (whence comes "Shangri-la") from the Kalachakra Tantra meditation.

- Sukhavati, realm of the Buddha Amitabha

- Zangdok Palri (the Copper-colored Mountain) of the Guru Padmasambhava who helped establish Buddhism in Tibet

- Tushita (*dga' ldan*), connected with the coming Buddha Maitreya, and with Tshongkhapa, the founder of the Gelug-pa sect.

The pure realms are all accessible through experiential meditation and trance, and through *sadhana* (*sgrub thabs*), visualizations that are described in various texts and oral teachings. The concepts of tantric visualization pervade Ladakhi Buddhist song texts of many genres, both at the court and village level. Many songs focus on a central figure, placing it in what can be characterized as either a mandala ('*khyil 'khor*—symbolic visualizations of a pure land) or a field of merit (*tshogs zhing*) in which buddhas, bodhisattvas and / or gurus are surrounded by their worshipers, disciples, and/or attendants.

Visualizations such as these derive from the threads of Bon and Buddhism combined in the Tantric traditions, which involved a combination of deep analytic philosophy, ritual, and various visualization meditations. According to Giuseppe Tucci: "individual deities, represented through their symbols, are brought into existence, that is made visible to the mystic, either externally, in an objectification in front of him, or within his own body. These divine forms are evoked not only for the attainment of salvation, but also for liturgical or magical reasons" (Tucci 1980, 32).

In subsequent chapters I examine these texts and show how Buddhist imagery permeated both court and village.

Chapter 2

Buddhism in Ladakhi Traditional Songs

The genres examined in this chapter exhibit varying emphasis on pre-Buddhist or Buddhist elements. The two are often inextricably intertwined, keeping with the syncretic nature of Vajrayana Buddhism, which has incorporated or co-opted native Tibetan/Ladakhi elements into its complex meditative visualization practices. The religious content in these songs reflects various facets of traditional Ladakhi society, and we can see how Buddhist practice, imagery, and philosophy were integrated into various sectors of that society. From the Namgyal court down to the village level we can see contradictions between orthodox Buddhist ideals and the realities of lay life.

Much of the variability in the relationship of pre-Buddhist and Buddhist elements relates to the function of the songs, and whether they originate in the royal court or in the villages, and to what extent the songs show monastic influence. We see representations of kingship characterized by militarism (a very non-Buddhist attribute), equating the king with the pre-Buddhist Gesar figure to enhance the personal charisma of the ruler. In the case of the Namgyal Dynasty, the depictions of the rulers as defenders of the faith are intertwined with representations of kingship inherited from the pre-Buddhist Tibetan traditions, including the Gesar epic. The monastic influence is noted in the detailed references to Vajrayana meditation visualization practices.

We also see contradictions between the realities of lay Buddhist life versus monastic ideals. As noted above, the militarism necessary to maintain Ladakhi independence was balanced against the Buddhist doctrines on doing no harm to other sentient beings. Another contradiction involves the consumption of *chang* (beer), or more specifically intoxication, which is prohibited for Buddhists, especially monastics, but is an integral part of lay life, and is celebrated in various song genres.

Before examining individual genres, I wish to present a brief introduction to Tibetan/Ladakhi Buddhist practices that inform the texts of these songs. Tantric/Vajrayana Buddhist practice is based on what is called the Three Mysteries: *mudrā, mantra,* and *maṇḍala. Mudrā* are symbolic or ritual hand gestures, or body postures. *Mantra* is sound, syllable, word, or group of words used to invoke mental transformations or invoke mental imagery (the word has been taken into English and will henceforth be used without italics). *Maṇḍala* (taken into English without diacritical marks) is both a generic term for any plan, chart or geometric pattern that represents the cosmos metaphysically or symbolically, and specifically a circle, inside of which is a square with four gates representing a temple or palace of a deity figure. An example is the sand mandala shown in figure 2.1, in which the central box represents *Yamantaka,* a wrathful protector, which in turn is surrounded by representations of twelve attendants.

The other commonly used configuration is called either a merit field or a refuge tree. A merit field (Tib. *tsogs shing)* is a representation in tree form of the Three Jewels (Buddha, Dharma, Sangha) and the *lama,* along

Figure 2.1. Sand Mandala for 13-deity Yamantaka, Likir Monastery 2001. *Source:* Author's photo.

with that teaching's lineage holders (Skt. *Vidyadhara,* Tib. *rig 'dzin),* such as *lamas* and disciples, and Dharma protectors (Skt. *Dharmapāla,* Tib. *chos-kyong),* which are supernatural beings that possess great spiritual power. This arrangement shows the interconnectedness of the various groups depicted and is symbolic of the totality of the idealized universe. Both mandalas and merit fields are Pure Lands or blessed abodes presided over by the central figure. Figure 2.2 is a refuge tree centering on the

Figure 2.2. Gelugpa Merit Tree. Fair use.

founder of the Gelugpa sect, Lobzang Dragpa, known as Je Tsongkhapa, situated in the blessed realm known as Tushita, which is the abode of the bodhisattva of wisdom, Manjushri, of whom Tsongkhapa is said to be an emanation. (Segment of wikimedia.org/wikipedia/commons/6/6f/ Thanka_-_Google_Art_Project_(434620).jpg).

The imagery and rhetoric describing both mandala and merit field carry over into representations of secular rulers, conflating the spiritual with the temporal. Rural representations of the world order are similarly informed by these monastic conventions, as all levels of Ladakhi lay Buddhist society have long been engaged in various forms of ceremonial and/or honorific activities, which are reflected in the texts of the various song genres we will now examine. I would like to examine four genres that reflect the variety of Buddhist themes in their lyrics:

- Tendel lu (*rten 'brel glu*)—songs of auspicious signs from the village repertoire

- Zhung lu (*gzhung glu*)—congregational songs from the old royal court

- Bagston lu (*bag ston glu*)—marriage songs

- Chang lu (*chang glu*)—beer songs

Tendel Lu—Songs of Auspicious Signs

The songs known as *stendel lu* or *tendel lu* (*rten 'brel glu*) originate at the village level, and are sung in groups, male and female, according to AIR staff artist Tsering Chorol (figure 2.3) and danced to during festivities that mark any auspicious occasions: weddings, childbirths, the Losar New Year, etc. (personal comm., July 31, 2012). These are often women's circle dances, with the slow footwork and subtle repetitive hand gestures typical of female dances. The right hand is held out in front at face height, palm forward, then closed as if picking a flower, then turned toward the dancer, and opened palm up offering the flower to the Three Jewels (Buddha, Dharma, and Sangha).

The texts specifically lay out a hierarchy starting in the heavens and extending down to the level of the common household and then to dancers in a dance courtyard. The word *tendel* has two meanings. The

Figure 2.3. AIR staff artist Tsering Chorol playing *daman*. *Source*: Author's photo.

more common is "good circumstance"; the other a more philosophical one, often translated as "transformation."[1] However, the lyrics of the samples collected by Tashi Rabgias himself in LYL do not directly support the more complex philosophical meaning. Instead, they more directly point at *rten 'brel,* meaning good signs or auspicious circumstances. Let us look at an example, referred to by Tashi Rabgias as "The Five Auspicious Signs" *(Rten 'brel lnga pa)* (Track 06).

> *ya gi shed dgung gnam sngon mo dgung gnam bsod nams can*
>   *zhig (2x)*
> *nyi zla ni gnyis ka kun bzhugs pa'i dga' ba la gzigs ang*
> *rgyu skar 'dzoms po kun 'khor ba'i skyid nyams la gzigs*
> *dga' ba'i rten 'brel gyi dang po mar yul gyi gzhung du 'khyil*
> *zag med rten 'brel gyi dang po drug ma nang du 'khyil.*
> [Behold yon strong blue sky, that blessed sky! (2x)
> Behold both sun and moon sitting in joy!
> Happily, behold the many constellations all around!

The blessed perfect first auspicious sign surrounds the center
　　of Ladakh,
The stainless first auspicious sign circles in the six-columned
　　chamber.]

ya gi shed chos grva gru bzhi chos grva bsod nams can zhig (2x)
yar 'dren gyi bla ma kun bzhugs pa'i dga' ba la gzigs ang
bu slob 'dzoms po kun 'khor ba'i skyid nyams la gzigs
dga' ga'i rten 'brel gyi gnyis pa mar yul gyi zhungs du 'khyil
zag med rten 'brel gyi gnyis pa ka drug ma nang du 'khyil.
[Behold that strong, square, blessed Dharma debate court! (2x)
Behold the lama guides joyfully seated!
Behold the many disciples surrounding (him) in happiness!
The blessed perfect second auspicious omen surrounds the
　　center of Ladakh,
The stainless second auspicious omen circles in the six-
　　columned chamber.]

ya gi shed sku mkhar mthon po sku mkhar bsod nams can
　　zhig (2x)
mi chen gong ma kun bzhugs pa'i dga' ba la gzigs ang
drag zhan dzoms po kun 'khor ba'i skyid nyams la gzigs
dga' ba'i rten 'brel gyi gsum pa mar yul gyi gzhung du 'khyil
zag med rten 'brel gyi gsum pa ka drug ma nang du 'khyil.
[Behold in yon strong high fortress, the blessed fortress! (2x)
Behold the great lords joyfully seated there!
Behold all the high and low officials happily surrounding them!
The joyous third auspicious omen circles inside Ladakh.
Let us be mindful of the stainless third auspicious omen circling
　　inside the six-columned chamber.]

ya gi shed dpal khang gru bzhi dpal khang bsod nams can zhig (2x)
yab yum pa ma kun bzugs pa'i dga' ba la gzigs ang
gnyen drung 'dzoms po kun 'khor ba'i skyid nyams la gzigs
dga' ba'i rten 'brel gyi bzhi pa mar yul gyi gzhung du 'khyil
zag med rten 'brel gyi bzhi pa ka drug nang du 'khyil.
[Behold yon noble square house, that blessed house!
Behold our mothers and fathers joyfully sitting there!
Behold the many kin happily surrounding us!

The joyous fourth auspicious omen circles the center of Ladakh
Let us be mindful of the stainless fourth auspicious omen
    circling inside the six-columned chamber.]

ya gi shed do ra gru bzshi do ra bsod nams can zhig (2x)
rje dpon chen po kun bzhugs pa'i dga' ba la gzigs ang
ya do mdza' bo kun 'khor ba'i skyid nyams la gzigs
dga' ba'i rten 'brel gyi lnga pa mar yul gyi gzhung du 'khyil
zag med rten 'brel gyi lgna ka drug ma nang du 'khyil.
[Behold that strong blessed square stage! (2x)
Behold the great lord joyfully sitting there!
Behold the helpers happily surrounding him!
The joyous fifth auspicious omen circles the center of Ladakh
Let us be mindful of the stainless fifth auspicious omen circling
    inside the six-columned chamber. (LYL, 6)]

Zhung lu—Congregational Songs

The *zhung lu* (*gzhung glu*) or congregational songs were composed in honor
of the kings, famous lamas, and other distinguished people, or in praise
of *gonpas* and places of social or religious significance (Shakspo 2008:
32). Trewin notes how *zhung lu* are part of a long tradition going back to
early pre-Buddhist Tibet, with various songs recorded on old documents
described as resolving tensions by praising the good deeds of others. Of
the Ladakhi genres classified as *zhung lu*, some are praise songs, some
are *chos-glu* (Dharma songs) intended as dedications to lamas, along with
various genres to honor the kings. There exists a particular class of praise
songs, sung in honor of the king, *gying lu* (*'gying glu*), which draw upon
the poetic imagery of the Gesar Epic, and place the king at the center of
the world order (Trewin 1995, 95). However, the Gesar imagery is not
restricted to *gying lu* but is used in *zhung lu* as well.

Ladakhi scholar Ngawang Tsering Shakspo writes that *zhung lu* were
originally performed in the royal palace on *Losar*:

On New Year's Day all the participants, including the local
gentry, ministers, and all their relatives, would come to the
palace in Leh bearing *kha-btags* (white silk scarves) as a mark
of respect for the king.

> Later in the day they would all proceed to the *thekchen* (the ceremonial dancing ground). Here a balcony was provided for the king and all his important guests. The rest of the audience would be seated around the dancing ground in a hierarchy that depended on social status. The *kharmon,* the palace musicians, would begin playing the music. Both the musicians and the dancers would sing the *gzhung-glu.* On this occasion the dances would be performed by a number of specially selected women dancers called *takshosma.* They came from families who were traditionally obliged by royal decree to provide a dancer for such occasions. This seems to have been as much a right as duty since other people required their consent if they wanted to participate in the dancing. These dances lasted for hours since every stanza of the song was followed by long periods of only music. (Shakspo 2008, 34–35)

Since the overthrow of the Namgyal Dynasty and its being relegated to a small palace in the village of Stok, this tradition has been discontinued. However, the *zhung lu* are still performed by common people during *Losar.*

Several themes in *zhung lu* reflect various aspects of the Buddhist worldview. These include representations of Ladakhi kingship, representations of Buddhist meditational and devotional practice, and Ladakhi patriotism. The Ladakhi kings are portrayed in *zhung lu* as protectors of the faith, often identified as either Buddhist protectors or semi-divine saviors (Skt. *Bodhisattva,* Tib. *byang chug sems dpa).* Initially a pre-Buddhist warrior hero, the Gesar figure was co-opted by the Buddhist lamas and transformed into an emanation of the bodhisattva of compassion, Avalokiteśvara (Tib. *spyan ras gzigs* [pronounced Chenrezig]). Avalokiteśvara in turn is an emanation of the compassionate Buddha Amitabha who rules over the blessed realm of Sukhavati. This rhetoric is notable in songs dedicated to King Sengge Namgyal.

What we witness in these songs is a complex set of meanings, with overlapping and interweaving symbols of spiritual and temporal power (figure 2.4).

In the following song, "The Highest Happiness Merit" (Track 07), the Gesar episode of the four conquests has been adapted to apply to Sengge Namgyal. The fanciful list of youthful conquests is interpolated with appeals to the king as Chenrezig and protector of the Dharma.

Figure 2.4. The Matrix of Royal Power. *Source*: Author's photo.

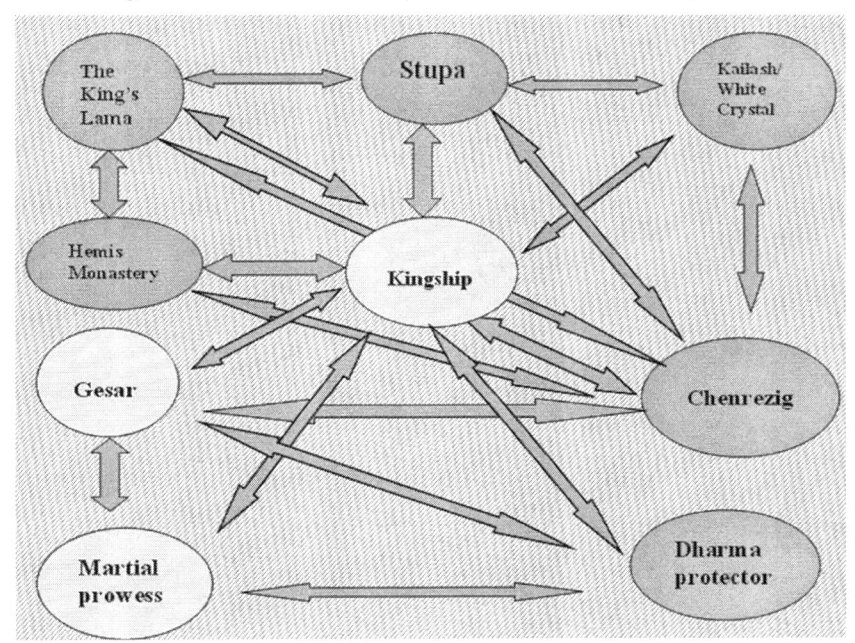

bsod nams mchog skyid (The Highest Happiness of Merit)

dang po bsod nams kyi mchog skyid po
bkra shis pa'i glu zheg len
sngar yang bsod nams kyi mchog skyid po
bkra shis pa'i glu zheg len.
[[to] the first highest merit, happiness,
Sing a song of auspiciousness.
Repeatedly [to] the happy blessing of merit
Sing a song of auspiciousness.]

gnya' khri btsan po yi gdung rgyud la
dpal bsam la lo 'dab rgyas (2x)
dpag bsam la lo 'dab po rgyas pa de ni.
[In Nyatri Tsanpo's lineage,
The leaves of the wish-fulfilling tree will blossom.[2] (2x)
The leaves of the wish-fulfilling tree will blossom.]

pa ma bzang po'i smon lam (2x)
tsan dan la lo 'dab po rgyas pa de ni
yab yum drang po'i smon lam.
[[It is] the good parents' prayer.
The sandalwood tree is growing.
[It is] the righteous parents' prayer.]

nyi ma dang bla ma dang pa ma gsum ga'i
sku drin po ci byas te 'khor (2x)
yab yum gnyis ka yi don de ru
ma ni bka' 'bum bzhengs
'di phyi gnyis ka yi don de la
yi ge ni drub ma bzhengs.
[The three: sun, lama, and parents—
How can I repay their kindness?[3] (2x)
For both my parents there,
Let 100,000 *manis*[4] arise.
In both this life and the next,
Let embroidered letters arise.]

nor bu de phyi na mi 'dug
nor bu de nang na 'dug
khyad nor de phyi na mi 'dug
khyad nor de nang na 'dug.
[It is not outside the jewel.
It is not inside the jewel.
It is not outside the chief wealth.
It is not inside the chief wealth.[5]]

nor bu de sa nang la stsal song zer na
sa gzhi po 'od kyis khengs
rin po che sa nang la stsal song zer na
nam mkha' po 'od kyis khengs.
[That jewel was said to be bestowed on the earth.
The earth was filled with light.
The precious one[6] was said to be bestowed on the earth.
The sky was filled with light.]

gong ma a lam kyi bdag po de
dbu 'phang lha bas mtho

chos rgyal ni ma rnam rgyal
dbu 'phang gnam las mtho.
[That highest king Alam[7]
Attains more glory than the gods.
The Dharma king most victorious
Attains glory in heaven.]

gso ma bzhengs pa'i sku mkhar pa'i nang na
a ma gces ma bzhugs
gso ma bzhengs pa yi sgo sgrig pa'i nang na
rma bya 'jol mo bzhugs.
[Inside the newly erected castle,[8]
His beloved mother lives.
Inside the newly erected gate put in place
The peacock[9] and nightingale[10] live.]

rma bya 'jol mo de bzhengs te
noo la dgongs pa stsal
rma bya 'jol mo de bzhengs te nas
tshul khrims la ngang ba stsal.
[The peacock and nightingale living there,
mind is bestowed on the prince.
By the peacock and nightingale arising
a swan[11] is bestowed on the virtuous one.]

noo yi dgung lo po bcu gcig pa'i nang la
la dvags kyi rgyal srid lon
tshul khrims kyi dgung lo po bcu gcig pa'i nang la
la dvags kyi rgyal srid lon.
[When the prince was eleven years old
The Ladakhi prince arrived.
When the virtuous one was eleven years old
The Ladakhi prince arrived.]

de dus thugs rje spyn rgyang nas gzigs shig
spyan ras gzigs kyi sprul pa mkhyen
de dus thugs rje spyan rgyang nas gzigs shel
'od gsal lha yi gdung rgyud mkhyen.
[Then looking around with compassion
Chenrezig, look at me with kindness.

Then looking around with compassion
Shining Deity of the Sky, see me.]

noo'i dgung lo po bcu gnyis pa'i nang la
bod rigs kyi nag bskor lon
tshui khrims kyi dgung lo po bcu gnyis pa'i nang la
bod rigs kyi nang bskor lon.
[When the boy was twelve years old
Tibet made offerings.
When the virtuous one was twelve years old
Tibet made offerings.]

de dus thgus rje spyan rgyang nas gzigs shig
spyan ras gzigs kyi sprul pa mkhyen
de dus thugs rje spyan rgyang nas gzigs shig
'od gsal lha yi gdung rgud mkhyen.
[Then looking around with compassion
Chenrezig, look at me with kindness.
Then looking around with compassion
`Shining Deity of the Sky, see me.]

noo'i dgung lo po bcu gsum pa'i nang la
kha che yul gzhungs gsum lon
tshul khrims kyi dgung lo po bcu gsum pa'i nang la
kha che yul gzhung gsum lon.
[When the prince was thirteen years old
Kashmir sent three kinds (of offerings)
When the virtuous one was thirteen years old
Kashmir sent three kinds (of offerings).]

de dus thugs rje spyan rgyang nas gzigs shig
spyan ras gzigs kyi sprul pa mkhyen
de dus thugs rje spyan rgyan nas gzigs shig
'od gsal lha yi gdung rgyud mkhyen.
[Then looking around with compassion
Chenrezig, look at me with kindness.
Then looking around with compassion
Shining Deity of the Sky, see me.]

What we see is a double legitimization of the king's authority: from the secular side by descent from the Tibetan Yarlung Dynasty, and identification with Gesar/Chenrezig on the religious side. As has been noted, the Gesar identity has multiple dimensions as a symbol of martial prowess, supernatural and spiritual power, and further links to Tibetan kingship. The rhetoric of tantric visualization is invoked in the generation of the mind of gratitude[12] to the triple nurturing of the sun, the parents, and the lama, followed by invocation of the mantra of Chenrezig. In effect this song is a visualization ritual (Skt. *Sadhanā*, Tib. *sgrub thabs*). The king, audience, singers, and dancers are participating in a communion, with an internalization of the imagery, as is common in such visualization yoga. The practitioner either becomes that figure or visualizes the object of meditation as being in their heart, on their head, or in front of them. In the following song, the listeners are explicitly told to offer praise (track 08).

bstod pa zhig 'bul (Offer Praise)

bstod pa zhig 'bul ang bstod pa zhig 'bul ang.
chos grva gru bzhi la bstod pa zhig 'bul ang.
dga' ba la gzigs ang yar 'dren gyi bla ma.
skyid nyams la gzigs ang lags bu slob 'dzoms po.
[Offer praise, offer praise.
To the square Dharma court, offer praise.
Behold with joy, the lama guide.
Behold with happiness, the gathered disciples.]

bstod pa zhig 'bul ang bstod pa zhig 'bul ang.
sku mkhar mthon po la bstod pa zhig 'bul ang.
dga' ba la gzigs ang mi chen gyi gong ma.
skyid nyams al gzigs ang drag zhan gyi 'dzom po.
[Offer praise, offer praise.
To the high castle, offer praise.
Behold with joy, the ancestors of the great lord.
Behold with happiness, the gathered officials.]

bstod pa zhig 'bul ang bstod pa zhig 'bul ang.
dpal khang gru bzhi bstod pa zhig 'bul ang.
dga' ba la gzigs ang yab yum gyi pa ma.
skyid nyams la gzigs ang lags ya do dang mdza' bo.

[Offer praise, offer praise.
To the square noble house, offer praise.
Behold with joy, the fathers and mothers of the parents.
Behold with happiness, the gathered helpers.]

ru thog kyung ru po mar dkar gyi 'brang rgyas.
khyung ru smug chung po mar dkar gyi 'brang rgyas.
la dvags kyi lha dmag de rtsi gu'i mar gyi rdzing bu.
Sengge rNam rgyal po rtsi gu'i mar gyi rdzing bu.
dga' ba la gzigs ang la dvags kyi lha dmag.
skyid nyams la gzigs ang Sengge rNam rgyal.
[Fort Garuda[13] Horn (is) a *'brang rgyas*[14] of white butter.
The small, dark Garuda Horn's *'brang rgyas*.
This Ladakhi army of deities (is) a pool of apricot seed oil.[15]
Sengge Namgyal (is) a pool of apricot seed oil.
Behold with joy, Ladakh's army of deities.
Behold with happiness, Sengge Namgyal.]

ru thog khyung ru po lcags dkar gyi rta sgo.
khyung ru smug chung po lcags dkar gyi rta sgo.
la dvags gas kyi lha dmag po pho lad (ngar lcags) kyi sgo gtan.
Sengge rNam rgyal po pho lad kyi sgo gtan.
dga' ba la gzigs ang la dvags kyi lha dmag.
skyid nyams la gzigs ang Sengge rNam rgyal.
[Fort Garuda Horn[is] a saddle of white metal,
The small, dark Garuda Horn's saddle is of white metal.
The Ladakhi chasm's army of deities' saddle is of steel,
King Sengge Namgyal's iron saddle.
Behold with joy Ladakh's army of deities.
Behold with happiness Sengge Namgyal.]

ru thog khyung ru po lha hor gyi du bag. (me mda')
khyung ru smug chung po la' hor gyi du bag.
la dvags kyi lha dmag de dmag chos kyi 'dzoms po.
sengge rnam rgyal de dmag chos kyi 'dzoms po.
dga' ba la gzigs ang la dvags kyi lha dmag.
skyid nyams la gzigs ang Sengge rNam rgyal.
[Fort Garuda Horn [is] Lahore's gun
The small, dark Garuda Horn

This Ladakhi army of deities is a gathered Dharma army.
Sengge Namgyal is the gatherer of the Dharma army.
Behold with joy Ladakh's army of deities.
Behold with happiness Sengge Namgyal.]

ru thog khyung ru po rta chos kyi 'dzoms po.
khyung ru smug de rta chos kyi 'dzoms po.
la dvags kyi lha dmag de rta pa yi me 'bar.
Sengge rNam rgyal de rta pa yi me 'bar.
dga' ba la gzigs ang la dvags kyi lha dmag.
skyid nyams la gzigs ang Sengge rNam gyal.
[Fort Garuda Horn [is] the gathered Dharma horses.
This dark Garuda Horn is a gathering of Dharma horses.
This Ladakhi army of deities' cavalry's guns,
Sengge Namgyal's cavalry's guns.
Behold with joy Ladakh's army of deities.
Behold with happiness Sengge Namgyal.]

ru thog kyung ru po bal 'jam gyi yun bu.
la dvags kyi lha dmag de skya phrug gi legs po.
Sengge rNam rgyal de skya phrug gi legs po.
dga' ba la gzigs ang la dvags kyi lha dmag.
skyid nyams la gzigs ang Sengge rNam rgyal.
[Fort Garuda Horn [is] of soft wool [yun bu]
This Ladakhi army of deities [is] the good of a young magpie.
This Ladakhi army of deities [is] the good of a young magpie.
Sengge Namgyal [is] the good of a young magpie.
Behold with joy Ladakh's army of deities.
Behold with happiness Sengge Namgyal. (LYL, 63–66)]

Other songs are informed by other meditational practices, such as the mandala offering. According to the noted Buddhist scholar and Tibetan translator Alexander Berzin, practitioners may engage in what is called offering of an outer mandala (*phyi'i dkyil-'khor*), which is a representation of a world system offered to a spiritual guide (Berzin 2003).

Berzin goes on to note that the world system represented consists of a system having four island-continents around Mount Meru in the center, with each island-continent having two smaller islands flanking it on the side facing away from Mount Meru (Berzin 2003).

Mount Meru or Sumeru is a legendary mountain in Hindu and Buddhist cosmology. It is sometimes replaced in the cosmology by the real-world Mount Kailash, which also has divine associations in Hinduism, Buddhism, Bon, and Jainism. It is said by the Hindus to be the abode of Lord Shiva and his consort Parvati. The Buddhists considered it to be the abode of the Buddha Demchok (Skt. *Chakrasamvara*) who represents supreme bliss.[16]

Mount Kailash has various attributes in the mythology of the region. In Tibetan the mountain is called *Gangs Rinpoche* (Precious Snow) or *Tise* (from the old Bon liturgical language Zhang Zhung, meaning "water peak"). *Kailāśā* means "crystal" in Sanskrit (Das 1902, 32). The crystal imagery is used in the song "Mt. Kailash's White Crystal Stupa," where the mountain is topped by a white crystal reliquary shrine or stupa (Tib. *Chorten*). White crystal is often used as a symbol for Chenrezig, who is frequently depicted with a white crystal rosary or represented by a white stupa.

In the *zhung lu* "*Tise shel dkar chod rten*" (The Crystal Stupa of Mt. Kailash) (Track 09) this cosmology is laid out quite clearly. In the second verse the reference to "storehouse of all types of grain" evokes the meditative practice of a mandala offering, in which rice is piled in a series of stacked circular vessels to represent the visualized world. In the text the sacred mountain and lake, Buddhist pilgrimage sites, are described in metaphysical terms. The area of Purang in Western Tibet was contested by Ladakh and Tibet during the late sixteenth and seventeenth centuries, but this poem shows no ambivalence, referring to Tibet, "the land of snows," as a holy place where "we are happy as gods."

Ti se'i shel dkhar mcod rten (The Crystal Stupa of Mt. Kailash)
ti se'i shel dkar mcod rten,
'dzam bu gling gi lte ba. (2x)
nang de na nang rten bzhugs yod.
ma rig mun pa kun sel
chos sku sang ba mtha' yas bzhugs
ma rig mun pa kun sel.
[The crystal stupa of Mt. Kailash,
The hub of the continent Jambudvipa. (2x)
When a religious relic resides inside there,
It dispels the darkness of ignorance.
The eternal, secret, Dharma body is there,
dispelling the darkness of ignorance.]

ti se'i g.yu mtso sngon mo,
klu rgyal 'jog po'i pho brang. (2x)
gcig tu rgyal nams yongs kyi,
'bru sna'i bang mdzod 'khyil.
spu rangs la lung chen mo'i,
ser mo nas kyi bang mdzod 'kyil.
[The blue, turquoise lake of Mt. Kailash,
Mansion of the naga king, Takshaka, (2x)
All together the kings come,
Around the storehouse of all types of grain,
To Purang, around the treasury
of the great valley's yellow barley.]

kha ba can gyi zhing khams de ni,
bde skyid lha dang mnyam 'byung. (2x)
[In the realm of the land of snow,
We become as happy as gods.] (LYL, 67–68)

Similarly, "The Hill Behind Red Rock Peak" uses the white crystal stupa image as a comparison to the meditation hut of one's root (true or principal) lama. The singers generate an aspiration for all those that help them to be reborn in the blessed realm of Guru Padmasambhava (Track 10).

gyab ri brag dmar gyi tse mo (The Hill Behind Red Rock Peak)
rgyab ri brag dmar gyi rtse mo de,
rtse mo shel dkar gyi mchod rten, (2x)
rtsa ba'i bla ma yi mthsams khang dang 'dra,
skyabs mgon ye shes kyi mtshams khang dang 'dra.
[That hill behind Red Rock Peak,
The white crystal stupa, (2x)
Is like the root lama's hermitage hut,
Is like the wisdom protector's hermitage hut.]

bdag cag 'gro ba rigs drug kun,
thugs rje lcags kyus zhungs shig,
drin can rtsa ba yi bla ma de mkhyen. (2x)
[We the six realms of sentient beings,[17]
Are in the center of the hook of compassion,[18]
Thanks to the kind root lama guide. (2x)]

nga dang ya do tshang ga pha ma mi gcig pa'i spun zla,
nga dang ya do tshang ga yab yum mi gcig pa'i spun zla,
zangs mdog dpal gyi ri bo ru skye ba shog cig. (2x)
[I and those that help, father and mother, people of the same
  family,
I and those that help, father and mother, people of the same
  family,
May we be reborn on the Copper Colored Mountain.[19] (2x)]

sa de mi yul gzhung na men rtse tshon sna 'dzoms po,
sa de dbu gtsang gzhung na men rtse tshon sna 'dzoms po,
tsa ba'i bla ma yi na bza' la 'bul,
skyabs mgon ye shes kyi na bza' 'bul.
[In that earth, my homeland, is a perfect many-colored top
  ornament[20],
In that earth in U Tsang[21] is a perfect many-colored top
  ornament,
I make offering to the root lama's robes.
I make offerings to the wisdom protector's robes. (LYL, 74–75)]

As was noted earlier, the Ladakhi royal dynasty claimed to be the
heirs of the Yarlung Dynasty after the disintegration of the Tibetan Empire
in the tenth century. Political fragmentation and conflict in Tibet continued
up until the mid-seventeenth-century re-unification under the Fifth Dalai
Lama and the Qosot Mongols under Gushri Khan.

Despite constant struggle in the sixteenth and seventeenth centuries between Ladakh and Tibet, the educated Ladakhi elite continued to
represent Tibet as a place of reverence and pilgrimage, with Ladakhis
traveling vast distances to circumambulate not only specific shrines, but
the entire city of Lhasa. The ambivalence of the Ladakhis toward Tibet
is shown in various songs, such as the following which demonstrates an
abiding loyalty to their homeland (track 11).

lha sa'i skor lam phra mo—Lhasa's Narrow Circumambulation Road

lha sa'i skor lam phra mo na mi tshogs mang tsam 'dug (2x)
skyes pa'i pha yul gyi mi po na chen gser las dkon'
gle chen dpal khang gi mi po rin chen gser las dkon.
[There are many crowds on Lhasa's narrow circumambulation
  road, (2x)

The great man from the land of my birth does golden work,
The great, precious man from great Leh's palace does golden
    work.]

chu de chu sna 'dzoms po mi yul gyi gzhung na 'dug,
chu de chu sna 'dzoms po lha sa yi gzhung na 'dug,
chang de a rag bdud tsi rang gi yul na 'dug,
skyems grang a rag bdud tsi gle chen dpal khang na 'dug.
[There is that perfect type of water in the homeland's center,
There is that perfect type of water in the center of Lhasa,
There is *chang, arak,* nectar in my own country,
There is cold, honored *chang* in great Leh's palace.]

rtsva de rtsva sna 'dzoms po mi yul gyi gzhung na 'dug,
rtsva de rtsva sna 'dzoms po lha sa yi gzhung na 'dug,
rtsva de rtsva sna 'dzoms po rang gi yul na 'dug,
rtsva de rtsva sna 'dzoms po gle chen dpal khang na 'dug.
[There is that perfect type of grass in the homeland's center,
There is that perfect type of grass in Lhasa's center,
There is that perfect type of grass in my own homeland,
There is that perfect type of grass in great Leh's center.]

shing de shing sna 'dzoms po mi yul gyi gzhung na 'dug,
shing de shing sna 'dzoms po lha sa yi gzhung na 'dug,
rigs bzangs lha shing shug pa rang gi yul na 'dug,
rigs bzang lha shug pa gle chen pal khang na 'dug.
[There is that perfect type of tree in my homeland's center,
There is that perfect type of tree in Lhasa's center,
There is the god cypress tree in my own land,
There is the god cypress tree in great Leh's palace.] (LYL, 73)

Bagston Lu—Wedding Songs

Wedding songs, or *bagston lu* (*bag ston glu*), offer a complex picture of
the common people's traditional worldview. The imagery is a mixture of
pre-Buddhist and Buddhist concepts, often conflated, as is characteristic
of Vajrayana Buddhism, and we see various contradictions between high
and small traditions in the observance of Buddhism in Ladakhi village life
very clearly illustrated in *bagston lu*. For example, the importance of beer

and drinking in Ladakhi culture in general contradicts injunctions against intoxication, although they are more strictly proscribed for monastics.

Other songs are sung by participants in rituals that stretch over weeks or months, beginning with the negotiations of dowry and bride price, which are basically beer songs meant to diffuse tensions in the negotiations. During the actual wedding there are mock battles over fetching the bride, other songs welcoming the bride to her husband's household, and so on (Ribbach 1985; Francke 1901, 1923).

It should be noted that marriage is not a religious sacrament in Buddhism, and clerical participation is not a prerequisite. Many of these songs are very close to liturgical in nature, invoking blessings on the participants; they are in part the domain of village song specialists called *nyer pon*,[22] although some are sung in groups by members of the wedding party that may know them. These blessing songs are collectively known as *tashispa lu* (bkra shis pa glu), or songs of auspiciousness because they begin with the formula, *om bkra shis par gyur cig. bkra shis bde legs dan ldan par gyur cig.*[23] The *nyer pon* might also lead songs to which people may dance at various points, either the groom's attendants or the wedding guests.

For example, during what Tashi Rabgias calls the "Mother's Libations Song," guests are welcomed with beer offerings made by the groom's mother to various universal and local deities by flicking drops of beer from the listeners' cups. Its invocation of blessings puts it into the category of a *tashispa lu,* and it would be sung by the *nyer pon.*

Prominent in the song are the *dakinis* (Tib. *mkha'dro*), female bodhisattvas that bestow wisdom and in part function like fairy godmothers: teaching, protecting, and at times chastising. *Dakinis* are a female embodiment of enlightenment energy and envisioned as "mothers" (guiding teacher) of the *nagas* (subterranean and/or water spirits). Offerings are also made to Indra, who was chief of the gods in the Vedic Hindu pantheon, co-opted as a significant guardian figure in Mahayana and Vajrayana mythology. These deities, in addition to the mother goddess of local *tsan* demons, are requested to avert misfortune from the celebrants and deflect it onto their enemies—a practical, if uncharitably non-Buddhist sentiment (track 12).

a ma'i dkar 'chol du—The Mother's Libation
Om bkra shis par gyur cig.
bkra shis bde legs dang ldan par gyur cig.
[Om, may there be auspiciousness.
May it be auspicious.]

lha gzhig gsol ma dan mkha' 'dro'i mchod
lha yi dbang po brgya byin zhal du mchod
la ru kha char bu yug ma stsal cig
kha char bu yug kun sdang ba'i dgra stsal.
[A god makes offering to the offering goddess/dakini.
I supplicate the sage of the gods, Indra of the hundred sacrifices.
May they not bestow rain and snowstorm over the passes.
May they bestow rain and snowstorm on angry enemies.]

btsan zhig gsol lo ma dang mkha' 'gro'i tshogs
btsan gyi a ma skyabs sbyin zhal du mchod
mi la snyun gzhi mgur cham ma stsal cig
snyun gzhi mgur cham kun sdang ba'i la stsal.
[One demon request of the assembly of dakinis
I supplicate the demon's blessed protective mother.
May they not bestow the pervasive four afflictions on people.
May they bestow the four affictions on our enemies.]

klu zhig gsol lo ma dang mkha' 'gro'i tshogs
klu yi ma dros gzi can zhal du mchod
rta la rgyu srin glang 'thab ma stsal cig
rgyu srin glang thabs kun sdang ba'i dgral stsal.
[The assembly of leaves and dakinis was requested by the
    nagas.
I supplicate the *naga* of the bright lake.
May they not bestow intestinal worms and stomach pains on
    the horses.
May they bestow intestinal worms and stomach pains on our
    enemies.]

mkhar ram gang du bzhugs pa'i rtse lha mchod
yul lam gang du bzhugs pa'i yul lha mchod
sa cha 'di la gnas pa'i gshi bdag mchod
gnya' bo spun dgu la skyob pa'i rabs lha mchod.
[I supplicate the god living in the high castle.
I supplicate the village god living in village and road.
I supplicate the protective god inhabiting the earth to this place.
I supplicate the protective god of the nine bride's attendant
    kin.] (LYL, 17–18).

What we see in this song is an invocation to all the deities in the environment: castle, village, road, and fields. The *nagas*, or local earth spirits, must be propitiated during weddings with offerings of *chang* (barley beer), as shown in the following song, offering beer to the whole world.

All my informants were unsure about how the generic blessing song (*bra shis pa'i* glu) melody, based on couplets, fits in with the three-line verse scheme of this text. The fact that the text ends with a quatrain adds to the mystery.

dkar 'chol spyir btang gi glu—Universal Libation song (LYL, 18–19)

Om bkra shis par gyur cig.
bkra shis bde legs dang ldan par gyur cig.
[Om may it be auspicious.
May it be auspicious.]

gser skyems gtsang ma zhig phud na mnyams par
gser skyems gtsang ma zhig steng gi lha la mchod
lha yi dbang po brgya byin zhal du mchod.
[All the golden *chang* is gathered as an offering.
All the golden *chang* is offered to the gods of the earth's surface.
I supplicate the sage of the gods, Indra of the hundred sacrifices.]

gser skyems gtsang ma zhig phud na ma nyams par
gser skyems gtsang ma zhig bar gyi btsan la mchod
btsan gyi a ma skyabs spyin zhal du mchod.
[All the golden *chang* is gathered as an offering.
All the golden *chang* is offered to the subterranean dakinis.
I supplicate the face of the mother of dakinis bestowing refuge.]

gser skyems gtsang ma zhig phud nas ma nyams par
gser skyems gtsang ma zhig 'og gi klu ma mchod
klu yi ma dro gzi can zhal du mchod.
[All the golden *chang* is gathered as an offering.
All the golden *chang* is offered to the dakinis above the earth.
I supplicate the face of the nagas' majestic mother dakini.]

mkhar ram gang du bzhugs pa'i rtse lha mchod
yul lam gang du bzhugs pa'i yul lha mchod

sa cha 'di la gsa pa'i gzhi bdag mchod
gnya' bo mi rta la skyob pa'i rabs lha mchod.
[I supplicate the god living in the high castle or anywhere else.
I supplicate the god living in the village or anywhere else.
Offering to the protective god inhabiting the earth to this place
Offering to the protective god of the bride's attendant kin.]

Pre-Buddhist traits are notable in the song contests known as "door songs" (*sgo lu*) (Francke 1923; Ribbach 1985). In a "door song," five friends of the groom, known as *nyao-pa* or *nyo-pa* (the word can also mean "witness") come to "purchase" the bride. This is one part of a marriage that is still viewed as iconic by contemporary Ladakhis, even if the ceremony is only a one-day affair. As described by Ribbach[24] in the early twentieth century, the bride's party is barricaded in the house and demands proof of the purchaser's identity. The *nyao-pa*

> claimed to be the sons of the gods of the high glacial mountains. The people in the house were suspicious. According to them no one could escape from that kingdom because it is guarded in all four heavenly directions (above, below, on the right and left) by four female animals. The guards are the white lioness with the turquoise mane (*senge dkar-mo gyu-ral-can*) above on the glacier, Goldeye the [female] fish (*nya-mo gser-mig*) below in the glacial stream, the queen of the wild birds (*bya-rgyal rgod-mo*) on the cliffs to the right and the giant tigress (*rgya-stag k'ra-mo*) in the sandalwood forest to the left. (Ribbach 1985, 65)

Sometimes the differences between pre-Buddhist and Buddhist cosmology are blurred, as in the following song listing Dharma protectors of the four directions as witnesses to and protectors of the wedding. These songs are sung by the *nyo pa,* who symbolize the Dharma protectors.[25]

tho glu—List Song (no melody known to my informants)
[Question] Is it not a miracle, this witness that appeared?
You came while whatever comes may come.
You go while whatever goes may go.
[Answer] I came, came from the East.
I go there to the North, to the realm of Orgyan.[26]

[Question] Since you come from the East,
What is the Eastern king like?
What are the servants like around him?
What are their manner and dress like?
[Answer] Since I come from the East,
The Eastern king is "He Who Guards the Country".
The servants around him are dressed in joy of the Dharma.
Their manner is like tattva[27]
If they question, they are inner questions.
I have unaffected speech.
[Question] Since you come from the South,
What is the Southern king like?
What are the servants like around him?
What are their manner and dress like?
[Answer] Since I come from the South,
The Southern king is "The High and Low One."
The servants around him are dressed in joy of the Dharma.
Their manner is like tattva.
If they question, they are inner questions.
I have unaffected speech.
[Question] Since you come from the North,
What is the Northern king like?
What are the servants like around him?
What are their manner and dress like?
[Answer] Since I come from the North,
The Northern king is "Watching Good People."
The servants around him are dressed in joy of the Dharma.
Their manner is like tattva.
If they question, they are inner questions.
I have unaffected speech.
[Question] Since you come from the West,
What is the Western king like?
What are the servants like around him?
What are their manner and dress like?
[Answer] Since I come from the West,
The Western king is "Son of Perfect Hearing."
The servants around him are dressed in joy of the Dharma.
Their manner is like tattva.
If they question, they are inner questions.
I have unaffected speech. (LYL, 38–40)

The question-and-answer format is quite common in Ladakhi songs, especially with the response coming either from or looking at phenomena of the four directions—again situating the listeners in the center of a mandala, specifically Orgyan, the mystical abode of Guru Padmasambhava, known also as Guru Rinpoche (the precious guru) who occupies a special place as one of the founders of Tibetan Buddhism. The kings are each surrounded by attendants dressed in joy of the Dharma, their manner conveying the meaning of ultimate reality. Drawing from the pre-Buddhist tradition, the singer professes his purity, claiming unaffected speech (cf. Francke 1901, 1923; Ribbach 1985).

Chang lu—Beer Songs

Chang (barley beer) occupies a significant place in lay Ladakhi culture, with a major portion of the barley crop traditionally going toward its production. Singing occupies an integral part of drinking bouts, both for entertainment and to diffuse conflicts brought about by lowering of inhibitions (Shakspo 2008, 58). These drinking bouts can be either exclusively male, or with men and women sitting on opposite sides of the kitchen that are the gathering place (*dzom sa*) in traditional Ladakhi homes—women traditionally both prepare and serve *chang*. The harsh Ladakhi winters are particularly a time when such sedentary activities occur.[28]

Many songs are about how the beer is made, and in many *chang* is described as *dud tsi* (*bdud-rtsi*), the nectar of the gods. Divine attributions notwithstanding, Ladakhis have had to reconcile strict Dharma practice which prohibits intoxication with the realities of lay life. The following song is a typical expression of this ambivalence (LYL, 55–58). It is sung to a sprightly dancelike tune in a seven-beat meter, broken into repetitive couplets (Track 13).

dri ba dri lan—Question and Answer
dri ba: chang ngas ni mi 'thung dgung la cha'in.
dgung sngon pang du len na chang yang 'thung.
[Question: I do not drink *chang*, I will fly into the sky.[29]
When the blue sky takes me in her lap, then I will drink *chang*.]

lan: dgung sngon pang du len mkhan nyi zla gnyis ka.
nyi zla gnyis ka dang 'o skol 'dra mdog med.

o los de 'dra rang ma gsungs skyems gang mchod.
gzhon pas de 'dra rang ma gsungs skyems gang mchod.
[Answer: The ones taken in heaven's lap are both the sun and
   moon.
We cannot compare ourselves with both the sun and moon.
O surely, don't talk like that; drink *chang*.
Oh, young one, don't talk like that; drink *chang*.]

dri ba: chang ngas ni mi 'thung brag la cha'in.
brag la phur pa rol na chang yang 'thung.
[Question: I do not drink *chang*, I will go to the cliff.
When I pierce the boulder with the *phurba*[30], I will drink *chang*.]

lan: brag la phur pa rol mkhan yar 'dren bla ma.
yar 'dren bla ma dang 'o skol 'dra mdog med.
o los de 'dra rang ma gsungs skyems gan mchod.
gzhon pas de 'dra rang ma gsungs skyems gang mchod.
[Answer: The one who pierces the boulder with the *phurba*
   is the lama guide.
We cannot compare with the lama guide
Oh surely, don't talk like that; drink *chang*.
Oh, young one don't talk like that; drink *chang*.]

dri ba: chang ngas ni mi 'thung chu la cha'in.
chu la lan bu lhas na chang yang 'thung.
[Question: I don't drink chang, I will braid the water.
When I am braiding the water, then I will drink chang.]

lan: chu la lan bu lhas mkhan nya chung gser mig.
nya chung gser mig dang 'o skol 'dra mdog med.
o los de 'dra rang ma gsungs skyems gang mchod.
gzhon pas de 'dra rang ma gsungs skyems gang mchod.
[Answer: One who braids the water is the little fish with the
   golden eye,
We can't compare ourselves with the little fish with the golden
   eye.
Oh surely, don't talk like that; drink *chang*.
Oh, young one, don't talk like that; drink *chang*.]

dri ba: chang ni mi 'thung spang la cha'in.
spang la me thog rol na chang yang 'thung.
[Question: I don't drink *chang;* I will go to the meadow.
When the meadow flowers bloom, I will then drink the *chang.*]

lan: spang la me thog rol mkhan dbyar zla gsum.
dbyar zla gsum po dang 'o skol 'dra mdog med.
o los de 'dra rang ma gsungs skyems gang mchod.
gzhon pas de 'dra rang ma gsungs skyems gang mchod.
[Answer: That which makes meadow flowers is the three
    summer months,
We can't compare ourselves with the three summer months.
Oh surely, don't talk like that; drink *chang.*
Oh, young one, don't talk like that; drink *chang.*]

dri ba: gser gyi gser skyogs kham pa de.
khyad nor de 'dra byung na chang yang 'thung.
[Question: That bluish gold ladle,
When I obtain that special treasure, then I will drink chang.]

lan: gser gyi gser skyogs kham pa de,
tsong dpon chen po gcig gi phyag na yod.
'o skol len du chas na sa thag ring.
'o skol nyo ru chas na ring thang che.
o los de 'dra rang ma gsungs skyems gang mchod.
gzhon pas de 'dra rang ma gsungs skyems gang mchod.
[Answer: That bluish gold ladle,
It is in the hand of a great master merchant,
When we are bringing it in a distant place,
Then we are buying it in a distant town,
Oh surely, don't talk like that; drink *chang.*
Oh, young one, don't talk like that; drink *chang.*]

dri ba: dza ti dmar po'i bag phor 'khyongs.
khyad nor de 'dra byung na chang yang 'thung.
[Question: You are bringing the groom's cup of red nutmeg
    wood;
When I obtain that special treasure, then I will drink *chang.*]

lan: dza ti dmar po'i pag phor de.
tsong dpon chen po zhig gi phyag na yod.
'o skol len du chas na sa thag ring.
'o skol nyo ru chas na rin thang che.
o los de 'dra rang ma gsungs skyems gang mchod.
gzhon pas de 'dra rang ma gsungs skyems gang mchod.
[Answer: That groom's cup of red nutmeg wood,
Is in the hand of a great master merchant,
When we are bringing it in a distant place,
Then we are buying it in a distant town,
Oh surely, don't talk like that; drink *chang.*
Oh, young one don't talk like that; drink *chang.*]

dri ba: tsan dan dmar po'i gsol cog 'khyongs.
khyad nor de 'dra zhig byung na chang yang 'thung.
[Question: You are bringing the table of red sandalwood.
When I obtain that special treasure, then I will drink *chang.*]

lan: tsan dan dmar po'i gsrol cog de.
shing mkhan mkhas pa zhig gi phyag na yod.
'o skol len du chas na sa thag ring.
'o skol nyo ru chas na ring thang che.
o los de 'dra rang ma gsung skyems gang mchod.
gzhon pas de 'dra rang ma gsungs skyems gang mchod.
[Answer: That table of red sandalwood
Is in the hand of a master carpenter's hand,
When we are bringing it in a distant place,
Then we are buying it in a distant town,
Oh surely, don't talk like that; drink *chang.*
Oh, young one, don't talk like that; drink *chang.*]

The singers are stating their contentment with the life of a layman, not seeking yogic attainment, not seeking riches. Drinking and having a good time are what matters.

The mandala or merit field format is occasionally used as well, although in a more diffuse form as shown in the song Tashi Rabgias calls "The Field of the God of the Blue Sky." It makes mentions of the wedding witnesses or *nya-bo,* so this also might be classified as a *bagston lu.* Nevertheless, the focus of the song is the drink.

dgung sngon po lha yi 'char gzhi—The Field of the God of the Blue Sky

A blue sky is like the spreading field of the god.

A high blue sky is like the spreading field of a fine lady.

Both the sun and moon are like a newly made white crystal offering cake.

The gathered stars are like a lovely display in a treasury. (2x)

We witnesses will be glad to take hold of the honored drink.

The nine witnessing kin will be glad to take hold of the honored drink.

A high castle is like the spreading field of the god. (2x)

A high adorned castle is like a lovely, spreading field.

A great old drink is like a newly made white crystal offering cake.

We witnesses will be glad to take hold of the honored drink.

The nine witnessing kin will be glad to take hold of the honored drink.

A high, empty meadow is like the spreading field of the god.

A high, adorned meadow is like a lovely spreading field.

A little black yak calf is like a newly made white crystal offering cake. (2x)

A herd of small yak calves is like a lovely display in a treasury.

We witnesses will be glad to take hold of the honored drink.

A high lake is like the spreading field of the god.

A golden eyed female fish is like a newly made white crystal offering cake. (2x)

An assembly of little messengers is like a lovely display in a treasury.

We witnesses will be glad to take hold of the honored drink.

The nine witnessing kin will be glad to take hold of the honored drink.

A square main house is like the spreading field of the god.

A happy square house is like a lovely, spreading field.

The parents are like a newly made white crystal offering cake.

The gathered kin are like a lovely display in a treasury.

We witnesses will be glad to take hold of the honored drink.

The nine witnessing kin will be glad to take hold of the honored drink. (LYL, 51–53)

Common with the *tendel lu, bagston lu,* and *zhung lu,* we have a mandala arrangement, although it is more specific to a rural Ladakhi setting, with a descending hierarchy of sky, castle, meadow, lake, and family house. The hierarchy differs from that of the *tendel lu* and *chang lu,* in that it is not an entirely social hierarchy, and does not explicitly reference Buddhism or Buddhist practice. The imagery is more nature-oriented, pre-Buddhist cosmology, with the concepts of the *drang-gyas* offering cake and white crystal prominent. Each level is occupied by its principal inhabitants with surrounding attendants. The reverence toward *chang* as an almost sanctified offering is a blending of Buddhist and Bonpo views.

Conclusions

Vajrayana Buddhism in Ladakh is a syncretic adaptation of Indigenous Himalayan religion by Tantric Buddhism. As such, we can characterize the religious content in these songs as having a varying emphasis on Indigenous/pre-Buddhist or Buddhist elements, with the two often inextricably intertwined. Much of the variability is related to the function of the songs, as well as the probable degree of formal Buddhist education of the composers/poets and audience. In the courtly *zhung lu* examples there are *sadhana*-like descriptions of a mandala hierarchy, mixed with pre-Buddhist elements relating to numinous entities such as the guardian animals.

The *tendel lu* are more straightforwardly Buddhist in their content, with no significant pre-Buddhist elements. The language and concepts are simpler, describing a simple hierarchical mandala progressing from sky, to monastery, to palace, to family home, to dance stage—from the universe down to the individual. Again, this is a typical mandala visualization progression. The meaning of *tendel* is a less sophisticated, more conventional one, as opposed to the subtle, ontological meaning of high Buddhist philosophy.

The *bagston lu* present the most complex picture, depending on what ritual stage a song is for. They vary from pure mandala visualizations that function as blessings, to the pre-Buddhist depictions of cosmology and the spiritual matrix in which people are situated. Many of the latter involve describing and propitiating local numina: demons, nature spirits/deities, as well as Buddhist figures that interact with them. In addition, these offerings often involve *chang,* a problematic substance for orthodox Buddhists.

The Buddhism/beer dichotomy comes to a head in the *chang lu,* whose raison d'être is drinking. A number of the songs recognize that it is impossible to follow a dedicated Buddhist asceticism and party at the same time, yet they mention the attainments of Buddhist yogins and equate *chang* with the food of the gods. Similarly, some *chang lu* will lay out a mandala focused more on the rural environment and its human and numinous inhabitants, propitiating the latter. There is no attempt at fully justifying *chang* from the point of view of high religion. This is lay life embedded in the matrix of the universe.

Figure 3.1. Map of Ladakh Trade Routes to Turkestan. *Source*: Barkley 1871. Public domain.

Chapter 3

Music in Muslim Communities

At Home and on the Silk Road

The various Muslim communities in Ladakh have had their own relationships with music, varying with history, geographic location, occupation, and sectarian philosophies. With much research yet to be done compared to the Buddhist community, it is still important to offer narratives that give a more balanced picture. This chapter will examine repertoires from the Sunni community of the Leh area and the Shia communities mostly concentrated in Kargil, parts of the Nubra Valley, and across the border in Baltistan—albeit with noticeable presence in and around Leh.

Extending the Geertzian concept of culture as webs of significance, Ladakh was clearly a nexus in multiple webs. The caravan routes fostered the flow of luxury goods in what was truly a global network. Indeed, silver mined in Mexico traveled across the Pacific to the Philippines, then to China, with some ultimately ending up as Ladakhi coins known as "chau" or "jau" (i.e., the price of tea) (Flynn and Giráldez 2002; Fewkes 2012; John Bray 2020). As noted by historian John Bray:

> The Ladakhi economy depended on a combination of agriculture, pastoralism and trade. The king was himself the most important trader in Ladakh, and customs duties formed a major part of his income. At a more humble level, villagers were able to supplement a precarious agricultural income by serving as porters on the trade routes between Kashmir, Tibet and Central Asia. The single most profitable trade good was

wool carried from the highlands of eastern Ladakh and Tibet to Kashmir. Arguably, the most important 'export product' of central and western Ladakh was the labour of porters carrying the wool. (Bray 2008, 44)

Kashmiri scholar Kulbhushan Warikoo commented on the richness of the trade going between India (via Kashmir) and Central Asia (with Ladakh being an important nexus):

Khotan was famed for jade, carpets and silken fabrics and hemp cords. Bukhara was noted for its carpets; Badakhshan for lapis-lazuli and rubies; Tibet for musk and pashm wool; Turfan for pashm wool and Kashmir for its saffron, fine shawls and calligraphed books. In short, these areas developed into important trading centres in this east-west trade which was carried through the « Silk Route ». Due to its geographical proximity to Central Asia and linkage with the Silk Routes system, Kashmir acted as an important transit emporium in the bilateral Indo-Central Asian trade. (Warikoo 1996)

In her 1999 book on Trans-Himalayan caravans, Janet Rizvi noted the importance of the Muslim traders, because the Central Asian markets would charge a tax on idolators, that is, Hindus and Buddhists. Thus, the Ladakhi Buddhist aristocracy would hire Muslim agents to maximize profits. So, when Muslim merchants from Kashmir and Turkestan began intermarrying with local Buddhist populations, this gave rise to communities such as the Ladakhi Arghon (literally, "hybrid") and Lhasa Kache (i.e., "Kashmiris ") in Tibet, they helped to form a cosmopolitan network linked by the commonalities of Sunni Islam and international trade. One should also note the presence of the surname Tibetbaqal (Tibetan trader) in Kashmir, including a famous family of *Sufiana Kalam* musicians. This has links to the Tibetan classical music known as *nangma* (derived from the Persian word for melody, *naghma*).

Members of the Arghon trading community loved music, as seen in nineteenth-century narratives that note how it lightened spirits on long trade expeditions. Two caravan drivers, famous for their travels in the late nineteenth and early twentieth centuries, were also known for their amateur connections to music: Ghulam Rassul Galwan and Kalam Rasul.

Both men distinguished themselves in guiding Europeans on arduous travels as far as Tibet, with Rassul Galwan being famous for writing a book, *Servant of Sahibs*, detailing his early life and travels. A translation of a song prefaces Rassul Galwan's main narrative:

Rassul's Song
The sun gave from east.
It is God's kindly.
Four side round made bright.
It is power almighty.
On poor boy look kindness.
On poor Rassul look kindness always.
Rassul not have work or money.
By kindly God get humble business.
If gave God, He not look
If wise or simple,
He not care
If big or little. (Galwan 1923, xix)

Unfortunately, the original lyrics in Ladakhi and the melody are not to be found.

Ghulam Rassul, describes how he builds what he calls a banjo in English (no doubt a Ladakhi *khopong* or *damnyan*).

One time I saw a boy play with a banjo, that had made himself, with own hand. His father was banjo-man in Leh.

That banjo look me very wonderful one thing for my play. But he not could give me. That was a spoon of wood, which the Ladaki people use for cook.

When I came home, I did find one old spoon which we had, and I did make me a banjo with own hand. But was little hard work; could not ready it in that day. I did keep it into the hole where I keep all my playthings all the time.

The following day I went to the meat-seller place, and bought a little piece of stomach of goat, and some horse-tail of hair. I did find that all thing. And I was very busy near the happy hole, in the work of my banjo.

That day was nearly done but could not get dry the skin.

He goes on to relate how he gets so involved in working on the instrument that he neglects to guard the chapatis his mother made for the Ramadan *iftar* (fast breaking), and the goats eat them. The ensuing chaos is memorable (Galwan 1923, 13–17).

Another notable caravan driver and horse trader was Kalam Rasul, later known as Baba Kalam. He was younger than Rassul Galwan and traveled with him to Tibet in the 1893 Littledale expedition, chronicled both by Galwan and St. George Littledale (Galwan 1923; Littledale 1894). Kalam Rasul's greater fame, however, rests on an abortive 1898 expedition to Lhasa led by two British officers, Neill Malcolm and Neill Wellby. Poor management and navigation led to the party going badly astray, leading to conflict between the British and the Argons. They separated on the Northern Tibetan plateau, with the four Ladakhis heading East toward China for reasons that were not completely clear. Ultimately one man died, and another joined a caravan heading to Lhasa, leaving Kalam Rasul and his younger brother, Juma Malik, who continued to Beijing. There, the Chinese authorities took charge of them and (no doubt thinking them spies) sent them under guard by caravan to Kashgar and thence back to Leh. They had been gone for four years, during which time their family had no news of them and had the prayers for the dead recited (Joldan 1985).

During his time far from home, Kalam Rasul wrote a song expressing homesickness (Track 14).

Kalam Rasul

nyima shar nas shar ba, shar gyi dron can nyima.
shar gsum shar nas shar ba, shar gyi dron can nyima.
nyima'i mdangs zer legs mo, skyes pa'i pha yul la phog.
mdangs zer od zer legs mo, gle chen dpal mkhar la phog.
[The sun rises in the West, the warm Western sun.
It rises in the precious West, the warm Western sun.
The good, radiant sunlight, touches the fatherland where I
    was born
The good, radiant light touches the great castle in Leh.]

butsha nga rang skye sa bo, gle chen dpal mkhar la skyes.
kalam rasul skye sa bo, gle chen dpal mkhar la skyes.
tshe sngon las kyi 'brel par, butsha rgya nag la bslebs.
tshe sngon las kyi 'brel par, ka lam ra sul mi yul la bslebs.
[I, the young man was born, was born by Leh Palace.
Kalam Rasul was born, was born by Leh Palace.

By fate the boy ended up in China
By fate Kalam Rasul ended up in China.]

'dug da ladvags kyi nang du, gnyen drung gnam gyi skar ma.
'dug da gle chen nang du, drag zhan gnam gyi skar ma.
skar ma skar yan la cha mkhan, butsha nga rang gcig gcig.
skar ma thor yan la cha mkhan, kalam rasul gcig gcig.
[By the stars read by the astrologer, Kalam Rasul is alone.
Now my family are in great Leh under a starry sky.
By the stars read by the astrologer, I, the boy, myself am alone.
By the stars read by the astrologer, Kalam Rasul is alone.]

'dug da ladvags nang du, sag chung gang gi mda' mo.
'dug da gle chen nang du, sag chung gang gi mda'mo.
mda' mo mda' yan la chag mkhan, butsha nga rang gcig, gcig.
mda' mo thor yan la chag mkhan, kalam rasul gcig gcig.
[Being there in Ladakh, at the moment of an arrow divination
Being there in great Leh, at the moment of an arrow divination
The arrow divination was done by an astrologer, I the boy
    am alone.
The arrow divination done by an astrologer; Kalam Rasul is
    alone.]

'dug da gle chen nang du, ma ni bo brgya bzhengs dangs stong
    bzhengs.
'dug da ladvags nang du, ma ni bo brgya bzhengs dangs stong
    bzhengs.
ha tsang rgyun de la bzhugs mkhan, mkhar og gi ma ni gcig gcig.
ha tsang rgyun de la bzhugs mkhan, mkhar og gi ma ni gcig gcig.
[Though the wide expanse of Leh
Has hundreds and thousands of Mani[1] built around,
In the whole of Ladakh there are hundreds and thousands of
    Mani built around,
The only one that this boy keeps seeing is the *mani* wall below
    the palace.
The only one that this boy keeps seeing is the *mani* wall below
    the palace.]

rgya nag gi lcang ra'i ka 'dug ste, butsha ngas tha mag kun
    yang bkangs.

rgya nag gi lcang ra'i ka 'dug ste, rasul gyis goraku 'thungs.
tha mag po rgya nag la 'thungs na, du ba bo rang yul la log.
gorakun mi yul la 'thung na, du ba bo gle chen la log.
[Smoking the pipe in foreign lands, smoke turned back to my
    dear Leh town.
Sitting on the Great Wall of China, I made the tobacco again.
Sitting on the Great Wall of China, Rasul drank some kora[2]
Smoking the tobacco in China, smoke turned to his own land.]

rgya nag mkhar gyi ka 'bing ste, kalam rasul dar ba'i lcog spar.
dar lcog rgya nag la spar pa, dar ka rang yul la log.
dar lcog ni yul la spar pa, dar ka po gle chen la log.
[Coming out of the Chinese castle's pillars, Kalam Rasul raises
    prayer flags.
The prayer flags raised in China, may the prayers flags return
    to one's homeland.
The prayer flags raised in one's own country, may the prayers
    return to great Leh.]
(Translation by Namgyal Angmo 2021)

What place did these caravan drivers occupy in the Buddhist-dominated
society around Leh? A cogent discussion is laid out by Dutch anthropologist Martijn van Beek in examining Rassul Galwan's book:

> We should also consider what may have been Galwan's own
> considerations in writing his account. While the readership
> could not have been intended to be primarily Ladakhi, as
> few people were literate in English, I would suggest that the
> audience Galwan intended for the *book* (rather than the *text* it
> contained) was indeed also a local, Ladakhi one. At the time
> of publication, Rassul Galwan was serving as *Aqsaqal* of Leh.
> As Mrs. Barrett, the editor, explains in her introduction to the
> book, this meant that Rassul was now the "chief native assistant
> of the British Joint Commissioner" who "is in authority over
> the traders meeting at Leh to exchange their goods" (Galwan
> 1923: xv). In spite of the obvious success of his career in the
> service of sahibs, Galwan was still from a poor family. His
> modest wealth hardly compared to that of the major trading
> families and landowning elite of Leh. Moreover, social status

in Leh to this day depends primarily on one's household background. Lacking the aristocratic (*sku.drag*) ancestry of the leading Buddhist families, the sacred superiority of religious leaders, and the economic power of the wealthier Argon trading families, Galwan sought to enhance his social standing by writing a book *in English*, the language of foreign and superior power. By addressing his 'Author's preface' to "King and Queen and ladies and gentlemen who will read this poor boy's book," Galwan put himself in the company, indeed in conversation, with the rulers of India, further stressing his position in that modern, colonial world where Ladakhi 'traditional' hierarchy carried little weight. (van Beek 1998, 61)

For the common folk of Ladakh, Buddhist and Muslim, there was the periodic liability of being pressed into *courveé* (unpaid, forced labor), known in Hindi/Urdu as *begar* and in Ladakhi as *khral*. As John Bray noted, "The word *khral* covered tax, tribute, duty and labour obligations. There were specific terms for particular types of tax (for example, *'bru khraL,* tax paid in corn; *dngul-khraL,* tax paid in silver), while the word for compulsory porterage was *'u-lag*" (Bray 2008, 43).

A style of song often associated with the Muslim populations, both Arghon and the Shia Purig-pa and Balti was the *ghazal*, which were often in the style of a narrative ballad. The song "Ali Khan" is from the point of view of a man, probably Sunni, having to fulfill his obligation to perform *begar* (Track 15).

Ali Khan
Zhag po la bltas te, Bu tsa nga byes (bes) la 'bing 'dug.
Skar bzang la bltas te,
Ali Khan byes la 'bing dug.
[Consulting the almanac
I, the young man, must perform *begar*[3]
Seeing the right date,
Ali Khan must go for his duty.]

Byes kyi byes 'go bo legs bcug,
Mthon mo mkhan bdag po'i sha ste.
Byes kyi byes 'go bo thon pa,
Kha chul gzhung gsum la 'bing 'dug.

[Let the duty pass as it will.
Someone who does his job well will earn the master's
    benevolence.
When the duty is over.
I am sent off to the three centers (ie. Srinagar)][4]

Kha chul gzhung gsum gyi nang na,
Gnyen dang drung po mi 'dug.
Kha chul gzhung gsum gyi nang na,
A ba dang a ma mi 'dug.
[In Kashmir's three centers
There are neither kin nor siblings.
In Kashmir's three centers
There is neither father nor mother.]

A ba dang a ma'i dod po la,
Baa baa ba kro mas jid,
Gnyen dang drung po'i dod po la,
A ma mdo bzhi lha mo.
[Instead of father and mother
There is Baba Bakro Masjid
Instead of kin and siblings
There is the mother goddess of Zoji-la.]

Srung ba skyabs pa mdzod dang,
Baa baa ba kro mas jid
Kha chul gyi yul dkyil la,
Baa baa ba kro mas jid.
[And it keeps safe the treasure of
Baba Bakro Masjid
In the center of the Valley of Kashmir
There is the Baba Bakro Masjid][5]

Baa baa ba kro mas jid nang,
Gser gyi bya pho gsum 'bos yod.
Gser gyi bya pho men tshug,
Kho zhva bulb ul yin tshug.
[Inside the Baba Bakro Masjid
Are the three secret golden roosters (or pigeons).

It is not a golden rooster.
Khozha is the *bubul* (Persian nightingale).] (Academy, Vol. I,
164–65)

The word *Khozha/Khoja* (master) can have a double meaning here—a
common thing in *ghazals*. In the spiritual sense it can refer to Baba
Dawood Khaki (1521–1585) a Kashmiri Sufi saint who earned repute for
his scholarship command of Islamic literature, *Hadith*, writing, calligraphy,
and poetry. The masjid mentioned may be his shrine. The other meaning
of Khoja may refer to the rich Arghon families that would have been
financing the caravan into which people were drafted as porters.

According to my research assistant, Namgyal Angmo, this song might
be considered a *ghazal* in the sense that it brings out individuality. She also
says that it might be a secular version of *Qasida* instead of strict *ghazal*.
Qasida are songs that women would gather to sing instead of going to
masjid or during Ramzan. They also are sung by men to wake the faithful
before dawn so they can eat the last meal before the day's fast.

Many of these songs comprise a repertoire generally known as
Balti *ghazal,* some of which are more akin to narrative ballads in form
and content, often praising local heroes. The subjects of these songs have
been forgotten by most people or can be vaguely guessed at. According
to Namgyal Angmo, the song "Ostad Man Mir" (Master Man Mir) may
refer to the chief of a group of mercenaries active in the Baltistan/Kargil
region (Track 16).

Ostad Man Mir

so ma steng khung gi gad pa na
rta pa mang po zhig yong ned
bu mo'i dun yad po yin min nam le
so ma steng khung gi gad pa na.
[In the new darkness above the cliff
Many horsemen came.
Is it not the girl's world, sir,
In the new darkness above the cliff]

rta pa mang po zhig yong ned
Os stad Man Mir gun yin min nam le
so ma steng khung gi gad pa na
rta pa mang po zhig yong ned.

[Many horsemen came.
Are they those of Ostad Man Mir?
In the new darkness above the cliff
Many horsemen came.]

bu mo'i dun yad min nam
so ma rta khang gi ha thog la
me tog sbrang bu'i skad tshor yod
bu mo'i dun yad min nam.
[It is not the girl's world.
In the new stable's ornament.
the flower buzzing is heard.
Isn't it the girl's world?]

me tog sbrang bu'i skad po ma yin
bu mo'i dun yad khyed rang dan nga 'dzoms te
bye ma'i yong kong 'phing 'dug
rang rang mgo'i heg mad min nam
[It is not the flower's buzzing.
You gather in the girl's world.
You come to the desert.
Doesn't each head have wisdom?]

Ostad Man Mir khyed rang dang 'dzoms te
chu med kyi rang 'thag skor 'dug
rang rang mgo'i heg mat min nam
stag shing um shing po skyur red
[Ostad Man Mir, you sir, have abundant glory.
A water mill lacking water is turning.
Doesn't each head have wisdom?
The birch tree, the revered tree is sour.]

la ling thang gi long dkyil la reg ged
gro bzang dang nas bzang po skyur red
ham zi gon ni so ba skob sbrag ged
rang rang gi mgo'i nyes pa min nam.
[He is in the center of the plain.
Good wheat and good barley are sour.

Along with the moldy, thick-shelled barley.
Isn't each head faulty?] (Academy, Vol. 1, 163).

The lyrics seem to indicate an ambivalent attitude toward this man, like the attitude toward the minister Pita Jogi discussed previously.

More in keeping with the style of Urdu *ghazal-s,* individual expression is seen in the song "Bu mo'i ming la Fatima" (The girl's name is Fatima), which takes place during what Ladakhis call the "Trade Period" prior to the closing of the borders. The protagonist is a poor Muslim farm girl who is socially ostracized, as indicated by not being able to get water, perhaps because the village well is off limits to her. This repeated reference to the "red rose" of her life also indicates her love interest who is the *tehsildar* (local government official). Her father is in Hardass Village in Kargil district where he gleans apples to sell. Her brother works in another village. A translation and audio are provided by my research assistant, Namgyal Angmo (Track 17).

Bu mo'i Ming la Fatima (The name of the girl is Fatima)
bu mo'i ming la pha ti ma
phan dil la gla' bcad de
sang ldang gi ja skol yod le
dmar po'i gu lab
[The name of the girl is Fatima.
I clean copper pots.
I have brewed wild herb tea.
Oh, the red rose of my life!]

yul mgo n yul mdug la
gu lab la chu btsal yod
gu lab la chu ma thob le
dmar po'i gu lab
[I went around the whole village.
Looking for water to water my rose shrub,
My poor rose didn't get water.
Oh, the red rose of my life!]

a pha har dras la yod
ka ka shin mgo'i ka na

jam shen du kan la you le
dmar po'i gu lab
[Father is stationed at Hardass
Brother is stationed at Shingo.
Jamshen is with the gleaners.
Oh, the red rose of my life!]

khi ri a ta drang po
na shi na dra mo
mig gis m thong le dga' mo
dmar po'i gu lab
[Your father is honest.
If I die, I will be blamed.
These eyes haven't seen a happy phase.
Oh, the ill-fated rose of my life!]

khyed rang yul gyi ta sil dar
nga shar sgo'i za min dar
ci byas pa'i hu kum yod le
dmar po'i gu lab
[You may be the Tehsildar of the town.
I am a rustic farmer.
What kind of order do you have for me?
Oh, the rose of my life!] (Academy, Vol. 1, 376).

Secular songs in the Shia communities have had the added scrutiny of theologians who question the moral correctness of music in general. Lois Ibsen al Faruqi, commenting on views of music in the Middle East, noted the general controversy about secular music genres, with serious vocal and instrumental music being deemed everything from *halāl* (legitimate), *mubāh* (indifferent), *makruh* (unfavored), to *harām* (forbidden) (1985, 7–12), and this argument is ongoing in the Shia communities in Ladakh and Baltistan. In a lengthy discussion with Prof. Nasir Shabani, an ethnic Balti from Kargil whose father is a *maulana* (Islamic scholar), he asserted that, excluding radical fundamentalists like Salafis and strict Iranian-influenced Shia clerics, folk music has generally been deemed acceptable. This includes pre-Islamic repertoires like the songs connected with storytelling of the Gesar epic known as *rgyang lhu* in Balti or *rgying glu* in Ladakhi. He shared an example by the great historian, journalist, storyteller, singer, and cultural/political activist Haji Master Hussain Silmo (track 18).

Nasir Shabani explains the narrative context of this song. One of the main parts of the story is that Bruguma/Duguma, the wife of the hero Gesar of Ling, has been held captive by the evil king of Hor (Mongolia?) along with a retainer. He goes on to explain that:

> Ling warrior Angara Ltzangspa in prison in Hor suddenly sees tents pitched at Tanbroq near Hor. Overjoyed, believing the same to be a sign of approach of Ling warriors invading Hor to rescue Duga ma and her retinue including Angara himself, he sings from inside the cage hung from the palace roof of the king Praghalde Rgyalpo:

Tan Tani Tanbrog (The Summer Place Tanbroq)
Behold! Yonder at summer place Tanbroq
Are seen tents of gold and silver pitched!
I fail to make out what it is,
O my king of Miracles!
The one with the golden dome is certainly Divine Son Kesar's
    tent!
Yea, the one with golden dome must
The Great Rgyalam's tent it be!
The one with sandal-wood life pillar
Is the great General's tent:
Tan Tani Tanbroq
Yea, the one with Sandal-wood life pillar
Is the Boy of the Gongmas, tent.
The one with ropes of pearl strings
is surely father Ldumbu's tent.
The one with coral stone hands atop
Is surely Princess Palmo's tent.
Not a plaything the Great Rgyalam is
But the very heart leaf of The New Queen:
Not an ordinary being The Divine Son is
But the very heart leaf of Graceful Dugu ma
Of hoping to join The Great Rgyalam again

Do I have the Pleasure now!
Of hoping to meet The Divine Son again
Do I enjoy the pleasure now,
O my exalted King of Miracles!
The divine army of Ling!
Let me pay my hand-folded homage, O king!
Not an ordinary army it is!
The divine army of Ling has
The warriors of Ling,
The ways of hurricanes (when rushing)
The warriors of Ling are never ordinary warrior.
A quiver full of piercing shafts they are!
(Translation by Prof. Nasir Shabani)

In an interview on the television program "Kargil Today" on December 16, 2020, Master Hussain discussed Muslim celebration of Ladakhi Losar, noting that this was one of the notable times when the Pan-Tibetan Gesar epic is recited and sung (Hussain 2020b). Thus, we see that wonderful conjunction of cultures where Balti, Purigpa, and Ladakhi share in celebration of Losar, each giving their own sectarian slant, but unified via the common Tibetic heritage. At the same time, the Persian spring New Year of Navroz is an important celebration for Kargil Muslims, with its own repertoires of song and dance, even if the more puritanical elements decry such public displays.

As noted above, theological acceptance of song and dance is a contentious issue. For example, the Ladakh academy of Art, Culture & Language, Kargil sponsored a Navroz celebration with exhibitions of song and dance. The event was recorded on video by several news outlets and posted on YouTube. The comments section varied from enthusiastic approval to condemnations such as, "in Islam dancing have no identity," or "in the holy month of Shaban dance and song are not allowed in our culture," or "the culture of dancing and singing is forbidden in Islam." On the other hand, one writer opined that Kargil is headed toward an ethnic vs. religious identity rivalry. He went on to add that religious scholars must understand that Kargili identity can't be exclusively religious but is a composite of both ethnic and religious, and that religious organizations are going to lose influence if they don't acknowledge this problem.

Shia Devotional Song Genres

Sung specifically during Muhurram, *marsiya* and *noha* are elegiac religious poems/songs commemorating the martyrdom of Husain and his comrades at Karbala. *Marsiya* originated in pre-Islamic Persia, picking up the Shia religious connotation, and spread to other Shia communities including the Deccan and Awadh in India, as well as Baltistan and other communities in the northwest of the Indian subcontinent.

Rohit Singh, in his 2016 PhD dissertation on religious practices in Ladakh, noted:

> Shi'is produce various oral and written narratives about Hussein's death. Collectively remembering the events at Karbala creates shared sentiments of grief and sorrow among Shi'is. To make sense of his death and cope with their sorrow, leaders and scholars deliver sermons concerning the purpose of Hussein's martyrdom, the legacy of Karbala, and the moral, theological, and political lessons which can be learned from the Karbala narrative. Shi'is in Leh receive these narratives predominantly from oral sources, such as public speeches during Muharram, or through the recitations of two forms of elegiac liturgy known locally in Urdu and Arabic as marsiya and nauha. (Singh, 2016: 213–14)

He goes on to note that "they also directly invoke episodes from the Karbala narrative when they recite nauha and marsiya in Balti or Urdu. Alongside these recitations, they weep, rhythmically beat their chests, and sometimes lacerate their bodies with whips and blades. These practices of self-laceration only take place during Muharram" (Singh., 215).

Marsiyas in Urdu first appeared in the sixteenth century in the Deccan kingdoms of India. They were written either in the two-line unit form, *qasida*, or the four-line unit form, *murabba*. Over time, the *musaddas* became the most suitable form for a marsiya. In this form, the first two lines of each stanza referred to as the *band* have one rhyme scheme while the remaining two lines referred to as the *tip* have another (Naim 2004, 1–2).

Nasir Shabani kindly supplied a recording of his cousin Mohammed Nasirul Mehdi Shabani singing a Balti *marsiya* lamenting the death of the infant Ali Ashgar, son of Hussein (track 19). The transliteration, commentary, and translation are his (personal comm., text, and audio via WhatsApp, August 8, 2023).

Elegy of Ali Asgar Infant Son of Husain Ibn Ali

The elegy denotes the occasion when Husain Ibn Ali brought back his infant son Ali Asgar back from the battle of Karbala. Husain Ibn Ali took his six-month-old son to ask the Yazid army for water to quench the infant's thirst; in return Umar Ibn Saad the commander-in-chief of the Yazid army ordered Hurmula (The arrow shooter) to kill Ali Asgar as discontent arose among the Yazid army. The elegy depicts the lament of Rabab, the mother of Ali Asgar, when the infant's corpse is brought back.

—Nasir Shabani

Marsiya Ali Asgar
Asgar Gyuray Imamis Ghobain Lzoqsay Khyongmana
Ngwedpa Zezi Si Rkoqmola Da Foqse Thongmana
Hrchik Chi Zeren Chi Laqpa Skoren Migi Oad Bula
Yari Di Skomfi Rkogmola Da Fangma Fod Sula
Paighambari Csari Chamani Mindogi Khaboo
Yaslong Maminma Shums Di Tha'ning Chadey Chhu
Ngomsa Mathongma Ni Buchoe Rdong Mikla Ni Darong
Shaqsna Diring Zizi La Skyurey Gyodpa Stong Na Strong
[When the leader (Imam) brought back Asgar's corpse lamenting
The mother cried seeing the arrow pierced through his throat.
Mourning in grief and distress for her son, the light of her eyes
Who could have shot the arrow through your dry and thirsty
     throat?
Oh! The one who is brought up in the progeny of Prophet
     like a bud of a flower.
Not allowed to nurture and slay in this land curbing water
     to drink.
Not seen my son's thirsty face quench of water today
If you depart leaving your beloved mother is thousands of
     regrets to me.]

This chapter is merely a preliminary look at the repertoires of the different Muslim communities in Ladakh. A more in-depth study will hopefully be forthcoming in the next volume.

Chapter 4

Music in a Changing Society

Performance Venues, Musicians, and Social Status

Venues for traditional songs have changed in the past 150 years. After the royal court in the Leh palace ceased to function as a center of temporal power with the 1842 Dogra conquest, songs such as *zhung lu* and *tendel lu* were primarily performed in village contexts, such as gatherings for festivals like the Losar New Year.

Bagston lu (wedding songs) are still performed, although the days of lengthy, multiday wedding negotiations and celebrations are mostly gone—no one has time anymore. What you often get are abbreviated rituals, keeping what people view as significant landmarks in the ceremonies, such as the song battles at the bride's door (*sgo glu,* "door songs"). This was described as a general trend by Ladakhi scholar Ngawang Tsering Shakspo (personal comm., August 6, 2009).

Prof. Sarah H. Smith of the University of North Carolina at Chapel Hill and her Ladakhi husband, Tonyot, described how his female relatives acted in place of her absent family (traditionally the male members) to barricade themselves in the house and act out the *sgo glu.* However, the entire celebration only took one day (personal comm., July 16, 2009). A similar experience was recounted by my friend, popular singer/songwriter Tashi Choesphel about his wedding in 2001 (personal comm., July 2009).

Back in 2001 I spent time in the village of Likir with the family of one of my students at Likir Gompa School. I was able to videotape them singing farmers' work songs as they harvested the barley. Nowadays, these songs have disappeared from common usage because farmwork is often performed by Nepali migrant labor instead of the traditional local farmers.

Private parties are another venue where both modern and traditional songs are sung. Noted singer Stanzin Dadul, during a video recording session of traditional songs, talked about performing *zhung lu* for parties and how they are often in demand (personal comm., July 27, 2009).

During the same recording session, I noted that for many lengthier *bagston lu* and *zhung lu* Stanzin Dadul would refer to a notebook filled with song lyrics. This seems to have been a common practice in Ladakh, in addition to oral transmission. Linguist Bettina Zeisler had been working for some years with an elderly singer/storyteller, the late Dhondrup Tsering of Achinatang Village, and has shared digitally scanned images of two of his extensive notebooks. Dating back as far as 1905, A. H. Francke collected versions of the Gesar saga from both oral dictations and manuscripts belonging to bards (Francke 2000 [1905–41]).

Erosion of traditional song and instrumental repertoires is also linked to rebellion against the caste system. As mentioned, the performers of the *surna* and *daman* who always accompanied songs and dances were the low-caste *Mon* who worked as subsistence farmers, carpenters, and musicians in the villages. Post–Indian independence, when the military and civil authorities embarked on public works projects to enhance infrastructure in the area, Mon chose to get a job and an education and give up being treated as subservient (cf. Trewin 1995; Rather 1993).

Lama Jamspal noted that this trend has been going on since his childhood in Basgo Village in the 1940s, where the Mon had "stopped beating." The village elders offered an abandoned farmstead to entice another Mon family to move to the village in exchange for their supplying music. However, he noted that some years later that family too "stopped beating" (personal comm., August 2001).

It is interesting to note how Lama Jamspal's comments indicate a strong association in many Ladakhis' minds of the Mon with the *daman*, as opposed to the *surna*. I had noticed this when talking about my research on the Mon with a couple of young Ladakhis who had immigrated to New York City. One of them didn't know who I was talking about, until his friend said, "You know, those funny guys who go 'taka taka taka' on the drums." Again, this was a manifestation of a certain indexing of *daman* to both the Mon and their musical activities: synecdoche, if you will.

This was also brought home to me in August 2001, during one of three summers when I was teaching English at Likir Monastery School. The novice monks, ages five to fifteen, all knew of my interest in Ladakhi music and had sung various children's songs for me. As part of my attempts to try to broaden their modes of expression, I asked them to draw pictures of scenes from their lives. One eleven-year-old boy named Lobzang Nyandak (a real smart-aleck whom my associate, Prof. Christian Haskett, nicknamed "Mr. Smiley"), drew what amounted to a cartoon, complete with speech balloons (figure 4.1). One of the speech balloons in the picture says, "Beat the *daman!*"—again, a clear indication of the iconic value of the *daman*.

This iconic value notwithstanding, the status of the Mon partakes of that liminal dichotomy between prestige product and despised agent that Trewin thoroughly examined in his PhD dissertation on *lha nga* ceremonial music (Trewin 1993). The Mon are still contesting their outcast status at the village level.

Various informants report on a significant confrontation that was precipitated by a former head of Leh District Department of Public Works Civil Engineering Department who was from a Mon family. At some public function in the 1980s no one was willing to sit next to him due to his unclean hereditary status—as opposed to his high professional status

Figure 4.1. "Beat the *daman!*"—cartoon by an eleven-year-old Buddhist monk. *Source*: Author's collection.

in the civil service. Quite reasonably, he was incensed at this insult, and organized a boycott by all Mon musicians for all events in Leh District. This was said to have lasted a couple of years, causing great dismay in the Buddhist population. Eventually something of a reconciliation with the Mon was achieved, albeit imperfectly. Part of what happened was that the Mon themselves missed playing for events and slowly came back.

Rebecca Norman, Volunteer Coordinator for The Students' Educational and Cultural Movement of Ladakh (SECMOL), had some cogent observations regarding the continued social upheaval and its impact on music:

> I think a lot of the Mons who have quit playing music have done so explicitly because of social caste discrimination in their villages. I have heard anecdotes from people involved about incidents of discrimination that led to Mons quitting music. I would too if I were them. One was a Mon kid who insisted on dancing along with the other kids at a New Year's party in Skyurbuchan. It was a modern party, teenagers dancing to recorded music. His family refused to submit to the punishment decided by the *goba* or villagers, and just quit relations with them, including music.[1]

Ms. Norman went on to note:

> I've had two experiences of people of middle caste in Sham picking up the Mon role of music. I attended a wedding in Skyurbuchan a few years ago, the year the Mons had quit, and middle-caste guys were playing the music. The *daman* sounded fine to me, but the surna was kind of funny. He mostly played recognizable song tunes like "Ali Yato" and "Shonkalimasho." It wasn't a proper big wedding, but a *paklok* (a redramatization of a bride-giveaway party years after the actual marriage).
>
> More currently, two middle-caste SECMOL staff members from Wanla, who were good at *daman* already, have been taking up the music at formal parties in their part of the village, Ursi. I went to a formal party with a /trhom/ there and they were playing the drums. The head dancers were paying them just as if they were real Mons, and they made a couple thousand

rupees. They are guys with enough social confidence in the first place to pull it off: "Yeah, we did the drumming, yeah, we got paid, ha-ha, what of it?"

Many villages have discontinued their traditional Losar activities because they don't have Mons able or willing to play the right music. I heard that in Nyemo they tried hiring Bedas from Leh but they didn't know the right tunes so it didn't work and the villagers just quit the next year. I understand the same has happened in many villages. Now, instead of the traditional Losar activities (horse racing, ice water bathing, historical re-enactments, whatever) there's just a youth party on New Year's with recorded music. (personal comm., email, January 12, 2010)

Until recently, modern Ladakhi young people have had an ambivalent attitude toward traditional songs. The language of genres like *zhung lu, bagston lu, tendel lu* is not colloquial modern Ladakhi, but instead a mixture of literary/religious Tibetan (*chos skad*) and colloquial speech (*phal skad*) in varying degrees—not easily accessible to common people. As one young tour guide, Tsewang Gyatso, commented, "I like them, but the language is difficult" (personal comm., July 2009).

Rebecca Norman noted that the erosion of the traditional song repertoire was most pronounced among upper- and middle-class youth living in Leh who may have had more exposure to mass media, although she speculated as to whether other socioeconomic factors might not come into play. In addition, local dialects are forgotten by urban youth who learn a generic Leh dialect, as well as Hindi and English. The net result was that the urban youth ended up being unable to speak to their village grandparents in their own language and are unable to enjoy the same music (personal comm., email January 12, 2010).

An added dimension to the linguistic mix is the repertoire of music performed in ethnic Dardic (otherwise known as Brokpa) areas in Western Ladakh. In villages like Dha, Hanu, Batalik, and Baima a significant amount of the population is bilingual in Ladakhi and Brokpa language (known in Ladakhi as *Brokskad*, otherwise known as Shina)[2], which is an Indo-Iranian language more closely related to Kashmiri. Even those self-identified Brokpa that no longer use *Brokskad* extensively are a musically conservative population, with more people continuing to cultivate the old Brokpa song, dance, and instruments (beyond the scope of the current study), as well as the majority Ladakhi repertoire. Various informants' comments are revealing in that they highlight linguistic change in Ladakh's history and the hegemony of the Tibetan Ladakhi language over Brokpa language and how this is linked with mainline Ladakhi songs.

My close friend Dawa Tsering is from the remote Brokpa village of Hanu, but his daughter, Skarma Yudon, is typical of the trend among urban youth. She went to a prestigious boarding school in Leh, was a straight-A student, and speaks good English, Hindi, and Leh-dialect Ladakhi. She spent holidays with her father's parents out in Hanu, 150 kilometers from Leh. She notes: "I don't know any *zhung lu*—when I go to my village only the old people sing them and only for functions. The language is very hard to understand" (personal comm., August 4, 2012). On the other hand, sixteen-year-old Deskyong Nyima Namgyal from Yangthang Village in the Sham Valley (near the Brokpa area) said he didn't sing these songs but mentioned that he did really like them. He thought they referred to Ladakhi history. He understands the words and does not find them to be difficult, even though he doesn't know Tibetan (personal comm., August 12, 2012). He recognized my interest in songs while hanging out at the internet cafe in Leh that his relative Stanzin Motup ran and brought me a CD of *zhung lu* he recorded from the radio and other sources—quite an extensive collection—most of them by Dorje Stakmo.

I spoke with adults thirty years old and older who came from a variety of villages and found a general appreciation and understanding of the music and lyrics. In fact, I got consistent descriptions of the songs' importance in affirming Ladakhi historical and cultural identity. My friend Dawa Tsering noted that his native village of Hanu and surrounding villages (five to seven hours drive from Leh) are very musical places, with many people that still either play instruments and/or sing. He said that in some villages there are Mon who specialize in instrumental music and are repositories of songs; in others the musicians are just ordinary villagers. I asked him what he thinks of *zhung lu*, does he understand the words, and are those words important? Dawa expressed very clear opinions:

> People like *zhung lu*, but these days after hearing two or three the young people put on the disco music. Part of the problem is that they don't understand the language. This comes from modernization, the moment a village has electricity they put on the TV in the evening. When I was young in my home village

(Hanu) people would gather in my house or some other house at night and my grandmother would tell stories, sing songs, tell riddles. The other people would too. People would know *zhung lu* because they were there—not just for functions, but for all the long wintertime. These days only the old people know them, and they are going.

When you hear *zhung lu*, you can hear it again and again. The melody is so special, and the words have such special meaning.

In some places, Shams side [i.e., the Shams Valley], like Skurbuchan, people are still knowing them. It is in the villages, not in Leh, that people know them. It is the Mon that were supposed to know all the words to the songs, but some old people know them very well, like my father. He can't sing very well, but he knows all the words of many songs. He was having a contest with his cousin who is a singer, and he was winning, knowing so much more of the words. When he was young, he had a contest with a village Mon and defeated him, and the guy left the function. (personal comm., August 4, 2012)

It should be noted that Dawa is college educated (Hindu College, Delhi University—equivalent to an Ivy League school), as well as being educated in spoken and literary Tibetan and Buddhist philosophy. He is Lama Jamspal's "nephew," being related on their maternal sides to the *Lonpo* (ministerial) family of Saspol Village—*skudrag*. Ladakhis in remote villages like Hanu are likely to be familiar with and appreciate *zhung lu*. For example, Dawa's assistant manager at the travel agency, Thinles Dorje, who is also from Hanu, had something revealing to say:

It [i.e., *zhung lu*] indicates the history of Ladakh, especially about the kings, about the monks, who have . . . discovered Ladakh. It is very nice to hear when you completely know about them—the language—when you know the meaning of the song, then it's very nice. It is always a meaningful one, regarding the places, the kings, and monks. . . .

My village is especially known for the *zhung lu because* they were the first origins of Ladakh [i.e., the Dards or *Brok pa*], and brought all the songs to Ladakh—the ancestors.

I then asked Thinles Dorje whether his twelve-year-old son knew *zhung lu*, and he said, "Yes, a little bit, but not much." Dorje admits with some chagrin that his son prefers more modern Ladakhi songs. I asked him whether he was unusual in knowing *zhung lu,* and he said many people in Hanu know them. However, he thought that people in villages closer to Leh might not know them so much (personal comm., August 4, 2012).

Other men and women I spoke to, ages thirty through sixty, repeated variations on this trope of *zhung lu* representing or symbolizing Ladakh.

I had a long conversation with a tour guide and driver, Rinchen Namgyal, a young man from Hanu in his mid-twenties:

> Hanu is a musical place. Particularly, what you see in Hanu is that it is a Brokpa place—you know that. Dha, Baima, Karponat are still Brokpa, but in Hanu it was converted to Ladakhi [language] by a king, and then the king imposed full men in Ladakhi songs on that place [meaning men who had full knowledge?]. The king asked them to sing that kind of song. So, there are so many songs originating from the kings—they are still there. *Zhung lu*—and there's another kind of song—shon lu.[3]

When asked whether he knows *zhung lu*, he said:

> In my village there are still so many functions in the winter—at least twice in a week. And then there are so many *zhung lus*—some of them compete with each other and they have to sing in the same tone. If they are supposed to compete with each other, first I would sing in one tone [i.e., drum rhythm], then another guy would have to sing in the same tone and sing another song.
>
> And though the king had changed the entire language of the village, because first they spoke in Brokpa, and then it was converted to Ladakhi. In Hanu it is now completely Ladakhi, but there are still four or five villages that speak Brokpa. (personal comm., August 5, 2012)[4]

So, what I am told is that in more remote villages, there are people who still sing *zhung lu,* whereas in the town of Leh the presence of radio, cassette players, TV, and later, CDs, DVDs, and the internet, etc. has oriented many people toward a passive mode of music consumption, as opposed to the pretechnological production/consumption of earlier times. In many villages only a few people are known for their singing ability; in some more remote villages, singing and playing music as a pastime is more prevalent. For instance, I have been told by Tsering Anchuk Ralam that many people sing in Skurbuchan village. Some also play *surna* and *daman*, instead of relying on Mon or Beda, and suffer no stigma. This is like performance patterns in the remote area of Zanskar, where there also are no instrumental specialists (personal comm., July 2011). Angchuk Ralam went on to note that most people who sing in Skyurbuchan don't have a good knowledge of complicated congregational songs from the old royal court (*zhung lu*), often singing them imperfectly in terms of melody and rhythm, and often inserting nonlexical syllables that distort the meaning of song texts.

Preservation and Promotion of Ladakhi Language and Music

Given the availability of radio, TV, and recorded media, even in remote villages, Ladakhis are increasingly exposed to mass media in Hindi. Nevertheless, there is also increasing Ladakhi language media production including radio, TV, music CDs, movies, and music videos, the last distributed both on video CDs (VCDs) and the internet.

Mass media exerts an influence on traditional songs, with those versions aired on radio or recorded on cassette and CD or posted on the internet being canonized as the standard or "correct" versions. What appears to be happening in Ladakhi mass media and in popular and scholarly discourse is a folklorization of Ladakhi music.

The English term "folklore" was coined in 1846 by British antiquarian William John Thomas, who defined it as "the manners, customs, observances, superstitions, ballad, proverbs, etc., of the olden times" (cited in Bauman 1992). This concept, which originated in nineteenth-century romanticism and nationalism, became a subject of concern among "individuals who felt nostalgia for the past and/or the necessity of documenting the existence of national consciousness or identity" (Dundes 1980, 1).

In a 2002 paper on preservation of intangible cultural heritage (ICH) Peter Seitel defines folklorization as "re-styling the expressions of ICH so that they become less complex aesthetically and semantically. They thus reify the notion of a dominant culture (the one whose knowledge informs and is developed by official administrative and educational institutions) that folklore is not as complex or meaningful as the products of high, elite, or official cultural processes" (Seitel 2002, 5). This last definition might be applied to Ladakh, in that the elite in scholarly, entrepreneurial, and media circles collect, categorize, and package traditional culture, such as music and dance, to promote a modern concept of Ladakhi identity. However, in contrast with folklorization controlled by an outside hegemonic culture, Ladakhi discourses on traditional song are primarily a reflection of internal changes in that society, in terms of both language and performance venues.

Colloquial Ladakhi was not written until the late 1800s and has only been commonly used in print media since the 1970s. Efforts to collect, codify, and propagate the language and literature have been conducted by academics such as Gen Tashi Rabgias and the Ladakh Cultural Academy, media organizations such as the local branches of All India Radio (AIR) and Doordarshan TV (DDTV), and grassroots organizations such as the Ladakh Ecological Development Group (LEDeG), the Ladakh Arts and Media Organization (LAMO), and SECMOL.

One can draw parallels with the fading of North American folk musics and their revival in the 1940s through 1970s. Although the roles played by those such as Tashi Rabgias, Morup Namgyal, AIR, and the Cultural Academy are not the same as those of John and Alan Lomax, Pete Seeger, and Folkways Records and the Smithsonian, one now sees a similar level of energy in Ladakhi preservation efforts. However, as in North America, standardization of the repertoire seems a likely outcome, given the pervasive nature of modern mass media.

The very use of the English word "folk" song is fraught with colonialist and/or classist bourgeois connotations (cf. Keil 1978; Henderson 2003). The dichotomy between poor, rural, mountain village life and the more prosperous life in lowland urban centers has been examined in other Himalayan contexts in Garhwali India and Nepal (Fiol 2011; Henderson 2003).

In the case of multiethnic Nepal, David Henderson and Paul D. Greene noted the government policy during the Panchayat period of presenting radio broadcasts of folk music from all regions, but in polished arrangements translated into the common Nepali. Nevertheless, such *lok gīt* are represented as being from the various regions (Henderson 2003). These *lok gīt* broadcasts and recordings (audio and video) target the educated urban populations of the Kathmandu Valley who are several generations removed from village life. *Lok gīt* are viewed as indexical to village life and evoke nostalgia for rural simplicity.

Henderson identified two main audiences for folk songs on Radio Nepal. First, many people living in the city grew up in villages and came to Kathmandu to work. Despite the hardships of village life, he found these people often talked about how folk songs remind them of life in a closely knit community full of shared pleasure. People who have lived all their lives in Kathmandu enjoy folk songs for their evocation of simpler times that are seemingly still available in village life. This nostalgia is not rooted in actual extensive experience of village life, but rather memories of the folk songs themselves combined with village images drawn from mass media (Henderson 2003, 8).

In post-Panchayat Nepal, Anna Stirr observed that the mono-lingual, mono-ethnic model had transformed in the production, marketing, and circulation of popular folk music. Various ethnic organizations view their sponsoring audio and video productions in terms of heritage preservation, emphasizing rural hill society (Stirr 2018).

There are differences between the Nepali urbanites and those living in Leh. Ladakhis are, for the most part, rarely more than a generation removed from village life, with many people still having relatives living in rural areas. Secondly, Leh is nowhere near the size of the sprawling urban center that is Kathmandu and does not isolate people in the same way an all-encompassing metropolis does. Thirdly, the outer trappings of tradition are still considered to be important, for example wearing *gon-chas* (men's Tibetan-style robes) and *sulma* (women's pleated overdress) on formal occasions such as when important lamas are present. Finally, as mentioned, songs in many genres have not been translated from local dialects into "colloquial modern Ladakhi" (*pal skad*). This contrasts with the Nepali language standardization of *lok gīt* during the Panchayat period noted by Henderson, which more clearly illustrates Seitel's characterization of folklorization as a restyling of regional musics.

Stefan Fiol's studies of Garhwali *Baddī* trance and festival music offer a view of a different dynamic. No state policy has been at work to preserve this repertoire, and the lowly social position of the *Baddī* (low-caste musicians) has led many of them to abandon music in favor of construction and other less stigmatized occupations. Nevertheless, a few artists continue to perform and have been recorded in academic settings as well as on commercial recordings. The picture is complicated by commercial appropriation and co-option of the *Baddī* repertoire and image, distorting, misrepresenting, exoticizing, and eroticizing them. The *Baddī* are part of the Garhwali self-image and are objects of nostalgia—not that this is enough to sustain them financially or relieve them of the burden of low status (Fiol 2010a, 2010b, 2011). This dynamic is somewhat like that of the Mon and Beda in Ladakh. By contrast, the Ladakhi repertoires, although less utilized in their traditional village contexts, are being cultivated in the new venues of mass media and tourist-oriented performances. They are performed by Mon and Beda, as well as by cultural activists who are not traditional musicians.

Ladakh differs from Nepal and the Garhwali region in several very significant ways. Firstly, it has traditionally been far less accessible to the rest of India, and even now is cut off from road traffic for almost half the year due to snow and landslides. Secondly, it has a much sparser population. These factors have not been conducive to significant urbanization or commerce that would support a native recording industry.

Furthermore, mainstream Indian media had little interest in Ladakh until the late 1990s. The various border conflicts with Pakistan brought it into prominence in several Bollywood movies—all with no Ladakhi music in them! Ladakh is portrayed as a rugged, exotic landscape in which life-and-death military struggles are played out. It was not until the 1990s that any commercial Ladakhi media production started, aided by the access to affordable cassette technology (cf. Manuel 1993).

The question of agency becomes important in terms of examining musical preservation and revitalization in Ladakh. Increased migration of educated Ladakhis to either Leh or urban centers in the south, such as Jammu, Chandigarh, or Delhi, creates the grounds for nostalgia. This nostalgia manifests itself in several ways in Ladakhi mass media. In the case of traditional music, images of rural life or historical scenes are portrayed in music videos, album covers, etc. Popular music videos often show scenes of rural life with shifting views of modernity versus tradition, especially in matters of clothing.

Relating to this discourse is an issue of terminology that has arisen at least since the publication of *Ladvags gyi yul glu* in 1970. The term *yul*, meaning nation, village, or countryside, is used by Tashi Rabgias to be equivalent to "folk." This seems to be a Tibetan usage (*yul glu* or *yul gzhas*), probably also influenced by the Hindi *lok sangeet* (people's music) or *lok geet* (people's song). However, this term is not widely recognized, or used in common speech; instead, the term *zhung lu (gzhung glu)* (traditional songs) is used. The other definition of *gzhung*, meaning "center," "gathered," or "congregational," refers to a specific song genre sung during traditional gatherings in the old royal palace in Leh. The more general "traditional" label covers virtually anything that is not commercial popular music.

I am more inclined to classify the *zhung lu* sung in the royal palace as art songs—a view shared with Mark Trewin and Susan Stephens (Trewin and Stephens 1987). I base this classification on the following criteria. Firstly, we have their cultivation by the aristocratic elite. According to Basgo musician Tsering Sonam Lagachirpon (figure 4.2), the lyrics for *zhung lu* were customarily submitted to the palace for approval and subsequent setting to music by the *khar mon*. He gave the impression this was more a literary critique issue than a censorship issue—one hoped one's lyrics were judged worthy to be performed before the king (personal comm., August 7, 2011).

The sophisticated literary evaluation places *zhung lu* in the continuum of pan-Tibetan, high literary culture, separating them from any small local oral traditions. This leads to the second point regarding music theory. While there is no large body of music theory comparable to that

Figure 4.2. Tsering Sonam Lagachirpon playing *khopong*. *Source*: Author's photo.

of Indian classical musics, the texts are governed by criteria arbitrated by the aristocracy and scholars from the point of view of classical Hindu and Buddhist esthetic theory.

Musical Preservation and Revitalization

There was concern as to whether the de-stigmatization of playing the instruments would catch on and lead to a reversal of repertoire loss. To address this issue, cultural advocacy groups started teaching traditional songs and musical instruments to keep them alive. One of the first was SECMOL. According to their website (www.secmol.org): "The Students' Educational and Cultural Movement of Ladakh (SECMOL) was founded in 1988 by a group of young Ladakhis to reform the educational system of Ladakh. Over the years our activities have been varied and are now mainly focused on activities for Ladakhi youth." One of SECMOL's main raison d'être was the continual neglect of Ladakh's educational system by the Jammu and Kashmir central government. Again, according to the SECMOL website: "In 1998, 95% of Ladakhi students failed the state 10th class exams every year, so we concluded that it was necessary to change the educational system. In 1994 SECMOL launched the Operation New Hope movement to improve education in Leh District, in collaboration with the Education Department, the local government and the village community members." In addition to its strong focus on education SECMOL publishes children's books, textbooks, and magazines in English and Ladakhi, as well as Ladakhi dictionaries, grammar books, and books on Ladakhi culture. SECMOL has a school campus in the village of Phey where daily activities support Ladakhi language and culture. Among these is the sharing and singing of traditional songs by resident staff and students. According to Rebecca Norman: "We sing /zhunglu/ after dinner every day at SECMOL so that the Ladakhi youth get a chance to learn these songs—otherwise, many young Ladakhis today don't know any zhunglu at all" (personal comm., email, November 2009).

SECMOL began running summer camp programs at their campus in Phey where traditional songs are an important part of the activities. Other workshops were run in different locations throughout Ladakh by the Youth Wing of the Ladakh Buddhist Association and the Young Men's Buddhist Association, recruiting notable musicians such as Tsering Stanzin of Skurbuchan as teachers.

These training programs have helped to foster local performance ensembles. One notable group was centered around Basgo village, one of the old royal capitals, informally headed by pharmacist Tsering Sonam Basgo Lagachirpon, pictured with Tsewang Paldan Wanda Yokmapa (Figure 4.3). The singers in the group are Sonam Wangdus Zasnapa, a carpenter and farmer and Stanzin Namgyal Zopa, a farmer (Figure 4.4). Other members of the group came from the neighboring villages of Ngey, Tia, and Wanda. Tsering Sonam said that prior to his first attending the SECMOL workshops, many of the musicians didn't really know each other well or know that the others sang or played (personal comm., August 7, 2011). The ensemble plays both on the radio in Leh and for various festivals, both locally and further away, and gets paid for it.

Other groups have been springing up. An acquaintance of mine, cultural activist Sonam Gyaltsan, was involved in a Leh-based ensemble whose members primarily learned surna and daman from Tsering Sonam Lagachirpon. Sonam Gyaltsan remarked how various Beda complained that his group takes away jobs from them. He counters that music is everyone's to learn, perform, and enjoy. One may note parallels between

Figure 4.3. Surna players Tsewang Paldan Yokmapa and Tsering Sonam Lagachirpon. *Source:* Author's photo.

Figure 4.4. Basgo Village Singers Sonam Wandus Zasnapa and Stanzin Namgyal Zopa. *Source:* Author's photo.

this case and that of Indian middle-class Brahmin co-option of Hindustani and Carnatic classical music, and the subsequent disenfranchisement of low-caste and/or Muslim and/or unmarried female performers (*tawaifs* and *devadasis*) (cf. Bakhle 2005; Srinivasan 1985).

Further grassroots musical education began at the Siddhartha School in Stok Village. Founded by Khensur Rimpoche Geshe Lobzang Tsetan, the abbot emeritus of Tashilhunpo Monastery, it is currently directed by his nephew Geshe Tsewang Dorje. Students learn songs, traditional dances, and how to play the *damnyan/khopong*, performing at public functions as well as at school.

As tourism becomes a dominant part of the local economy, traditional song and dance have undergone processes of commoditization and folklorization. Tourist-oriented performances occur at summer festivals in venues like the Leh Polo Grounds, as well as at NGOs like the Himalayan Cultural Heritage Foundation (HCHF) and the Ladakh Arts and Media Organization (LAMO). Hotels are springing up all over on land that was formerly cultivated fields, generating considerable wealth in certain sectors of the population. The larger, fancier hotels often arrange song and dance performances for tourists that employ musicians. According to conversations with people at the Ladakh Buddhist Association (LBA), one of the main points of their music workshops was to train young people so they can find employment as musicians for the tourist trade. They have similar programs to train people as monastery guides.

Broadcast Media

AIR broadcasts began in Leh in 1971 with a mixture of national programming transmitted in Hindi and local news and music programming in Ladakhi (Dolma 2009). Everyday programs of Ladakhi traditional songs are aired for thirty minutes, with either live performances or archived recordings. These broadcasts have allowed various singers to gain fame beyond their local audiences. Some vocalists come with their supporting party of musicians that may perform instrumental dance music as well.

AIR Leh has a small group of staff musicians that function primarily as supporting instrumentalists for vocalists. No staff musicians are exclusively vocalists, although many are fine, educated singers. Singers are remunerated according to a schedule of fees for casual artists of varying grades.

Funded by tourism, the blossoming of Ladakh's economy has led to increased cultural production. Now, Ladakhis in general are proud of who they are and where they live. This is compared to the economically depressed 1970s when everyone who could do so procured work in places like Jammu, Punjab, or Delhi. A branch of DDTV was set up in 1984 but was limited to national broadcast feeds in Hindi. Not until 1991 was Ladakhi language programming instituted consisting of news and cultural programs, including traditional music and dance (Dolma 2009).

Printed compilations of song lyrics have been part of song preservation in conjunction with radio and sound recordings. In the early days of AIR broadcasts from Leh, Morup Namgyal sang many songs with texts from LYL. As a result, these versions became somewhat canonized in many people's minds. When I first started doing research at AIR in 2009, the director, the late Tsewang Rigzin, kept a copy of LYL in his office.

As is common at media organizations throughout the world, politics, personalities, and random misfortune get in the way of music preservation. An unfortunate fire at the AIR studio some years ago led to the loss of irreplaceable archived reel-to-reel recordings of artists both living and dead. Former program director Morup Namgyal did all he could to save and/or re-record artists whose recordings had been lost, and deeply regretted the loss of valuable cultural treasures.

With recent modernizations of the AIR studio, efforts are being made to convert the archives to digital formats that can be backed up to avoid future mishaps. All current recordings are digital and backed up with archival CDs as well as disk drives. I myself was the beneficiary of this new technology when Tsewang Rigzin asked me to give a radio interview in Hindi about my research. The producer/host Stanzin Lodus was able to give me a copy of the MP3 file in short order.

The combined print and broadcast propagation of the LYL versions of the lyrics has had the effect of canonizing them in the minds of villagers and town dwellers. Mass media such as radio, TV, and commercial cassettes, CDs and the internet have led, as they have in most of the world, to an increased passivity in the consumption and production of music. This has been noted by Rebecca Norman: "Once the All-India Radio station starts playing a given version, or when somebody (mostly Morup Namgyal or Dorje Stakmo) releases a recorded version, everyone seems to think that is the "correct" version. . . . Between young people tending not to learn them and All India Radio standardizing them (usually to MN's version), it's likely that the local variations will quickly be lost" (personal comm., email, November 17, 2009).

This process has continued with the three-volume collection published by the Cultural Academy. In the editorial process a committee of scholars and performers took texts of songs previously published and subjected them to editorial scrutiny. This was in part intended to correct any textual contradictions that may have crept in via oral transmission. The net effect contributes to the further canonization of specific textual versions. Each book was accompanied by a CD with the first verses of most of the songs in each volume (some melodies were not available). This too may potentially lead to a canonization process. Nevertheless, the intention is to allow people to learn the songs, preserving them for future generations. The latest edition has replaced the CDs with QR codes that people can use to download the songs to their smartphones to allow for greater access.

Music Education

Through the combined efforts of the various NGOs and government institutions, education in song repertoire and musical instruments has grown. Individuals such as Tsering Sonam Lagachirpon, Mahammud Ali, Angdu Khigu, Tsering Stanzin, Kunzes Dolma (figure 4.5), and others have been offering classes in singing, surna, daman, *khopong* to young people in various settings both scholastic and outside. Recently, Tsering Sonam's student Angdu Khigu has been prominent in the revival of the khopong and, to a lesser extent, the piwang.

Angdu Khigu is an IT technician working for the district medical office and is not a full-time musician. Nevertheless, he has been active in music education and revival. He had a class in 2018 teaching *khopong* at the Buddhist Padme Druk Kharpo School in Leh. As a private teacher, he at one point early on had about twenty-five experienced and beginning students on *khopong*. He lamented the fact that he only has one *piwang* student, although that one was good, having previous experience playing guitar and drum. This has expanded as he has given various group courses under the auspices of the Cultural Academy and other institutions.

His teaching activities have increased dramatically; as he noted, he has had over a hundred students, past and present. He added: "I also provide classes even in out of Ladakh, last year was in west Bengal there I teach

Figure 4.5. Beda singer Kunzes Dolma. *Source:* Author's photo.

Khopong and flute to Monk in Darjeeling monestry. . . . no piwang students, because there is no one willing to make the instruments" (personal comm., June 6, 2023). Figure 4.6 is a screenshot of a video Angdu posted on Facebook on February 14, 2023, in which he is teaching khopong to a group of young people from Changthang. This class was offered free or at low cost to students. Angdu received a small fee from the Cultural Academy.

He has been so inspiring that some of his second batch of students were inspired to create a khopong academy (figure 4.7):

> Khopong institution means in Ladakh it's almost revive[d] and everyone [wants to] learn and play. Every day I get calls. I am very busy in summer and also in office. Therefore some students started commercial class in Choglamsar. . . . Jigmet is from Sakti village,he [is from] my second batch student.

Usually, instruments have been made by hand in Changthang by one or two people. It was significant that Tsering Sonam was kind enough to sell me his own instrument (pictured in figure 4.2) so that I could learn to accompany myself. With the explosion in the number of people learning the instrument, Angdu has outsourced mass production to Tibetan workshops in Delhi and Dharamsala in order to keep costs down and meet demand. Angdu added, "To date I supply more than 300 Khopong in Ladakh region without any profit, shape and quality is much better than

Figure 4.6. Angdu Khigu's khopong class for Changthang students. Fair use.

Figure 4.7. Khopong academy. Fair use.

Figure 4.8. Khopong production line. Fair use.

you have. All the instrument brought from Dharamshala, Delhi" Figure 4.8 shows the instruments in various stages of completion, with Figure 4.9 showing the finished product. Angdu pointed out that the leather and paint work were done in Leh.

With missionary zeal, Angdu has written a khopong primer, adapting the Indian *sargam* notation system. This volume (figure 4.10) was published at the end of 2022 by the Cultural Academy.

And if that weren't enough, he goes on to state: "Now my next destination is [to] revive the piwang instrument" (Ibid.).

Angdu has been almost singlehandedly responsible for reviving the Ladakhi version of the fiddle known as the *piwang*, which differs in shape from the Tibetan instrument of the same name. It has fallen out of use in Ladakh, even in Changthang. However, with the encouragement of people like Tsering Sonam Lagachirpon it was revived and reconstructed. Old derelict instruments were around in various village households, but no one played them—people only talked about old times. Angdu Khigu, already learning *khopong* from whomever he could, wanted an instrument with sustain that could accompany songs other than Changthang *zhabro*.

Figure 4.9. Finished mass-produced khopongs. Fair use.

Figure 4.10. Khopong primer by Angdu Khigu. Fair use.

A clue as to reconstruction was provided by Brown University PhD student Katie Freeze, who spent a year in Ladakh studying *khopong* as part of her broader study of Central Asian lutes. She shared a video with various people, taken in the neighboring Spiti Valley in Himachal Pradesh, showing a three-course fiddle built like the *khopong*. This supplied clues for reconstruction. Subsequently, Angdu also located a lone, eighty-five-year-old *piwang* player in Changthang who was able to demonstrate both a working instrument and playing technique. Working with a *khopong* maker, Angdu was able to reconstruct the shape and tuning, resulting in a four-string instrument tuned D-GG-d (Figure 4.11) This maker was not enthusiastic about making more of them, as they are more complicated than *khopong* and take longer to build. I asked Angdu if he could get the

Figure 4.11. Angdu Khigu playing *piwang*. Fair use.

gentleman to make me one, as I am a performer of Ladakhi vocal genres and want an instrument with more sustain. Short of the maker relenting, I am going to be obliged to build one myself.

Music Revitalization and Controversy in Kargil District

I have not spent any significant time in Kargil District, but through discussions with colleagues and recordings from that region, I can report on some of the cultural activities there. Differences in the majority religions—Shia and Naqshbandi Sufi—have shaped a different trajectory. I have previously mentioned the Balti *ghazal* repertoire popular in both Leh and Kargil towns. Other notable genres include the lengthy narrative ballads from the Gesar epic (Balti *rgyang lhu*), as well as instrumental music for outside events like archery, dances, and polo matches.

The influence of Shia puritanism inspired by the Iranian Revolution starting in the 1980s discouraged public performance of secular genres.

Nevertheless, religious genres connected with Ramadan, Eid al Fitr, Eid al Adha, and Muharram such as *Marsiya, Nauha,* and *Qasida* are popular with large public performances, both live and disseminated via broadcast media, sound recordings, and videos posted on YouTube.

According to writer, scholar, and educator Nasir Shabani there has been a resurgence in public performances of song and dance. This has carried over into education at all levels of primary, secondary, and post-secondary institutions (personal comm., June 1, 2023). He shared with me the YouTube video of the conference in Kargil commemorating the forty-first anniversary of the Suru Valley Public Higher Secondary School, where there were addresses from across Ladakh with videos in the background. These show students singing and dancing (figures 4.12 and 4.13)

In another video of the Mendoktsar Dramatic Club, Kargil, we see men and women singing and dancing to a Balti ghazal written by Fida

Figure 4.12. Kargil secondary school students singing and dancing (Sharbani 2023). Fair use.

Figure 4.13. Kargil secondary school girls singing and dancing (Sharbani 2023). Fair use.

Hussain Shamim Baltistani. They are accompanied by daman, harmonium, and a bowed instrument (not clearly visible) (figure 4.14). The comments are for the most part from both sides of the Line of Control between Kargil and Pakistani Gilgit-Baltistan) with the majority showing cultural pride and appreciation.

Nevertheless, there is some pushback from conservatives, as seen in comments. Criticisms include:

- It is not Islamic Balti culture.

- Bollywood culture has prevailed in Kargil; people have lost their own culture.

- Jinnah was right: he knew that this would happen in a Hindu dominant country.

- Girls and boys dancing in front of spectators in the name of culture is shameful.

Figure 4.14. Public Balti ghazal performance in Kargil. Fair use.

- They feel that the people of Baltistan and Skardu are following the right path (i.e., being more conservative and discouraging such performances).

Conclusions

This body of music has had a diminishing place in Ladakh as that society has profoundly changed since Indian independence in 1947. In part these changes were the result of Mon rejecting their despised position, leaving no one to perform on *surna* and *daman*. In part changes are the result of a shift to a faster-paced, more mobile economy where people do not have time for lengthy ceremonies like weddings, or the fact that farmwork is often performed by Nepali migrant labor instead of Ladakhi farmers.

The major transformation of Ladakhi society to a tourism-based economy, starting in the 1990s, has pumped a huge amount of capital into the economy and fostered a sense of regional pride that was lacking in previous decades. This has given rise to a market, both locally and for tourists, for recorded music and videos that depict traditional music and dance. The marketing of "tradition" is closely linked with images of rural costumes, agriculture, homes, and history. These resonate with the Ladakhi middle class that consumes mass media, reinforcing a sense of continuity with family back in the villages. Thus, we see a shifting back and forth between t-shirt and jeans to the *gonchas* (male robe), and between Punjabi-style *salwar-kameez* (women's baggy pants and tunic) and traditional *sulma* (pleated dress), as dictated by the formality of the occasion. Media presentations linking traditional images with song reinforce the sense of Ladakhi identity.

The seductively ubiquitous Hindi mass media presence has grown tremendously. Yet this same mass media has also allowed traditional songs to spread beyond their usual venues and is serving as a vehicle for preservation as well. This archiving and preservation have been accompanied by a renewed interest in the performance of traditional songs, and in young people learning traditional instruments as part of a dynamic revitalization at all levels of Ladakhi society.

On the other hand, the collection of song texts and broadcasts of recordings by singing stars has tended to create a folkloric canon of "official" or "correct" versions, to the detriment of local variants. Ngawang Tsering Shakspo has noted this trend, but casts it in an optimistic light:

> The fact that old songs are now being collected, and new ones composed, written and broadcast, implies that a process of standardization is probably occurring whereby regional variations are becoming less pronounced. The writing of the songs must itself be having a considerable effect on the nature of what was previously a purely oral tradition. It is obvious that the face of the folk tradition is changing quite rapidly in some respects and will probably continue to do so in the future. However, this is only possible because the tradition of song in Ladakh is so strong that such changes are both necessary and accommodated in its already rich cultural heritage. (Shakspo 2008, 75)

Given the current boom of Indian tourists flooding Ladakh, the seasonal demand for performing arts has increased dramatically. The growth of opportunities for income, coupled with increased ethnic pride, offer added incentive for music revival. With the uncertainty surrounding the splitting of Ladakh from Jammu and Kashmir, and the revocation of Article 370 of the Indian Constitution, the question of protected tribal status for Ladakh as a Union Territory is up in the air. Judging by all Ladakhi media discourse this is a hot topic, with Ladakhis being aggressively vocal about asserting their cultural integrity. The next few years will be fraught with danger but rife with possibilities.

Chapter 5

Songs and Cultural Representation in the Modern Market

Wandering around the music stores and stalls of Leh Bazaar in the late 2000s, I found that most cassettes, CDs, VCDs, and DVDs are Bollywood and Nepali popular music and videos. A couple of dozen selections were Ladakhi popular music, and another dozen or so are Ladakhi traditional music of various genres. Most recordings of both popular and traditional music have been produced in studios in Delhi or Jammu, with a few done in small Ladakhi studios.

In the 2010s, the number and sophistication of Ladakhi production facilities increased, with the top studios having multiple sound booths, digital mixing and editing, and sophisticated postproduction such as doubling of tracks for a fuller sound. Awareness of digital production techniques is becoming more common, especially among singers who have any contact with mass media facilities. In fact, while I was making field recordings, several notable singers requested CD or DVD copies, so they could do editing on computers owned by friends and/or family. This is hardly surprising where many farmhouses, even in remote rural areas, have solar photo-voltaic chargers for batteries and satellite television dishes. The most sophisticated example was when I spent several hours observing recording sessions run by singer/composer/producer Dorjay (Stakmo). His studio features PCs with Pro Tools and other editing software, with which he carefully lays down tracks.

Much of the economic dynamic has changed as digital copying has made piracy almost ubiquitous. CDs and DVDs are almost never produced anymore or are viewed only as advertisements for publicity to generate live performances. Much production has shifted online to platforms like YouTube, as musicians have become part of the digital world. The dividing line between traditional and popular musics has been blurring as younger artists produce arrangements that use nontraditional, Western, or African instruments like guitar, synthesizer, and djembe drum—not necessarily a bad thing if one views this as being a living art as opposed to a museum piece.

Representations of Tradition

Mass media representations of traditional culture in Leh District focus on images of rural life: clothing, farming, nomadic herding, mountain passes, as well as Buddhist iconography. These images have been used in the packaging and presentation of recorded music since cassette and CD technologies became locally available in the 1980s and 1990s. A detailed examination of various examples reveals several trends.

Morup Namgyal[1] (figure 5.1) dominated the Ladakhi music scene, both as AIR program director from the 1970s through the 1990s, and as

Figure 5.1. Morup Namgyal. *Source:* Author's photo.

a public performer and composer. His early access to recording studios allowed him to produce a variety of influential recordings, both of traditional and popular music. The cover art for his cassettes and CDs uses Buddhist iconography and scenes of rural life.

Both his 2003 CD Music Center *Folk Songs of Ladakh* (figure 5.2) and a cassette of the same name use images of rough-clad rural men and women for the covers. Before I met him in 2009, I had thought that the man on the cassette cover *was* Morup Namgyal, in part because his name is directly under the male image. It should be noted that both men on the CD cover are bearded elders in traditional rural costume. These images, aimed at the urban Leh audience and/or non-Ladakhi tourists, clearly use the tropes of age = tradition = rural = traditional songs. Other album covers feature a *surna* and *daman*. In the minds of many Ladakhis these instruments are emblematic of traditional music. This was summarized a couple of years ago when talking to pop singer/songwriter Phontsok Tsering Dhimbir. We were discussing the possibility of his touring the US to perform folk songs.[2] He speculated as to whether we could get *surna* and *daman* players as well. He noted that "it just isn't the same without *surna* and *daman*" (personal comm., June 2008).

It might be argued that these aforementioned covers are somewhat disingenuous in omitting Morup Namgyal's image, focusing instead on images that evoke rural authenticity. Like most Ladakhis, Morup Namgyal was born in a rural village (Wanla) but is educated and lives

Figure 5.2. Morup Namgyal CD: *Folk Songs of Ladakh*. Fair use.

as a sophisticated Leh urbanite, often wearing a jacket and tie for formal secular occasions. It is common for Tibetan and Ladakhi Buddhists to wear traditional male and female dress (*gonchas* and *sulma* respectively) for formal religious occasions, such as teachings by His Holiness the Dalai Lama (figure 5.3). Clearly, for many Ladakhis, traditional dress relates to auspicious occasions that have cultural significance, evoking thoughts of traditional life when seen in images.

This approach is also followed by the very popular singer/producer Tundup Dorje from Stakmo Village (commonly known as Dorjay Stakmo). He is shown in figure 5.4 in *gonchas*, with various mountain and meadow scenes in the background. Oddly enough, his female support singer, Tibetan Tsetan Lhamo, is apparently not in traditional costume but is shown in a smaller superimposed image, smiling beguilingly. This gives a mixed message of tradition and modern marketing of female image.

As we see in the album cover in figure 5.5, exoticism and sexual allure are used as marketing tools. In a strategy like Morup Namgyal's

Figure 5.3. Ladakhis in traditional dress awaiting the Dalai Lama, Leh 2009. *Source:* Author's photo.

Figure 5.4. Dorjay Stakmo Jaabro CD. Fair use.

album covers, Dorje Stakmo is not even shown. Instead, we see images of a demure young Ladakhi girl, wearing the traditional *perak* (festival headdress decorated with massive amounts of turquoise). The use of the violin image in the background may be construed as showing that the producers are global sophisticates, yet still authentically Ladakhi—either that or some graphic designer gratuitously chose a stock image relating to music.

Figure 5.5. Dorjay Stakmo CD. Fair use.

Some earlier cassettes from the 1990s presented a more conservative bare-bones packaging. The AWA production group cassette recording (figure 5.6) features older traditional singers: Tsering Stanzin, Padma Dorje, and the late Tseschu Lamo (awarded the Sangeet Natak Academy Award for folk music, and referred to as the Lata Mangeshkar of Ladakh).

The Ladakh Ecology Development Group (LEDeG), in addition to its focus, worked with Gen Tashi Rabgias, publishing several of his collections of poems, as well as books of song texts in a similar vein as LYL. They have also published a few cassettes of traditional Ladakhi music. The

Figure 5.6. AWA production—Zhung-lu. Fair use.

LEDeG cassettes were packaged as part of the general agenda for cultural development and preservation, with cassette covers having simple designs showing women in traditional *sulma* and *perak*.

Video and the Portrayal of Tradition

The advent of video has allowed for richer semiology, a dimension that Dorjay Stakmo has been exploring extensively. In his video CD, *Zhung lu: First Folk Video Album of Ladakh* (figure 5.7), he presents five vignettes as settings for individual folksongs. Each depicts totally traditional rural settings; all with Buddhist themes. An analysis of two of these videos is revealing.

The first song, *rgya nag po tho shes na* (If You Know the Chinese Altar), is from the Gesar saga, with a text listing his childhood conquests, similar to those mentioned in previous chapters. There follows a series of scenes that portray Gesar's connections with Chenrezig/Avalokiteswara and his miraculous deeds.

As the action proceeds, we see the king perform a series of acts of devotion, manifesting magical/spiritual power. He offers a *khatag* (prayer scarf) at a shrine and then carves the Chenrezig mantra, *Om mani padme hum*, on a rock—a common devotional practice. Through the magic of video technology, we witness the miraculous appearance of a *khatag*, followed

Figure 5.7. Dorjay Stakmo's first VCD album cover. Fair use.

by a cup of tea. We then see an arrow shot into the air becoming a ball of blessed light. The song ends with a bow to the buddhas, dedicating the merit of his actions for the benefit of all sentient beings—again, common Buddhist practice.

The next video on the CD is a setting of the *zhung lu Thiksey Gompa*. The opening scene is a Ladakhi dinner party in a traditional kitchen. The men are seated at *chogtse* (low Tibetan tables), with the women on the other side of the kitchen. The hostess is serving, and as she salutes the guests, we see the kitchen that is the social center of rural homes, with the dishes in glass-fronted cabinets and the brass decorated iron stove (figure 5.8) that is the home for its own tutelary deity, the *thab lha* (stove god).

A Mon enters the room announcing that he and his group will supply music. Oddly, the actor/musician has a stammer. The question I have is this: Is it just incidental, or does this play into some stereotype, perhaps of Mon being inbred? The members of the dinner party then decide that they want to hear the song about the famous Gelug-pa monastery.

The actor playing the host then lip-synchs the song sung by Dorjay Stakmo to the sound of the *surna* and *daman*. At various stages, the other

Figure 5.8. Women sitting behind the stove. Fair use.

men display outpourings of emotion and devotional feeling and gently stroke or cup each other's faces in displays of camaraderie. We see this type of male bonding in other videos produced by Dorje.

The song itself is structured as a mandala with praise to the various levels of the world and human society, connecting them to Thiksey Gompa as the center. The images go through a visualization, starting with a long exterior shot with the row of stupas in front of the complex (figure 5.9), to the interiors of the temples and prayer halls with the assembly of monks. The focus finally shifts to the central icon of the founding Thiksey Rinpoche[3] on the altar. The scene then ends with a close-up of the current Thiksey Rinpoche,[4] leading the prayers. The views then reverse, ending up back at the distant view of the monastery.

Dorjay Stakmo's next *zhung lu* VCD weaves the songs into a continuous story depicting images of village life with little dramas and stresses, resolving into heartfelt rural harmony. In this VCD Dorjay employs songs

Figure 5.9. Thiksey Gompa. Fair use.

in a similar way to Bollywood movies, using them interspersed and/or simultaneous with the action. He also uses a broader variety of instruments, substituting the *lingbu* (transverse flute) for surna for the most part. The traditional ensemble is not used for most of the songs but for the most part plays faintly in the background. It is used more actively in a fight scene in which a village rowdy is rampaging, underscoring the action with a dramatic, urgent motif.

As seen from the cover (figure 5.10), the double whistle flute (*sakling*) figures prominently in accompanying songs. Both it and the single *ling bu* are associated with herders and are deeply associated with rural life. The mixing of flute and *daman* is innovative, but still clearly indexes to traditional village life. From a musical production point of view, it has the advantage of being less overwhelming than *surna* in conjunction with the solo voice of Dorje. Clearly his experience as a popular and traditional singer, as well as a recording engineer and producer, has allowed him to make such an artistic choice and have it enthusiastically received by the Ladakhi public.

Oddly enough, the choice to use the flute was an accident, precipitated by the moist climate in Delhi where the sound recordings were made, rendering the daman very muffled. To compensate for the lower volume, he substituted the flute tracks, played by the renowned Tibetan flautist Nawang Kechog.

Many of these videos have been uploaded to YouTube, giving artists greater exposure, given that the new economics have turned the videos

Figure 5.10. Dorjay Stakmo's VCD. Fair use.

into purely promotional materials with little hope of monetizing them. Millennials and Gen X, as digital natives, have wholeheartedly embraced the new venue. As previously mentioned, depictions of tradition have a strong appeal.

In addition to Angdu Khigu, a host of young artists have come to prominence. One of the rising stars of both traditional and popular music is Dorjay Stakmo's student, vocalist Padma Dolkar (born 1998). In the video depicted in figure 5.11 she is shown in a traditional kitchen (the center of social life in Ladakhi households) accompanied by Angdu Khigu playing *piwang*. Except for Angdu's sunglasses, their dress is all evocative of "the good old days" (https://www.youtube.com/watch?v=evb5KUZRlmo accessed July 7, 2023).

The Dashugs Band takes a slightly different, more popular approach to light genres like *ghazal* and *zhabro*. Their instrumentation is a mixture of the traditional: *khopong* and *daman,* with steel string acoustic guitar and quiet electric bass, and the now very popular African *djembe* drum. In the video pictured in figure 5.12 the guys are all wearing traditional *gonchas*, although the guitarist is wearing a Western-style cowboy hat, which is very common among nomadic Tibetan and Changthang popu-lations—and sneakers! (https://www.youtube.com/watch?v=6sbTMC9Vfpg accessed July 8, 2023).

Musically, they keep very close to the original performance style of *zhabro*. The *djembe* is subordinate to the daman, which plays the typical three-against-two hemiola pattern. The guitar plays a subdued A-minor/G-major ostinato elaborated by the bass. The energetic dance tempo and

Figure 5.11. Padma Dolkar, vocal and Angdu Khigu, piwang. Fair use.

Figure 5.12. The Dashugs Band performing a zhabro. Fair use.

mixed visuals produce a polysemic fusion of youthful modernity and eternal traditions.

Given the nonremunerative nature of making recordings in the modern digital world, these videos are the logical successors of the prior physical media. The distribution through social media such as YouTube and Facebook generates social capital that can translate into paid live performances. The careful curation of public image allows these artists to establish celebrity both in Ladakh and in the target audience of tourists who may look for "authentic" experiences when they come to the region.

Chapter 6

Other Song Genres

In this chapter I wish to examine a few of the other notable song genres in Ladakh. These are primarily songs from either agrarian villages or the nomads of the Changthang Plateau that leads into Tibet. Compared to the complex meters of the song types examined so far, other genres are based around simpler rhythmic patterns: binary, ternary, and the occasional compound seven-beat meter (3-2-2). In the case of ternary meters, there is a frequent use of hemiola. The latter is a common feature in Kashmiri, Balti, Afghan, Nepali, and Garhwali musics. For instance, among the nomads on the Changthang Plateau, who are musically and linguistically more akin to the Tibetans, one of the most popular song and dance genres is *Zhabro*. Unlike the better known Tibetan version, the Changthang versions are primarily in ternary meter. Like Tibetan *zhabro,* the most iconic instrument accompanying this genre is the *Damnyan* or *khopong* lute. One of the most famous *zhabro* is "The Damnyan Tashi Wangyal." (Track 20) (Cultural Academy III).

> *sgra snyan nga la zer ba'i bla ma mi 'dug ma sems.*
> *sgra snyan bkra shis dbang rgyal la bla ma mi 'dug ma sems.*
> *sgrub chen thang stong rgyal po sgra snyan nga yi bla ma. 2x*

> [Don't think to tell me that my damnyan does not have a lama.
> Don't think that the damnyan Tashi Wangyal does not have a
>   lama.
> The great spiritual attainer Thangtong Gyalpo is my damnyan's lama. 2x]

sgra snyan nga la zer ba'i yab chen mi 'dug m sems.
sgra snyan bkra shis dbang rgyal la yab chen mi 'dug ma sems.
shing de shing rgyal rgyal po de sgra snyan nga yi yab chen yin. 2x

> [Don't think to tell me that my damnyan does not have a big father.
> Don't think that the damnyan Tashi Wangyal does not have a big father
> That wood of the king of the giant-tree is my damnyan's big father. 2x]

sgra snyan nga la zer ba'i yum chung mi 'dug m sems.
sgra snyan bkra shis dbang rgyal la yum chung mi 'dug ma sems.
sha ba yu mo'i pags pa sgra snyan nga yi yum chung yin. 2x

> [Don't think to tell me that my damnyan does not have a little mother.
> Don't think that the damnyan Tashi Wangyal does not have a little mother.
> That skin of the female deer is my damnyan's little mother. 2x]

sgra snyan nga la zer ba'i spun mched mi 'dug ma sems.
sgra snyan bkra shis dbang rgyal la spun mched mi 'dug ma sems.
tse tse ra ma'i tsi ri de sgra snyan nga yi spun mched yin. 2x

> [Don't think to tell me that my damnyan does not have siblings.
> Don't think that the damnyan Tashi Wangyal does not have
>   siblings.
> The intestines of the she goat are my damnyan's siblings. 2x]

sgra snyan nga la zer ba'i chos grogs mi 'dug ma sems.
sgra snyan bkra shis dbang rgyal la chos grogs mi 'dug ma sems.
phyag mdzub bcu po tsang ma sgra snyan nga yi chos grogs yin. 2x

> [Don't think to tell me that my damnyan has no Dharma companions.
> Don't think that the damnyan Tashi Wangyal has no Dharma
>   companions.
> All my ten fingers are my damnyan's Dharma companions.]

(Ladakh Cultural Academy 2014, III: 1, trans. ND).

The use of metaphor is striking in this and other songs in the genre. Again, we see a hierarchy of relationships depicted: lama, parents, siblings, and fellow spiritual practitioners. The use of nature imagery is common, such as in these lyrics from a *zhabro* recorded by David Lewiston in 1977 (Lewiston 1977).

You are the high sky
You are the sun and the moon
We did not think of meeting before
But we met in the home today
There is nothing as happy as that.

Reflecting the nomadic origins of the genre, equestrian themes are not uncommon, as seen in the *zhabro*, "*rta pho zing zing khrol khrol*" (The Stallion's Bells Go Zing Zing) (Track 21) (Cultural Academy, II: 65–67).

rta pho zing zing khrol khrol—The Stallion's Bells Go Zing Zing
(Cultural Academy, II: 65–67) (Track 21)

rta pho zing zing khrol khrol 2x
rta pho rang gi lus de la 'bab byung
rag chung yi lus la 'bab byung.

    [The stallion's bells go "zing zing" 2x
    The stallion's own body therefore gallops
    The small copper colored one's body gallops.]

ljags pa gser gyi a long 2x
rta nga ran gi lus de la 'bab byung
rag chung nga yi lus la 'bab byung

    [The honored one's golden earring 2x
    The stallion's own body therefore gallops
    The small copper colored one's body gallops.]

mthur 'go ya ma ya zur 2x
rta pho nga ran gi lus de la 'bab byung
rag chug nga yi lus la 'bab byung

    [A pair of reins at his temples 2x
    The stallion's own body therefore gallops
    The small copper colored one's body gallops.]

gser srab lu gu rgyud 'dra 2x
rta pho nga rang gi lus de la 'bab byung
rag chung nga yi lus la pam byung

[The bridle's ornaments are like a chain 2x
The stallion's own body therefore gallops
The small copper colored one's body gallops.]

na 'jam shu gu rgya shog 2x
rta pho nga ran gi lus de la 'bab byung
rag chung na yi lus la 'bab byung

[Like smooth Chinese paper 2x
The stallion's own body therefore gallops
The small copper colored one's body gallops,]

do gom pad ma'i 'dab brgyad 2x
rta pho nga rang gi lus de la 'bab byung
rag chung nga yi lus la 'bab byung

[Step like an eight-petal lotuses 2x
The stallion's own body therefore gallops
The small copper colored one's body gallops,]

sa li skar ma babs 'dra 2x
rta pho rang gi lus de la 'bab byung
rag chung nga yi lus la 'bab byung

[Like a fiery star descending to earth 2x
The stallion's own body therefore gallops
The small copper colored one's body gallops,]

chibs sga nyi ma'i rang shar 2x
rta pho nga rang gi lus de 'bab byung
rag chung nga yi lus la 'bab byung

[The saddle is the rising of the sun 2x
The stallion's own body therefore gallops
The small copper colored one's body gallops,]

glo chen dgu bcu go dbu 2x
rta pho nga rang gi lus de la 'bab byung
rag chung nga yi lus la 'bab byung

    [The great saddle girth has ninety studs 2x
    The stallion's own body therefore gallops
    The small copper colored one's body gallops,]

'ob chung nyi zla gcig 2x
rta pho nga rang gi lus de la 'bab byung
rag chung nga yi lus la 'bab byung

    [A pit and sun and moon are all one 2x
    The stallion's own body therefore gallops
    The small copper colored one's body gallops.]

ga gdan 'ja'mtshon sna lnga 2x
rta pho nga rang gi lus de la 'bab byung
rag chung nga yi lus la 'bab byung

    [The seat cushion has five types of rainbow-hued symbols 2x
    The stallion's own body therefore gallops
    The small copper colored one's body gallops.]

mi bo smug chung zil 'dra 2x
rta pho rang gi lus de la 'bab byung
rag chung nga yi lus la 'bab byung

    [The man is like a brilliant medicinal herb 2x
    The stallion's own body therefore gallops
    The small copper colored one's body gallops]

cu ti nag po dbu slas 2x
rta pho nga rang gi lus de la 'bab byung
rag chung nga yi lus la 'bab byung.

    [He has a braided black pigtail. 2x
    The stallion's own body therefore gallops
    The small copper colored one's body gallops]

Like *chang lu* and some marriage songs, an antiphonal verse structure is common, in this case between men and women, such as in the *zhabro* "chu bzang shar gyi phyogs" (At the East Side of Chuzang) (Track 22).

chu bzang shar gyi phyogs—At the East Side of Chuzang

chu bzang shar gyi phyogs na 2x   *ci'i sgo mo shig shig/ 2x*
chu bzang shar gyi phyogs na 2x   *chos kyi sgo mo shig shig/ 2x*
de 'dra'i chos sgo 'bad mkhan//   *skyabs mgon rgyal ba'i zhab phyi//*
chu bzang lho yi phyogs na// 2x   *'bru yi sgo mo shig shig/*
de 'dr'i chos sgo 'bad mkhan//   *skyabs mgon rgyal ba'i zhabs phyi//*
chu bzang nub kyi phyogs na 2x   *sman gyi sgo mo shig shig/*
de 'dra'i chos sgo 'bad mkhan//   *skyab mgon rgyal ba'i zhabs phyi//*
chu bzang byang gyi phyogs na 2x   *ci'i sgo mo shig shig/*
chu bzang byang gyi phyogs na 2x   *mtshal gyi sgo mo shig shig/*
de 'dra'i chos sgo 'bad mkhan///   *skyabs mgon rgyal ba'i zhabs pyi//*

[At the east side of Chuzang 2x   What gates are waving? 2x
At the east side of Chuzang 2x   The gates of Dharma are waving. 2x
The person that strives for the   The Victorious Lord's[1] servant//
    gates of Dharma//
At the south side of Chuzang // 2x The seed gates are waving/
The person that strives for the   The Victorious Lord's servant//
    gates of Dharma//
At the north side of Chuzang 2x   The medicine gates are waving/
The person that strives for the   The Victorious Lord's servant//
    gates of Dharma//
At the west side of Chuzang 2x   The vermillion gates are waving/
The person that strives for the   The Victorious Lord's servant//]
    gates of Dharma//

(Cultural Academy, III)

What is interesting about this song that the references are to Chuzang Monastery, which is all the way in Eastern Tibet in what is now in China's Qinghai province. This monastery was an important center of activity by Je Tsonkhapa, the founder of the Gelugpa sect of Tibetan Buddhism. The words are not of high literary content but do show a devotional spirit—a festive side of Buddhism.

As noted previously, *ghazal* is another notable genre popular in Kargil and in Leh towns. Again, the usual prestige accompaniment of *surna* and *daman* figures prominently. Originating in Baltistan, the texts are generally romantic, playful, or sentimental in nature. Melodically, they tend towards syllabic settings with minimal melismatic ornamentation. One famous song, was introduced to me by Kunzes Dolma, is "Ache Nyima Zangmo" (Elder sister Nyima Zangmo) (Track 23).

a ce nyi ma bzang mo, sgo gang gi g.yu zhung.
Ban dha nyi ma bzang mo, sgo gang gi g.yu zhung.
De 'dra sgo gan khyong mkha, kho ba yi a jo.
De dra gyu zhung khyong mkhan.

> [Big sister Nyima Zangmo has a turquoise on the middle of her
>   door
> Miss Nyima Zangmo has a turquoise on the middle of her
>   forehead
> Whoever brings it, elder brother, is like,
> Whoever brings the turquoise is like the chief of a great treasury
>   from the capital.]

a ce nyi ma bzang mo, yo gor bog chung.
ban dha nyi ma bzang mo, yo gor bog chung.
de 'dra bog chung khyong mkhan, yo gor bog chung.
de 'dra bog chung khyong mkhan, sde pa phyag mdzod chen mo.

> [Big sister Nyima Zangmo has a small gemstone in that place
> Miss Nyima Zangmo has a small gemstone in that place
> Whoever brings the gem, elder brother, is like,
> Whoever brings the gem is like the chief of a great treasury from
>   the capital.]

a ce nyi ma bzang mo, brang gang gi bod shel.
ban dha nyi ma bzang mo, brang gan gi bod shel.
de dra bod shel khyong mkhan, kho ba yi jo.
de dra bod shel khyong mkhan, sde pa phyag mdzod chen mo.

> [Big sister Nyima Zangmo has a Tibetan crystal on her breast,
> Miss Nyima Zangmo has a Tibetan crystal on her breast

Whoever bring the Tibetan crystal is like,
Whoever brings the Tibetan crystal is like the chief of a great
treasury from the capital.]

A ce nyi ma bzang mo, dung lag gi rta mig.
A ce nyi ma bzang mo, dung lag gi rta mig.
De dra dung lag khyong mkhan, kho ba mi yi a jo.
De dra dar mig khyong mkhan, sde pa phyag mdzod chen mo.

[Big sister Nyima Zangmo, has a conch-shell ornament on her
arm
Miss Nyima Zangmo has a conch-shell ornament on her arm
Whoever brings it, elder brother, is like,
Whoever brings the "silk eye" is like the chief of a great treasury
from the capital.]

A ce nyi ma bzang mo, si kim sked rags.
A ce nyi ma bzang mo, si kim sked rags.
De dra ske rags khyong mkhan, kho ba mi yi a jo.
De dra ske rags khyong mkhan, sde pa phyags mdzod chen mo.

[Big Sister Nyima Zangmo has a sash from Sikkim.
Miss Nyima Zangmo has a sash from Sikkim.
Whoever brings the sash, elder brother, is like,
Whoever brings the sash is like the chief of a great treasury from
the capital.]

A ce nyi ma bzang mo, sog lham gyi phur ma.
A ce nyi ma bzang mo, sog lham gyi phur ma.
De dra sog lham khyong khan, kho ba mi yi ajo,
De dra sog lham khyong khan, sde pa phyags mdzod chen mo.

[Big Sister Nyima Zangmo has Mongolian boots with a border
Miss Nyima Zangmo has Mongolian boots with a border
Whoever brings Mongolian boots, elder brother, is like,
Whoever brings the Mongolian boots is like the chief of a great
treasury from the capital.]

(Cultural Academy, 2014, III, 354–355).

The text here is similar to various rural genres such as *chang lu* (beer songs) and *bagston lu* (marriage songs), and *stod lu* (praise songs) (Rabias 1970, Dinnerstein 2013a, *Ladakh Cultural Academy 2014)*. According to the 2014 Cultural Academy collection, this song is classified as a *gar zha glu* (Song from Lahaul)—further indication of the crossroads hybrid nature of Ladakhi music. Many *beda* families such as that of Tseschu Lhamo and Kunzes Dolma originally came from Lahaul and Spiti and may originally be related to *baddi* families from Himachal Pradesh and Uttarkhand. As opposed to the court genres, the genres with simpler meters have affinities with musics of neighboring regions. Ternary meters with hemiola may be seen as a stylistic link with musics of other regions, such as Changthang *zhabro*.

Songs such as "Ache Nyima Zangmo" which enumerate gifts, or the attributes of something or someone are common. What is noteworthy in this text—as in texts from marriage songs in particular—is the descriptions of material goods from other areas along the caravan routes: Tibetan quartz crystal, Sikkimese cloth goods, conch shell from India. The Mongolian boots are a style of cloth boots with embroidery and upturned toes, inspired by the Mongols' cavalry boots.

Some Ladakhi/Balti *ghazals* are more similar in textual style to Urdu *ghazals*, with romantic or sentimental lyrics. However, unlike the Urdu *ghazal*, there are rarely double meanings in texts mixing spiritual with worldly.

Another well-known rural genre is *tsig glu* (literally, "word songs"). These are short quatrains sung as sarcastic banter between the sexes, especially when young people are out tending flocks. They are sung acapella or accompanied by the *gling bu* (duct flute) or the *ska gling* (double duct flute). There are a few stock melodies that fit most verses, an example of which is given here in a recording of a single verse (Track 24).

> *khang bu de ci byed?*
> *dar lcog g.yon nam mi 'dug.*
> *rang sems nag te ci byed?*
> *mi sems nag ste me 'dug.*

>> [What is the use of that little house?
>> Prayer flags do not waver.
>> What is the use of one's own black mind?
>> People's minds are not black.]

Other verses sung to the same melody are given here.

rang sems shel gyi bum pa,
phyi gsal na gsal 'dug pa.
mi sems rja ma'i bum pa,
phyi 'thib nang 'thib 'dug go.

> [The crystal pot of one's own mind,
> Is transparent.
> The earthen pot of people's minds,
> Outside are dull, inside are dull.]

sems pa dkar dang mi dkar,
dkar yol nang gi oma.
rang sems brtan dang mi brtan,
ku lig nang gi gze ma.

> [Thoughts clear and unclear,
> Milk in a china cup.
> One's own thoughts, stable and transitory,
> A key in a lock.]

skyid ong rgyags ong bsams nas,
rgya shar la bsgyur pa yin.
gru la gru log long ba,
snang ba'i gru la ma shar.

> [Happiness comes, and satisfaction comes, from thinking.
> I will be at the main gate in the east.
> Look at the corner.
> Look for illumination in the east.]

zhim po za yin bsams nas,
tshas la u sub tab pa yin.
ngon tsha med pa'i u su,
mgo mjug log ste skyes song.

> [Tasty food is thought of
> When coriander is planted.

> Without modesty, the coriander
> Sprouts do not come up.]

(Cultural Academy III: 292–293)

As we see from these verses, there is reference to Buddhist concepts of mental clarity, with metaphors of crystal versus earthenware similar to those of more literary genres.

The intent here is not to give an exhaustive catalogue of all Ladakhi song genres. What I have done is present notable rural and urban genres to give an overview of these rich musico-literary traditions.

Chapter 7

Musical Characteristics of Traditional Ladakhi Song

This chapter adopts a more analytical approach, focusing primarily on the four representative genres: *rten 'brel glu, bag ston glu, chang glu,* and *gzhung glu.* I do, however, look at other genres represented in LYL to give a wider overview of rhythm, melodic structure, form, and text setting. I employ Western staff transcriptions to quantify some of these musical phenomena.

Francke noted that "the Ladakhi music and art of dancing is so entirely different from Tibetan music and dancing that non-Tibetan influences must be suspected" (Francke 1904, 366). Ladakhi melodic style is more likely derived from Kashmiri and Indian melodic models, although showing strong pentatonic usages similar to the Tibetan. Ladakhi songs in many genres are shaped by the complex isorhythmic drum cycles on *daman* and *daf,* employing a single fixed, repeating rhythmic pattern, which indicate an overlay of Kashmiri, Balti, or Central Asian instrumental style. This is in contrast to most genres of Tibetan music, which do not have a strong emphasis on drumming and have nothing analogous to the rhythmic cycles that govern so many Ladakhi genres.

Song Rhythms

Although there is no explicit music theory such as the Indian *tala* system, there does exist some vocabulary to describe rhythm in Ladakhi music. This terminology may be viewed as implied musical theory to the extent that songs (including instrumental dances) are grouped together according to common rhythms that Trewin reports as being called *glu rtsas* (Trewin 1995, 354). None of these has a name, such as *teental, dadra etc.*, but songs are identified as being in the same rhythm.

The issue of terminology is of interest here. The word *rtsas* (or *btsas*) can mean a seed or to give birth to something, indicating the songs come from a common root. There are other words used to describe common rhythms. Lexicographer Rebecca Norman lists the word *sas*, meaning "rhythm" (Norman 2011, 225). Tsering Angchuk Ralam feels the correct word is *tshang*, meaning a nest (i.e., where a family of birds lives) and refers to the common rhythm itself. Others assert it is the actual groups or suites of songs performed in such common rhythms that are referred to as *glu tshang*-s and that the actual rhythm performed is the *lu sas* or *lu btsas*.

Each repetition of the basic rhythmic cycles is known as *ldab*, meaning times (e.g., *gsum ldab*= 3 times), or *skyor*, meaning to repeat. Each *ldab* consists of a series of beats (*rdung*) that do not vary as to number and length. They are internally organized according to a systematic variation of pitch, stress, resonance, and timbre. Each cycle starts on the principal beat or "heel" (*rkang*)—somewhat analogous to the *sam* in Indian music. Melodies often start on the *rkang*, but in practice singers will often lead up to it with anacrusis (a pick-up, as it were) utilizing nonlexical syllables. Examples of these usages are shown in figures 7.1–7.3.

Trewin noted that the internal organization of strong and weak beats is not always so clear. He points out that in simpler divisive meters with symmetrical beat groupings, such as those in 8 or 12, main beats are marked by clear accents of pitch or stress. The cycles are divided into two

Figure 7.1. Anacrusis leading to *rkang* in *rgyab ri brag dmar gyi tse mo*. *Source:* Transcription provided by the author.

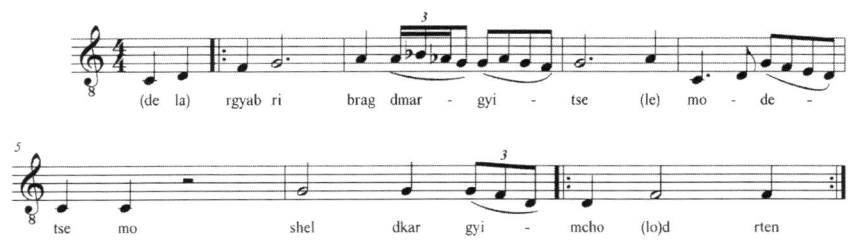

Figure 7.2. Anacrusis leading to *rkang* in *ri bo g.yang can*. *Source:* Transcription provided by the author.

Figure 7.3. Anacrusis leading to *rkang* in *ti sei shel dkar mchod rten*. *Source:* Transcription provided by the author.

halves that are often marked by pitch plateaus with drum strokes being played on either the high, "female" drum (*mo skad*) or the lower "male" drum" (*pho skad*), as in figure 7.4.

However, with asymmetrical additive meters there often is an ambiguity in the drumbeats with accents of stress and pitch conflicting with agogic (duration) ones, as, for example, in the following rhythm (figure 7.5).

Figure 7.4. Pitch plateaus in symmetrical meter. *Source*: Transcription provided by the author.

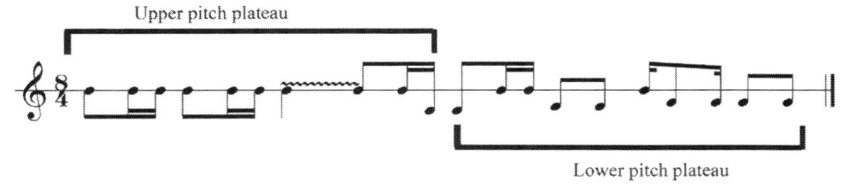

Figure 7.5. *Daman* rhythm with ambiguous accents. *Source*: Transcription provided by the author.

Trewin points out in this example how there is a conflict between a grouping of 2-2-2-3 and 2-2-3-2, with a pitch accent occurring on the seventh beat and an agogic accent on the eighth beat. He notes that depending on the context, such as the pattern of melodic movement or dance steps, one would interpret the groupings one way or the other (Trewin 1995, 354–58).

I note this ambiguity as seen in transcriptions (here done in 9/4 instead of 9/8) of two different songs set in the same *lu tshangs*. In *kaba rinpoche* (The Precious Pillar) (figure 7.6, Track 25), we seem to have a shifting back and forth between a phrasing of 2-2-2-3 (measures 2, 3, 4, 7, 8) and 2-2-3-2 (measures 1 and 5).

There is far less rhythmic ambiguity in *dgom pa gser gyi bya skyibs* (figure 7.7), which primarily follows the 2-2-2-3 pattern. (Track 26—full song as *gad pa gser gyi bya skyibs*)

I myself performed this song at the dedication of the new library of the Ngari Institute of Buddhist Dialectics and noted two different rhythmic patterns in the *daman*. When I was singing, the rhythm was simpler and more regular as in figure 7.8A below. When the *surna* was playing there

Figure 7.6. *Ka ba rin po che*. *Source*: Transcription provided by the author.

Figure 7.7. *Dgon pa gser gyi bya skyibs* transcribed as sung by Ali Mahmud. *Source*: Transcription provided by the author.

Figure 7.8. 9-beat *daman* patterns. *Source*: Transcription provided by the author.

was mixed rhythmic ambiguity and tension in the *daman* rhythm, as in figure 7.7B and figure 7.5 above.

What is interesting to note in Figure 7.8 is the fluidity of rhythm, with a quarter and two eighth notes pattern in line A interchangeable with quarter note triplets in line B. Trewin noted similar patterns that are interchangeable with two eighths, with agogic accents shifting and becoming "smoothed out" as tempo increased (figure 7.9) (Trewin 1995, 356).

Figure 7.9. Rhythmic shift with tempo. *Source*: Transcription provided by the author.

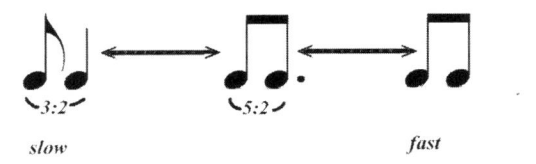

Rhythmic complexity and ambiguity do *not* generally carry over to the same degree into song melodies, which follow the basic landmarks of the rhythm in terms of beat groupings and stress. This difference between drumming and melody might suggest they may have different origins, with a more local melodic style being juxtaposed with the complexities of an elite instrumental style.

I have noted a similar use of isorhythmic cycles in recordings I've heard of Balti *surna/daman* ceremonial music. In them, rhythms are simple—either duple, triple, or a simple additive cycle of seven—with nothing analogous to the more complex additive meters seen in Ladakhi examples. There are similarities between Ladakhi and Balti rhythms in some of the alternating patterns of low/high/low/high/drum roll, as in the excerpt shown in figure 7.10 (http://www.youtube.com/watch?v=5RcIaPErusM, accessed March 7, 2013). The *surna* melody is tied to the drum cycle, played on a *daman* and a bass drum called *gring jang*, although there is a meandering quality to the melody that is more akin to the ceremonial Ladakhi *lha rnga* music where the drumming is the important element. As in some of the Ladakhi examples, the melody seems to exhibit some ambiguity between 3-3 and 2-2-2.

In contrast to the Balti example, melodies in genres such as *rtendel glu, chang glu,* and *gzhung glu* more obviously follow significant landmarks

Figure 7.10. Balti instrumental piece for *surna, daman,* and *gring jang* Festival of *Jashn e Ghanche. Source*: Transcription provided by the author.

in the rhythms. In the transcription of *rten 'brel gsum pa* (figure 7.11) (Track 27) the correspondence of melodic line to the *daf* rhythm is quite clearly 2-2-3-2-2-3.

While learning to sing some of the more complicated songs, I was admonished to listen to the flow of the *daman* by a number of people who were not specifically musicians but were educated listeners. On the other hand, I noticed that when most people sing more complicated songs a cappella, they tend to be loose with the rhythm and have difficulty matching it to *daman* when singing with accompaniment—a common problem with guest singers at AIR.

The rhythms on *daman* in particular are taught using mnemonics that are similar to those used to convey Middle Eastern rhythmic modes—"dim" and "tang." These are played on the low drum (*pho-skad*, male voice) and high drum (*mo-skad*, female voice) respectively. This is the method I most heard when my various informants were reciting a rhythm. In his 1995 PhD dissertation Trewin noted a more complex tonal

Figure 7.11. *Rten 'brel gsum pa* with *daf* rhythm—Tsering Chorol. *Source*: Transcription provided by the author.

system analogous to Indian *naqqara* (kettle drums) using the following sounds (Trewin 1995, ch. 7, table 4) (figure 7.12).

I have not heard this system being discussed by artists at AIR or elsewhere, but it may have currency among the traditional specialists in the ceremonial *lha rnga* music that Trewin was studying (Trewin 1995, 349). In the same study Trewin also noted some of the common song rhythms (Trewin 1995, ch. 7, musical example 2), which do occur with considerable variation (figure 7.13).

Figure 7.12. Seven syllables for *daman* sounds. *Source*: Transcription provided by the author.

Bol	drum	pitch	resonance	timbre (location of stroke)	stress
NĀ/RĀ	mo-skad	high	open	near rim	relatively stressed
TĀ	mo-skad	high	open	between rim and center	heavily stressed
TĪN	mo-skad	high	open	3-5 cm from rim	fairly heavily stressed
GHE	pho-skad	low	open	center	variable
KA	pho-skad	low	closed	center	relatively light

DHĀ = NĀ or TĀ + GHE

DHĪN = TĪN + GHE

Figure 7.13. Some common song rhythms. Fair use.

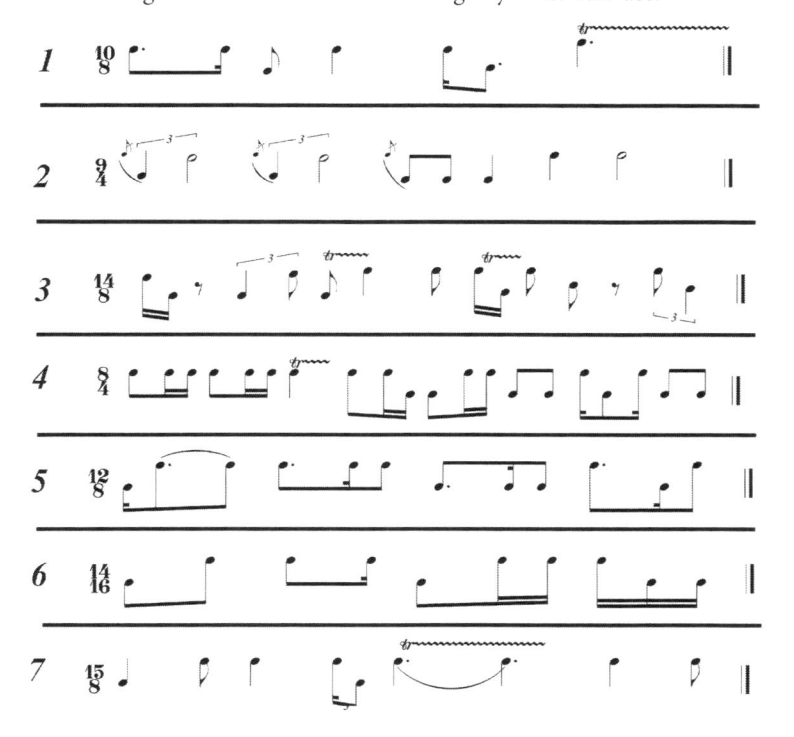

Rhythmic Taxonomy of Songs

According to Tsering Sonam Lagachirpon, most *lu tshangs* have no name, except for one which is called *chopo glu* (big song), which he demonstrated as having fourteen beats. He says it is used for songs of Gesar such as *dering nyid milam bo* and *baru dzong yi lam go*, which is a song from Kargil (personal comm., August 8, 2011). This rhythm seems to correspond to Trewin's example 3 in figure 7.13 and the rhythm used in *rten 'brel gsum pa*.

Nevertheless, Ladakhi musicians can state quite definitively which songs belong to a given *glu tshangs*. Based upon this body of common knowledge, I have attempted to construct a taxonomy of the songs contained in LYL. Working with Tsering Chorol at AIR, we went through the entire list of songs in LYL, with her singing them while either banging out the *daman* rhythm on a desk or playing them on the *daf*. Starting at the beginning, each time we hit a *glu tshang* previously not encountered, we established that song as the base line (no pun intended) with which similar songs were grouped. Some songs neither she nor Ali Mahmud were able to perform, but in total we identified melodies for around one hundred of the texts.

What follows are primarily transcriptions of some of the rhythms performed by Chorol, along with her assessment of which songs belong in each of those *glu tshangs*. In addition, I include the transcription of the first song in the book in which she encounters each rhythm, followed by a table of songs that conform to that rhythm, listing the page number of the lyrics and the genre of each song. In some cases, I note that Chorol commented on how a song or genre not represented in LYL is grouped in each rhythm.

rten 'brel gsum pa (2-2-3-2-2-3)

A transcription of the song with *daf* accompaniment is shown in figure 7.11. This is the rhythm that Tsering Sonam Lagachirpon referred to as *Chopo glu* (long song) (figure 7.14).

rten 'brel lnga pa A (2-2-2-3)

In general flow it has much in common with the Turkish *Aksak*/Greek Karsilama rhythm, although this is always played in a fast tempo.

— — — ∪ ∪ ∪
D-kk T-kk D-kk T- T- t-

Figure 7.14. Rhythm for *rten 'brel gsum pa* as played on *daf* by Chorol. *Source*: Transcription provided by the author.

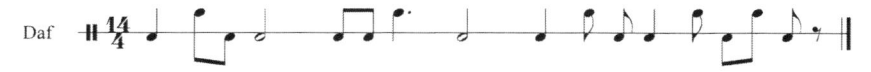

In terms of tempo, it resembles the Hindustani Matta Tal:

+			2		0		3	4		||
1	2		3	4	5	6	7	8	9			
Dhin	**tirakita**	|	**dhin**	**na** |	**tin**	**na** |	**dhin** |	**dhin**	**na**	**||**

The question yet to be answered is what the origins of this rhythm are. I speculate a blending of elements, perhaps a cycle like Matta Tal with the penultimate drum roll motive derived from Baltistan.

Figure 7.15 (a repeat of Figure 7.7) is a transcription of *daman* renditions, version A when performed with voice, B the more complex version performed with *surna*.

Figure 7.15. *Rten 'brel lnga pa* A rhythm—*daman* version. *Source*: Transcription provided by the author.

Figure 7.16 shows variants played by Chorol on *daf*. The third and fourth systems show the basic 2-2-2-3 structure very clearly.

Figure 7.16. Rhythm of *rten 'brel lnga pa* A, showing variations played on *daf rten 'brel lnga pa* (Full recording with surna and daman for this book—track 06). *Source*: Transcription provided by the author.

Daf

Figure 7.17a. Transcription of *rten 'brel lnga pa* sung by Chorol and Yangchan with *daf* accompaniment by Chorol. *Source*: Transcription provided by the author.

Figure 7.17b. Transcription of *rten 'brel lnga pa* sung by Chorol and Yangchan with *daf* accompaniment by Chorol. *Source*: Transcription provided by the author.

rten 'brel lnga pa B (2-2-2-2)

A full transcription of this is shown in figure 7.19 with a recording with *surna* and *daman* (Track 29).

Figure 7.18. *Daf* pattern for *rten 'brel lnga pa* B as played on by Chorol. *Source*: Transcription provided by the author.

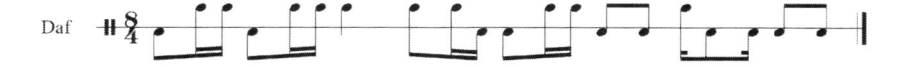

Figure 7.19. *Rten 'brel lnga pa* B—Chorol and Yangchan, Chorol on *daf.*

rten 'brel lnga pa C (2-2-2-2)

In another recording session, I was able to get more examples, shown in figures 7.20–7.21.

Chorol commented that this rhythm is used in *chabs skyems yi glu,* a type of dance song where men dance with pitchers of *chang* balanced on their heads, and various *bagston sgo glu* (wedding door songs).

Figure 7.20. Daf patterns for *rten 'brel lnga pa* C as played by Chorol. Author transcription.

Figure 7.21. Other *daf* patterns for *rten 'brel lnga pa* C as played by Chorol.

Figure 7.22. *Rten 'brel lnga pa* C—sung by Chorol and Yangchan, Chorol on *daf*.

Figure 7.22b. *Rten 'brel lnga pa* C—sung by Chorol and Yangchan, Chorol on *daf*.

rten 'brel rdun pa—2-2-2-2

This is a more syncopated variant of the previous rhythm.

This is illustrated in transcription 7.24 and the *surna* and *daman* rendition in Track 30.

chang glu pattern 3-2-2-3-2-2

This is one of the archetypal patterns in Ladakhi music, and is used not just in *chang glu*, but in many dance songs, such as those associated

Figure 7.23. Daf patterns for *rten 'brel rdun pa* as played by Chorol. *Source*: Transcription provided by the author.

Figure 7.24. *Rten 'brel rdun pa*—sung by Chorol with *daf. Source*: Transcription provided by the author.

Figure 7.25. *Chang glu* rhythm as played by Chorol. *Source*: Transcription provided by the author.

with the dance of the *nyao pa*-s (groom's attendants) in weddings. It resembles meters used in India such as *rupak tal* and *pushto tal*, as well as cycles in Baltistan, Kashmir, Afghanistan, and the Middle East. Interestingly enough, the Arabic name for this cycle is *Dawr Hindi* (cycle of India). It can be viewed as being in 14 rather than 7, as there are usually symmetrical halves to the melody and rhythm. In the song *bzo thabs* (The Skill

Figure 7.26. *Bzo thabs*—sung by Chorol and Yangchan, Chorol. *Source*: Transcription provided by the author.

of Brewing), the fourteen-beat phrasing is seen primarily in the melody, which is the same as "dri wa dri lan" (Question and Answer, Track 13).

Shon glu or *zhabs ʻbro*—3-3 against 2-2-2

This rhythm is used primarily in two dance song genres: *shon glu*, for the festival *shondol* dance and *zhabs ʻbro* (pronounced zhabro or jabro), a type of circle or line dance of the Changthang Plateau nomads. A transcription of an example is shown in figure 7.27

According to Ngawang Tsering Shakspo, these genres originate outside Ladakh, the *Shon glu* in Gilgit, Baltistan, and the *zhabs ʻbro* in Tibet (Shakspo 2010, 201–3). However, the best-known Tibetan *zhabs ʻbro* are in duple meters, so it may be that the Changthang version, while danced in ways similar to the Tibetan version, may have adopted the triple meter from further west. In *zhabs ʻbro* the use of tabla, harmonium, *daman* and *sgra nyan* (Tibetan lute) or the Ladakhi version known as *khopong*, are further indications of a syncretic genre. In both *shon glu* and *zhabs ʻbro* the use of hemiola, either with 3 against 2, or 3-3 alternating with 2-2-2, is prevalent in the percussion parts.

Figure 7.27. *Zhabs ʻbro* melody with *daman* rhythms recorded in AIR studio 29 July 2012. *Source*: Transcription provided by the author.

Form in Traditional Song Genres

In Tibetan songs, the basic unit is the stanza (Crossley-Holland 1967, 12). I have found the same to be true in Ladakhi traditional song, with stanzas having four, six, or eight lines. The relationship of lines in a stanza to rhythmic cycles varies depending on how syllables are set (i.e., purely syllabic, melismatic, or having nonlexical interpolations), the speed of cycle, as well as the number of syllables in each line. The stanza can be broken up according to a few different schemes. Figure 7.28 gives a transcription with the first stanza of the famous "Lha sa'i skor lam phra mo" (Lhasa's Narrow Circumambulation Road) (Full recording, track 11).

Each line of the stanza has the same music, consisting of parallel phrases, with an open ending on the fifth in the first, closed ending on the tonal center in the second. In the case of the first stanza, the first line is repeated, with different third and fourth lines, giving a music/text relationship of AAA_1A_2, and subsequent verses $AA_1A_2A_3$, where the subscripts indicate that the same music has different lyrics.

A different music/verse relationship is seen in *dgom pa gser gyi bya skibs*

(The Monastery of the Golden Cave) (figure 7.29). In the full recording (track 26) you will hear the correction "gat pa gser gyi bya skibs" where *gatpa* is a cliff, instead of the incorrect, but commonly sung, *gompa* (monastery).

Figure 7.28. *Lha sa'i skor lam 'phra mo*—1st stanza. *Source*: Transcription provided by the author.

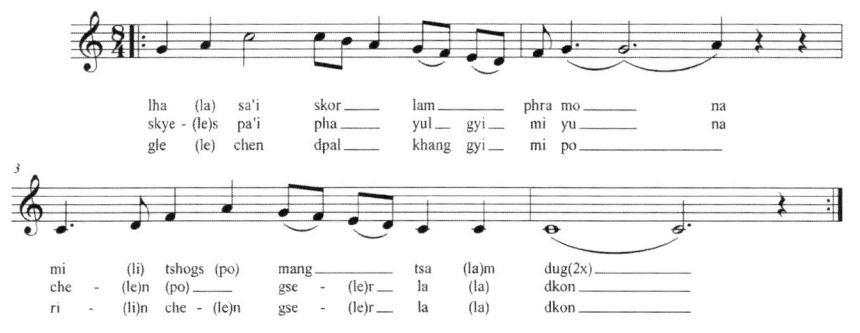

Figure 7.29. *Dgom pa gser gyi bya skibs*. *Source*: Transcription provided by the author.

dgon pa [gat pa] gser gyi bya skyibs
ma bzhengs pa yi dgon pa x2
ma 'gyur btsan po ru bzhugs song zer na
dgon pa de bzhengs pa bas mtshar

'gyur med brtan po ru bzhugs song zer na
dgon pa de bzhengs pa bas mtshar.
[The Monastery of the Golden Cave
The monastery not built (by human hands) x2
When someone says the unchanging king dwelt there
The monastery was built by a miracle
When someone says the unchanging king dwelt there
The monastery was built by a miracle.]

g.yas phyogs kyi gangs ri dkar po
ma bshams pa yi rtsam tshug x2
ma 'gyur brtan po ru bzhugs song zer na
rtsam tsug de bshams pa bas mtsar
'gyur med brtan po ru bzhugs song zer na
tsam tsug de bshams pa bas mtshar.
[The white snowy mountain at the right side
How healing is that which was not arranged x2
When it is said the unchanging king dwelt there
It was arranged by a miracle
When it is said the unchanging king dwelt there
It was arranged by a miracle.]

g.yon phyogs kyi mtsho mo ma pham
ma ltems pa yi yon chab x2
'gyur med brtan po ru bzhugs song zer na
yon chab de ltems pa bas mtshar x2
[On the left side is the invincible lake[1]
An uncontrollable water offering[2] x2
When it is said that king that grew strong dwelt there
It is a miraculously controlled water offering x2]

mdun gyi can dan gyi sdong po
ma btsugs pa yi lag tshug x2
ma 'gyur brtan po ru bzhugs song zer na
lag tshug de btsugs pa bas mtshar
'gyur med brtan po ru bzhugs song zer na
gser lcang de btsugs pa bas mtshar.
[In front of the tree of eternity
Not planted by human hand x2

When it is said the unchanging king dwelt there
It was miraculously planted x2]

'a jo rang gser rkyang gi thod dar
no mo nga dngul rkyang gi pu ri x2
a jo rang gi thugs sems la ma babs song zer na
no mo nga yis lha chos zhig byed. x2
[The elder brother's[3] own golden wild ass has a head ornament
My, the girl's, silver wild ass has a saddle x2
When it is said that elder brother's own compassion is not
    encountered
I, the girl, have encountered the sublime Dharma. x2]

The first two lines are repeated in both the music and the lyrics, again
with a parallel phrase structure in the melody, but there is a second
melodic section with a paired phrase structure that is used for the third
and fourth lines: AAB_1B_2.

Another music/stanza scheme is seen in *"Stod rGyad Gar"* (Above
is India) (figure 7.30) with pairs of lines in a parallel phrase relationship,
the first phrase (mm. 1–2) ending on the first note of the scale, and the
second phrase (mm. 3–4) ending on the fourth.

Crossley-Holland found several of the Tibetan examples he studied
had some sort of refrain, either repeating words or nonlexical syllables
(12). None of the 128 songs in LYL has evidence of a refrain. However, one
point of similarity between the repertoires is the use of strophic pairing of
stanzas with antiphony. Crossley-Holland noted these occurring especially
in songs of labor, dance, and love (12). I have previously discussed antiphonal structures in the type of marriage songs known as "door songs" (*sgo
glu*), with their challenge and response. We also see a similar format in
the performance of sarcastic/teasing songs between groups of young men
and women (*tsig glu*), although the stanzas are not specifically paired, and
are thrown out in response to whatever was sung by the opposite side.
The statement/response or question/answer format is also used in several
chang glu as well—very apt for social activities like drinking.

I found another example of statement/response structure in the
genre known as classification songs (*'byed 'dzug*) (LYL, 222), which uses
a complex variant with alternating sides singing couplets or single lines,
with the two parties singing a couplet together inviting everyone to dance.
Unfortunately, I have not found an informant who knows the exact melody,

Figure 7.30. *Stod rgyad gar*-sung by Ali Mahmud and Tsering Angchuk Ralam. *Source*: Transcription provided by the author.

but Tsering Chorol described the singing of it (personal comm., July 22, 2012). The flow, with Q for question, A for answer, T for together, 1 for a single line, 2 for a couplet is as follows:

Q2 A2 Q1 A1 Q1 A1 T2 | Q2 A2 Q1 A1 Q1 A1 T2 | Q2 A2 Q1 A1 Q1 A1 T2 |

Of examples in LYL the use of T2 comes closest to a refrain.

A song that does make clear use of a refrain structure is the neo-traditional song *Ali Yato le*, attributed to Aba Tsewang Dorje, ca. 1960 (figure

7.31)—probably the most famous song in all Ladakh. It is not included in LYL but is considered by all Ladakhis to be "traditional." Measures 9–12 in the transcription are a refrain that is repeated with each verse. Here are the full lyrics:

Introduction:
byar kha la kha thon pa de la,
'brok sa bde mo yod,
spang dang me tog pa lu sru li,
dri zhim 'thul 'thul yod,
g.yag dang 'bri dan ra ma lug gi,
khyu chen khyu chung yod,
mar dang o ma da ra phyur phe,
bshon chu 'di ri ri.

Figure 7.31. *Ali Yato le*, Introduction, chorus, first verse. Author transcription.

[Summertime on the high pass; there's a beautiful summer
    pasture
Grass and *palu* flowers; it's full of wonderful smells
Yaks, goats, and sheep; we've got big flocks and small
Butter, milk, buttermilk and cheese; dairy products flowing
    freely]

Chorus:
He yi a li ya do le
He nyi bcu rtsa lnga le 2x
[Hey-hey! Aha, my friends, hey; twenty-five, hey!]

Verse 1:
Byen byen byen la bcag ste 'khyir, a li ya do le,
Thur thur thur la bcag ste 'khyir, a li ya do le
[Up-up-up this way; aha, my friends!
Down-down-down that way, my friends!]

Chorus:
Verse 2:
Mdang 'de ring sang skyid po med, a li ya do le,
Mdang 'de ring sang ga mo med, a li ya do le
[There's not a happier time than this, my friends!
There's not a happier time than this, my friends!]

Chorus
Verse 3:
Skyid po rang ngis ma byo na, a li ya do le 2x
[If you don't make yourself happy, people will make you suffer.
Chorus] (Norman 2001, 59–60).

Melodic Characteristics of Ladakhi Songs

Ladakhi/Tibetan terminology used in discussing music is not as detailed
as the terminology of either Western music or Indian classical music.

Native terminology does not make the kind of distinctions that
are made in Western music culture: the term for monastic music

instrumental music, *rol-mo*, is also used to describe non-monastic instrumental music, as well as music in general; the term for monastic chant, dbyangs, is similarly used to describe non-monastic song. If there is a need to make any kind of distinction, or to clarify the level of reference, then music as a general category, rather than monastic instrumental music in particular, may be referred to as *rol-mo-dbyangs* ("instrumental music and song"), or song as a general category. rather than monastic chant in particular, may be referred to as *glu-dbyangs* ("vocal melody"). (Trewin 1995, 85–86)

The thirteenth-century Tibetan scholar Sakya Pandita characterized the singing of "far Westerns" (i.e., of Tibet) as "neighing, sing[ing] with knots (*mdud-pa*)" (Ellingson 1979, 235). Rather than referring to a constrained vocal style, as Ellingson suggests, Trewin feels this description perhaps reflects the tumbling quartal and quintal patterns, frequently in chains of interlocking sequences characteristic of Ladakhi melody (Trewin 1990b). An example of a "tumbling quartal/quintal pattern" can be seen in my marked transcription in figure 7.32.

Picken noted the differential features of Ladakhi vocal music in ascent and descent (1957:141), which he attributes to border conditions, that is, mixing of pentatonic ascent with hepta- and hexatonic descent. For example, in figure 32 above we see a pentatonic 1-2-3-5-6 structure in measures 1-2 and a 6-5-4-3-2-1 descent in measure 3. Similarly, in example 30 there is a consistent ascending pattern of

1-<3-4-5<7-1 and a descending 1-<7-6-5-4-<3-2-

Figure 7.32. "Tumbling quintal and quartal patterns." *Source*: Transcription provided by the author.

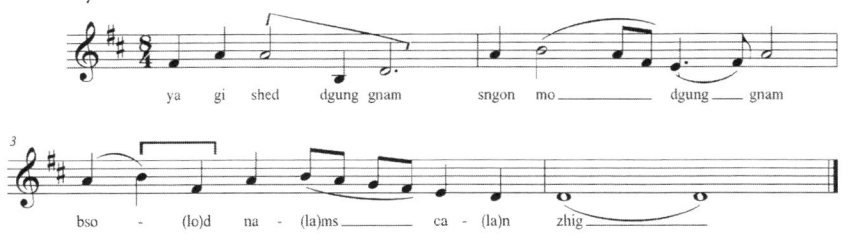

Scale Patterns in Ladakhi Song

In their 1987 study of Ladakhi music, Trewin and Stephens examined over one hundred songs and identified certain common melodic characteristics. Firstly, they noted that the majority are based around ahemitonic pentatonic scales, mainly on a scale similar to the Indian Bhupali scale of 1-2-3-5-6-1. While this is certainly a common melodic structure, it should be added that in an examination of the 128 songs in LYL, I have found other common patterns as well. I would like to examine some examples of transcriptions from my field recordings and other *Sources*. I was not able to locate melodies for all 128 texts, but of approximately 100 songs I identified 76 unique melodies that break down into the following main patterns with their variations: 1-2-3-5-6-1.

The best-known song that fits this "Bhupali" pattern is *Ali Yato Le*, shown above in Figure 4. An older example of this pattern is found in the *chang glu, bzo thabs* (The Skill of Brewing) (figure 7.33).

It is not a pure pentatonic melody, having the descending 1-7-6-5. **1-2-4-5-6-1** (Similar to Hindustani Raga Durga), for example, *dgom pa gser gyi bya skibs* in figure 29 above. **1**-flat **3-4-5**-flat **7-1**, similar to that of Hindustani ragas like Dhāni or Bhimpalasi. Examples are *stod rgya gar* (figure 7.33 above) and *nyi lza dbang mo'i glu* (The song of Nilza Wangmo") (figure 7.34) (track 3, full recording).

1-2-4-5-flat **7-1**, similar to Hindustani Raga Madhyamat Saranga. Many songs have heptatonic descents. Trewin has also noted this pattern and finds it suggestive of contact with Indian music (Trewin 1995, 205–6). The song *Tisei shel dkar mchod rten* (Mt. Sumeru's White Crystal Stupa) shows this pattern with some passing tones (figure 7.3 above). A striking

Figure 7.33. *Bzo thabs* as sung by Ali Mahmud and Tsering Angchuk Ralam. *Source*: Transcription provided by the author.

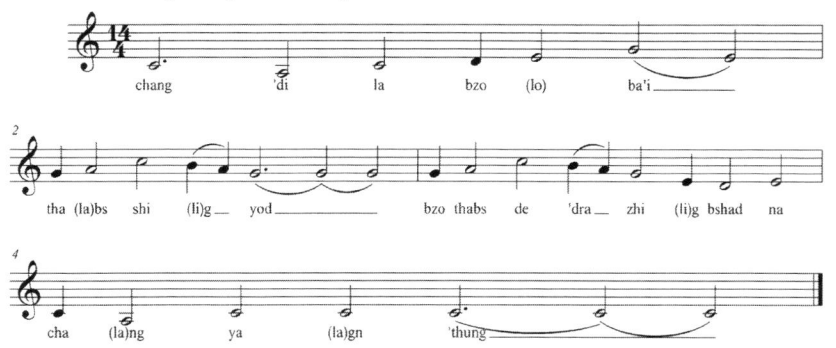

Figure 7.34. *Nyi lza dbang mo'i glu* as sung by Chorol and Yangchan. *Source*: Transcription provided by the author.

example of a probable Hindustani influence is the use of the fourth and first scale steps as major cadential points, such as in *stod rgya gar* (Above is India) (figure 7.30 above).

Another example is *shel ldan g.yu mtsho* (The Crystal and Turquoise Ocean) (figure 7.35) (track 28).

Figure 7.35. *Shel ldan g.yu mtsho-*as sung by Ali Mahmud and Tsering Angchuk Ralam. *Source*: Transcription provided by the author.

Pitch Range and Melodic Movement

When sung with *surna* the tonic of songs is generally around E—rather high for male voices. Without *surna,* singers can pitch their voices lower. We can hear this in some of Dorje Stakmo's commercial recordings, where he uses flutes or synthesizer instead of *surna,* allowing him to sing in a more baritone range. For the sake of clarity in transcriptions, I have usually set the pitch at C but have varied this depending on the range of the song and the readability of the notation.

The general range of songs is an octave and a fourth (as in figure 7.36 below). Many begin on the lower fifth, with a common opening pattern being 5-6-1 (e.g., figure 36). Trewin has characterized many Ladakhi songs as having a double arch with the melody rising to a large interval drop of a fifth, sixth, or octave, followed by a second rise and a more incremental descent to the tonal center (1995). Examples are given in figures 7.35 to 7.38.

Figure 7.36. Dgon pa gser gyi bya skibs—A section. *Source*: Transcription provided by the author.

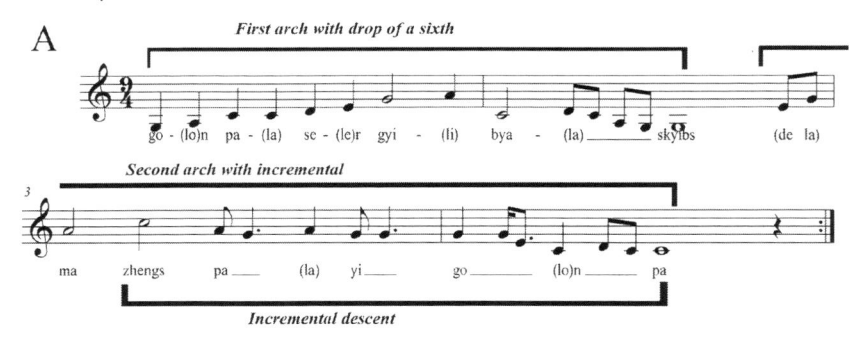

Figure 7.37. *Nyilza Wangmo*-A section. *Source*: Transcription provided by the author.

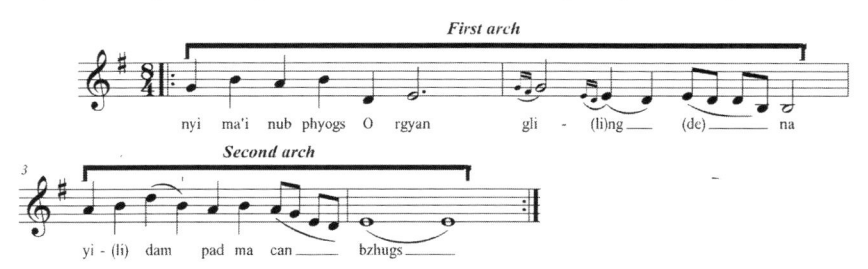

Figure 7.38. Bsod nams mchog skyid. *Source*: Transcription provided by the author.

Text Settings in Various Genres

In general, Ladakhi songs tend toward syllabic settings. As mentioned earlier, oral tradition states that texts were composed, submitted to the Leh palace, and subsequently set to music by the *mkhar mon*. The melodies might not fit the words precisely, and thus require stretching either with melismatic passages or interpolating additional grammatical particles into the text.

In the case of melismatic passages, we note the practice in songs like *gzhung glu* of interpolating nonlexical syllable extensions (usually with an /l-/ sound) in long melodic passages, (e.g., *mchod rten -> mcho-(l)od rten*.) What is this technique called, if anything, by singers at large? In a 1991 article on rhythm in Ladakh song and dance, Mark Trewin refers to it as *tsig lhad* (word interpolation) but gives no references as to where he got this term. After some searching, I found reference to this technique in Walter Kaufmann's book on Tibetan Buddhist chant where it is used in very slow tantric chants to both allow for articulation and obscure the meaning to keep it from the uninitiated (Kaufmann 1975, 4–14). I suspect Trewin got the term from someone informed by monastic practice (Gen Ngawang Tsering Shakspo or Gen Tashi Rabgias). Morup Namgyal's daughter Tsering Chorol was also familiar with the term. According to SECMOL volunteer coordinator Rebecca Norman,

> Tonight we started a new zhunglu song after dinner, and had reason to mention the "la" syllables in it. I called them the "la-li-lu" things, and asked if anybody had ever heard a name for them, such as /tshiglat/. It seemed pretty clear that nobody had, and we've got students from all regions of Leh District, and Chiktan and Wakha in Kargil. It's possible some had but were too shy to say so, or didn't bother, but I think really nobody had ever heard any word to label those syllables.

We sing /zhunglu/ after dinner every day at SECMOL so that the Ladakhi youth get a chance to learn these songs—otherwise, many young Ladakhis today don't know any zhunglu at all. I have never heard a particular term for the extra syllables. When I'm typing them in the computer and asking whether I should type them or remove them, I refer to them as /la-la-la/ or /la-li-lu/ and am understood, and have never noticed anyone saying any particular word for them. However, /tshiglat/ would be a plausible word for them, or more likely, /tshiglak/. Sham /lhakcas/, Leh /lakces/ means to be extra, to be left over. Compounds can include the syllable Sham, Nubra /lhak/, Leh, Upper Ladakh /lak/ to refer to extra or left over things. So /tshiglak/ or /tshiklhak/ is plausible for this meaning. (personal comm., November 17, 2009)

The insertion of "filler" between words consists of additional grammatical particles as such as:

"*po*" or "*bo*"—postpositions that signal agency, masculine gender, or are equivalent to "the" (usually not specified in Tibetic languages),

"*de*"—a continuative particle or indicator of participles. More often in song texts it has the meaning of "it," "that," "that one," "he," "she," or "the."

"*zhig*"—postposition meaning "one" or "some" or as an imperative particle after verbs.

An example of the use of additional grammatical particles can be seen in figure 7.28 above in Tsering Chorol's rendition of *Lha sa'i skor lam 'phra mo*.

It should be stressed that these various types of interpolation do little to obscure the meaning of the song texts. This contrasts with the use of *tsig iad* in various styles of Tibetan Buddhist chant, where the interpolations serve not merely as aids to melodic articulation, but as means of making it harder for noninitiates to understand the meanings and potentially come to harm through misunderstanding or misuse of the rituals, while still allowing them to gain the blessings of hearing a given ceremony (Kaufmann 1975).

The only songs that seem to have a strongly melismatic texture are some of the wedding songs, such as in the *sgo glu* (door song) transcribed below in figure 7.39. The fact that these songs are meant to be sung a cappella and have pre-Buddhist texts may indicate a musical origin that predates the introduction of *surna* and *daman* rhythms.

The short melismas that are present in some melodies are treated in different ways. For example, I transcribed two versions of the well-known song *ka ba rin po che* (The Precious Pillar) performed by (1) Ali Mahmud and Tsering Angchuk Ralam and (2) Dorje Stakmo (Figure 7.40) (Track 25).

Figure 7.39. *Sgo glu* (Door song) as sung by Stanzin Dadul, 27 July 2009. *Source*: Transcription provided by the author.

Figure 7.40. Comparison of two version of *ka ba rin po che. Source*: Transcription provided by the author.

In both versions the primary word settings are syllabic, with short two-beat melismas. The performance by Dorje has more elaborate melismas, as well as using various types of tremolo, much of which is very hard to notate. I speculate that these ornaments might be a manifestation of an Indian-influenced style that was characterized to me by the late Tsewang Rigzin as the Muslim Purig Style, which he described as being cultivated by Morup Namgyal (personal comm., July 13, 2011).

Characteristics of Song Genres

I offer some notes summarizing the characteristics of the four genres featured in this study.

RTEN ʻBREL GLU

These are all in moderate tempi. The text settings are all syllabic. The melodies are more conjunct than g*zhung glu* with an occasional leap of a fourth or fifth. *Ten ʻbrel glu* are all strophic, with either an antecedent/consequent or AABB binary form. Some are meant to be dance tunes, while others are sung in large groups at religious gatherings, such as when important lamas give teachings. They are not as complicated as *zhung lu,* apparently deriving from and/or being geared toward less skilled performers.

BAG STON GLU

Most songs are sung a cappella, although instrumental dances and dance songs are also considered by some to be part of the repertoire. As mentioned before, *rten ʻbrel glu* are sung at weddings and other important occasions.

Many songs are of the sub-genre known as *bkra shis pa glu* (*tashis pa lu*—auspicious songs), which, for the most part, uses one basic melody, with variations. The more usual version is shown in Figure 7.41 and a transcription of a more ornate version by Morup Namgyal in Figure 7.42. Both have the same blessing intonation at the beginning, and the same strophic, syllabic setting in a simple 6/8-type rhythm.

CHANG LU

Chang lu seem to be predominantly simple, strophic songs in a seven- or fourteen-beat rhythm, with syllabic settings. Melodic motion is conjunct

Figure 7.41. Tashis pa lu. *Source*: Transcription provided by the author.

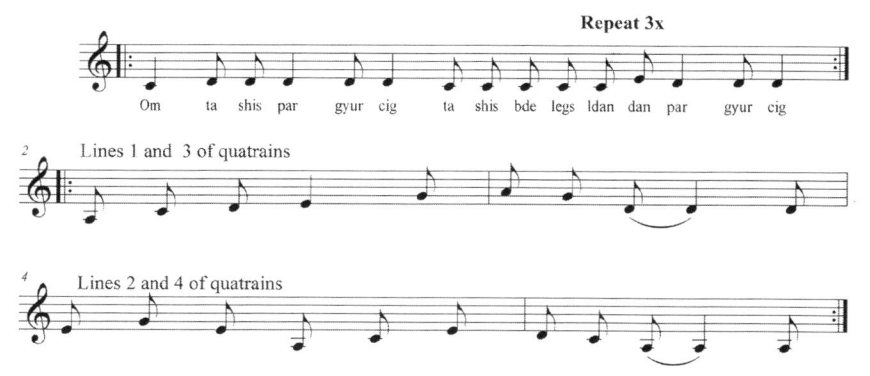

Figure 7.42. *Tashis pa lu*—ornate version by Morup Namgyal. *Source*: Transcription provided by the author.

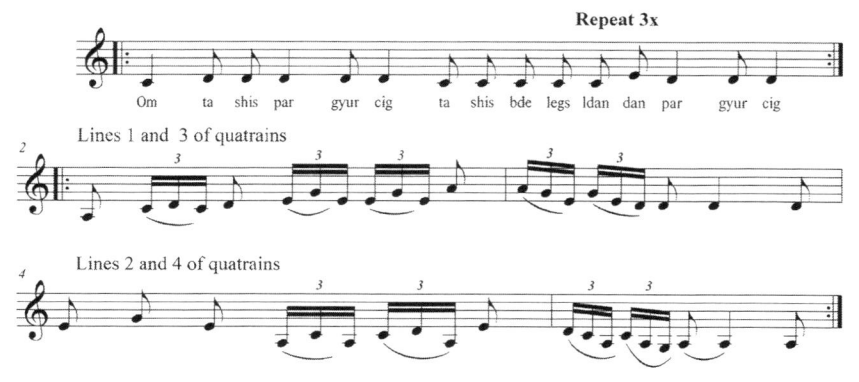

with few jumps and shows a simple antecedent/consequent structure. Many use the *bzo thabs* melody (figures 7.26 and 7.33 above).

Zhung lu

Most of the characteristics of *zhung lu* have been discussed in detail elsewhere in this chapter, but in summary, the repertoire is characterized by rhythmically sophisticated melodies with combinations of conjunct motion and wide leaps. The rhythmic cycles are more complex than in simpler genres like *chang glu*, or most *bag ston glu*, with the melodies varying from simple antecedent/consequent couplets to multisection compositions spanning several drum cycles. They are invariably strophic in form, often with lengthy literary texts. The text settings are almost exclusively syllabic, with syllables being extended by the addition of various lexical and nonlexical particles.

Chapter 8

Concluding Summary

While living in a time of rapid technological, economic, and social change, Ladakhis remain connected to village life and a sense of history and legend. The songs texts I have examined show how figures like King Gesar, King Sengge Namgyal, and Lama Stagtsang Raspa still loom large in Ladakhi consciousness. A sense of common history is evoked for all Ladakhis, both Buddhist and Muslim, with the old songs continuing to resonate across generations, although when and where they are performed, and by whom, has changed.

By the early 1950s, the closing of the borders with Pakistan and Chinese-ruled Tibet and Turkestan (Xinjiang) brought the traditional caravan trade to a halt, impoverishing the region. Military tensions with both India's neighbors brought a large Indian army presence that necessitated changes in local infrastructure and created a demand for public sector labor offering nontraditional venues for employment. Many of the traditional village instrumental musicians, the *Mon*, have taken advantage of growth in the nonagricultural sector to reject their low-caste occupations and not play music anymore. This has led to loss of repertoire, even though the *Beda* have attempted to move into the niche.

The Ladakhi economy has been expanding since the opening of the area in the mid-1970s, and even more since the tourism boom began in the 1990s. This has increased demand for traditional music, with new venues developing, such as upscale hotels and public events that celebrate local ethnic pride. Organizations like the Cultural Academy, SECMOL, LAMO, and HCHF have been working to collect and teach songs, as well as *surna, daman*, and *khopong*, increasing the number of performers of traditional repertoire.

The advent of mass media has been a mixed blessing with Ladakh being bombarded with Hindi- and English-language TV, radio, movies, and recordings. Being part of modern India, Ladakhi youth, especially in Leh and Kargil, are active consumers of popular music of all sorts: Bollywood, Nepali pop, and *lok pop*, as well as Anglo-American genres of all types. This is in addition to the growing Ladakhi pop music scene with its syncretic mixture of all the genres mentioned above.

At the same time, the media have been a means of cultural *preservation*. AIR and Doordarshan TV offer opportunities for regional artists to perform *zhung glu,* and local producers are publishing audio and video recordings of traditional songs. Additionally, there is a growing internet presence. Catchy, modern arrangements of *zhung lu* by Dorjay Stakmo and young Ladakhi urbanites such as Padma Dolkar, Angdu Khigu, and the Dashugs Band are increasingly being posted on the digital crossroads of YouTube.

From a music analysis point of view, we can characterize the position of Ladakh as a crossroads culture in terms of melodic patterns, rhythmic systems, and the use of *daf, and* the prestige *surna/daman* ensemble, all instruments of Western Asian origin. The hybridity of Ladakhi traditional songs is even more notable when considering the song lyrics, which are part of a pan-Tibetan cultural continuum containing both pre-Buddhist local traditions and literary high culture. The songs themselves are part of the matrix of the old Ladakhi life cycle: seasonal festivals, farmwork, beer drinking, and other activities, as well as more significant life-cycle events such as weddings and the birth of children. Thus, as performative phenomena the songs' musical settings are inextricably linked with the language and content of the lyrics.

བསྔོ་བ་ (bsngo ba) — Dedication

For those readers who were familiar with this music before, it is hoped that this book and its recordings have served to enrich that knowledge. For those who found this an unfamiliar repertoire, I hope to have shared something of the wonder I've experienced these past twenty-five years. I offer this work out of love and respect for my teachers, colleagues, and friends in Ladakh, and, to paraphrase the Seven-Limb *Puja* (liturgy), "may the merit gained in my acting thus, go to the alleviation of the suffering of all beings."

Glossary

Avalokiteśvara (Tib. Spyan ras gzigs [pronounced Chenrezig]): bodhisattva of compassion,

Bagston lu (*bag ston glu*): marriage songs.

Beda: itinerant, low-caste musicians.

Bodhisattva (Tib. *byang chug sems dpa*): Buddhist protector or semi-divine savior.

Bon: Pre-Buddhist religion containing a mixture of shamanistic and animistic traditions, at times combined with the belief in the personage of a divine king. The adjective is Bonpo—also a practitioner of those beliefs.

Brokpa (*'brogs pa*): Dardic speaking peoples that live in the western part of Ladakh, thought to be the main inhabitants of the area prior to colonization by Tibetic speaking people.

Buddha: Sanskrit for "Enlightened One" (Tib. *sangs rgyas*). It can either be a title, as in "The Buddha," referring to the historical Prince Gautama Siddhartha Sakyamuni, or it can be used generically in lower case to refer to any enlightened being.

Chang: barley beer.

Chang lu (*chang glu*): beer songs.

Dakini (Tib. *mkha''dro*): female bodhisattva that bestow wisdom and in part function analogously to fairy godmothers.

Daman: double kettledrums.

Dharma: Buddhist teachings or law.

Ding jang (*gring jang*): large barrel drum used in Baltistan and the Brokpa area of Ladakh.

Geshe: Buddhist monastic degree equivalent to combined Ph.D. and Doctor of Divinity.

Gompa (*dgon pa*): Monastery.

Gonchas: men's Tibetan-style robes.

Khatag: blessing scarf.

Khar mon (*mkhar mon*): palace musicians.

Lama: (Skt. guru): Buddhist teacher, often a monk.

Lha nga: (drum of the gods) ceremonial/processional music played on *surna* and *daman.*

Lok gīt: Folkloric versions of Nepali folk songs.

Maṇḍala: generic term for any plan, chart or geometric pattern that represents the cosmos metaphysically or symbolically.

Mantra: sound, syllable, word, or group of words used to invoke mental transformations or invoke mental imagery.

Mon: low-caste musicians, carpenters, and subsistence farmers.

Mudrā: symbolic or ritual hand gesture, or body posture.

Nagas (Tib. *klu*): local earth or water spirits.

Puja: Ritual or liturgy.

Rol mo: Tibetan Buddhist music, or music in general.

Sangha: The body of Buddhist practitioners, or the body of monks and nuns.

SECMOL: Students' Educational and Cultural Movement of Ladakh. It is a cultural advocacy group and school with headquarters in Phey Village, founded in 1988 by a group of young Ladakhis with the aim to reform the educational system of Ladakh.

Sgo glu (door song): subgenre of marriage songs in which there is a contest between the bridegroom's party outside the bride's house and the bridal party barricaded inside.

Sku ṭag (*sku drag*)—families of aristocratic origin.

Stupa (Tib. mchod rten): reliquary shrine or tumulus.

Sulma: women's pleated overdress.

Surna: Double reed shawm.

Tendel lu (*rten 'brel glu*) songs of auspicious signs—also pronounced *stendel lu.*

Tsig lu (*tsig glu*): literally "word songs," gently sarcastic or satirical songs sung in a free rhythm.

Tsig lhad/*tsig lad* (word interpolation): interpolation of nonlexical syllables in song texts.

Vajrayana: Sanskrit for "Thunderbolt Vehicle." School of Buddhism that utilizes the tantric techniques of mudra (gesture or image), mantra (sound formula), and mandala (symbolic diagrams) to reach enlightenment more quickly.

Yul lu (*yul glu*): songs of village, countryside, or the nation.

Zhabro/jabro (*zhabs 'bro*): song and dance genre from Changthang nomads and Tibet.

Zhung lu (*gzhung glu*): (a) general term for traditional songs; (b) specific genre of congregational songs connected with the Namgyal Dynasty court.

Appendixes

Appendix A

THE ORTHOGRAPHY AND PRONUNCIATION OF LADAKHI

Ladakhi and Tibetan words are transliterated according to the standard system of Wylie (1959) with the exception that, as with the Tibetan script itself, no letters are capitalized. Following Tibetan orthographic practice, I represent each syllable as separate, as opposed to the other common practice of hyphenating lexical units. As shown in the following table, the Tibetan writing system comprises an alphabet of thirty consonants and four vowel signs. This alphabet also functions as a syllabary: most phonemes in Ladakhi occur as syllables that may be simply represented by basic letters plus vowels, with only a few being represented by certain combinations of letters in syllable-initial clusters.

TIBETAN LETTER TRANSLITERATION PHONEMIC/
PHONETIC PRONUNCIATION

Transcription

VOWELS

ཨ or འ	a or ‘	/ə/	[a~ə]	initially/medially, as in "ago";
			[a]	finally, as in "bar"
ི	i	/i/	[i]	as in "beet" (short)
ུ	u	/u/	[u]	as in "boot" (short)
ེ	e	/e/	[ɛ]	initially/medially, as in "bet";
			[e]	like Spanish "e"

	o	/o/	[ɒ]	initially/medially, as in "hot"
			[o]	finally, as in "boat"

PLOSIVES

པ་	p	/p/	[p]	as in "pill"
ཕ་	ph	/ph/	[ph]	as in "uphill"
བ་	b	/b/	[b]	as in "bill";
			[ɓ]	fricative after /r/ or /l/
ཏ་	t	/t/	[t]	as in "stand"
ཐ་	th	/th/	[th]	as in "right-hand"
ད་	d	/d/	[d]	as in "damned";
			[ɗ]	fricative after /r/ or /l/
		/ʈ/	[ʈ]	retroflex [t] in some initial positions, as in Hindi *khāṭ* ('cot')
		/ʈh/	[ʈh]	retroflex [th] in some initial positions, as in Hindi *ṭhik* ('OK')
		/ɖ/	[ɖ]	retroflex [d] in some initial positions, as in Hindi *ḍar* ("fear')
ཀ་	k	/k/	[k]	as in "scanned"
			[x]	retracted in absolute final position
ཁ་	kh	/kh/	[kh]	as in "backhand"
ག་	g	/g/	[g]	as in "gander"
			[ɡ]	fricative after /r/ or /l/

AFFRICATIVES

ཙ་	c	/tʃ/	[tʃ]	as in "chill"
ཚ་c	h	/tʃh/	[tʃh]	as in "church-hill"
ཛ་	j	/dʒ/	[dʒ]	as in "Jill"
ཙ་	ts	/ts/	[ts]	as in "pizza"
ཚ་	tsh	/tsh/	[tsh]	as in "it's hot"
ཛ་	dz	/dz/	[dz]	as in "adze"

FRICATIVES

ས་	s	/s/	[s]	as in "seat"
ཤ་	sh	/ʃ/	[ʃ]	as in "sheet"
ཟ་	z	/z/	[z]	as in "zebra"
ཞ་	zh	/ʒ/	[ʒ]	as in "leisure"
ཧ་	h	/h/	[h]	as in "heat"

TRILLS

| ར་ | r | /r/ | [r] | as in "rat" |
| | | | [r̥] | voiceless in some initial positions before /ts/ |

LATERALS

ལ་	l	/l/	[l]	as in "lap"
			[l̥]	voiceless in some initial positions before /p/, /t/ or /d/
			[ɬ]	murmured [l] in some initial positions, like Welsh "ll".

NASALS

མ་	m	/m/	[m]	as in "map"
ན་	n	/n/	[n]	as in "nap"
ཉ་	ny	/nj/	[nj]	as in "new"
ང་	ng	/ŋ/	[ŋ]	as in "sing"

SEMI VOWELS

| ཝ་ | w | /w/ | [w] | as in "ward" |
| ཡ་ | y | /y/ | [y] | as in "yard" |

Unlike many Tibetan dialects, stress, duration, and tone have no phonemic value in Ladakhi, and therefore have no bearing upon musical settings. However, free variation at phonemic and sub-phonemic levels, especially between voiceless/voiced and unaspirated/aspirated consonant pairs and between the vowels [a~e~o ~ə], seem to be especially prominent in song, compared to speech.

As in Tibetan, the prefixes, g, d, b, m and ', are not usually pronounced, except in some cases where they follow an open syllable, e.g., the m in rna-mchog ('ear'). The special combinations involving d before b are pronounced as in Tibet, i.e., db as /w/, and dby as /y/; thus dbang ('power') is pronounced [waŋ] and dbyangs ('tune') as [yaŋs]. Additionally, in Ladakh, dp has the value /sp/ or /ʂp/; e.g., dpyid [the season 'spring'] is pronounced [spit] or [ʂpit].

Unlike Tibetan, the head letters, r, s and l, that may surmount certain basic letters always affect Ladakhi pronunciation. In general, these consonant combinations have the expected sound values resulting from the combination of the component phonemic units, subject to the small phonetic changes given in the table; thus /r/+/d/ =/rd/ [rd], as in rdung, the verbal stem meaning '(to) beat' (e.g., a drum), which is pronounced [rd̪uŋ]. Exceptions to this general rule are:

> r above k, m, n,ny and ng becomes /ʂ/ [ʂ], giving /ʂk/ [ʂk],
> /ʂm/ [ʂm], etc.
> s above b, d and g becomes /z/ [z], giving /zb/ [zb], etc.
> l above ts becomes /r/, giving /rts/ [r̥ts]
> l above t becomes /ʂ/, giving /ʂk/ [ʂk]
> l above b becomes /r/, giving /rb/ [rb]
> l above k gives /ɬ/ [ɬ] Note that, in the absence of a prefix,
> the pronunciation of head letters may be preserved when
> following an open syllable; thus lha-rnga is pronounced
> [ɬarŋa] whereas rnga ('drum') is pronounced [ʂŋa].

In dialects of Upper Ladakh (including Leh), the subjoined y has the same effect as in Tibetan, thus:

> y below m gives /njy/ [njy]
> y below p gives /tʃ/ [tʃ]
> y below ph gives /tʃh/ [tʃh]
> y below b (except when prefixed by d, see note 2)
> gives /dʒ/ [dʒ]

The Subjoined r or l, however, affects Ladakhi pronunciation somewhat differently:

> r below k, t and p gives /ʈ/ [ʈ]
> r below kh, th and ph gives / ʈ h/ [ʈh]
> r below g, d and b gives /ɖ/ [ɖ]
> r below s, h and sh all gives /ʂ/ [ʂ]
> r below m becomes /ʂ/, giving /ʂm/ [ʂm]
> l below k, g, b, r and s gives /ɬ/ [ɬ]
> N.B. l below z gives /lz/, not /d/ as in Tibetan

As a general rule, the pronunciation of final letters is preserved in Ladakhi. The letters b, g, and d tend to become voiceless plosives (i.e., /p/, /k/ and /t/), especially when followed by an extra final (always s and always pronounced) (Trewin 1995, 17–21).

Appendix B

Additional Songs with Transcriptions and Translations with Commentary

This is a compilation of additional songs from *Ladvags gyi yul glu*: *stendel lu, bagston lu, chang lu* and *zhung lu,* with their translations, and notated transcriptions of the melodies (when a recorded example was not available). I have annotated the texts, occasionally giving an occasional explanatory preface for clarification. Where available, I have included recordings of the songs. I include the Wylie transliteration, and translation for the fullest appreciation of the word-music relationships.

As in Indian music, there is no concept of key in Ladakhi music. When sung with *surna,* most melodies are centered on E, but I put the transcriptions in whatever key makes the notation more readable. When sung *a cappella* they are pitched to suit the singer. Textual interpolations, both lexical and nonlexical, are shown in parentheses.

To help the reader more clearly understand the song transcriptions, I list the rhythmic cycle of each song—if I could determine it. In cases where a song's rhythm is unclear, I leave the transcription in free rhythm. I list the rhythms in figure B-1:

Figure B.1. List of Song Rhythms. *Source:* Transcription provided by the author.

ཪྟེན་འབྲེལ་གྱི་གླུ།

rten 'brel gyi glu—Songs of Auspicious Omens

rten 'brel gsum pa—The Three Auspicious Signs
(Track 27)—Rhythmic cycle 1
dgung gnam bzhengs pa skar tshogs su mang byung (2x)
'bur du mtho ba de nyi ma dang zla ba
mdangs su gsal ba de nyi ma dang zla ba
dga' ba'i rten 'brel dang po de dang zungs shig
zag med rten 'brel dang po zungs shig.
[In higher relief are the sun and moon
There shine brightly sun and moon.
Let us be mindful of the joyous, first auspicious omen.
Let us be mindful of the stainless first auspicious omen.]

gling bzhi bzhengs pa mi tshogs su mang byung (2x)
'bur du mtho ba de rgyalpo dang bla ma
mdangs su gsal ba de sengge dang stag tshang
dga' ba'i rten' brel gnyis pa de dang zungs shig
zag med rten 'brel gnyis pa de dang zungs shig.
[In the four continents, many assemblies of men arise (2x)
There in higher relief, king and lama
There shines brightly the lion and tiger nest[1]
Let us be mindful of the second auspicious omen.
Let us be mindful of the stainless second auspicious omen.]

skyes pa'i pha yul la ni tshe dbang gi bum pa
gle chen dpal mkhar ni tshe dbang gi bum pa
'bras dkar dbol bo spungs pa dang 'dra byung
dga' ba' rten 'brel gsum pa de dang zungs shig
'o ma'i rdzing bu 'khyil gsum pa de dang zungs shig
zags med rten 'brel gsum pa de dang zungs shig.
[In the homeland of happiness, the vessel of long life
    empowerment
In Leh's noble castle, the vessel of long-life empowerment
It is like white rice piled high.

Let us be mindful of the third, surrounded as by a lake of milk.
Let us be mindful of the stainless third auspicious omen.]
   (LYL, 2)

rten 'brel lnga pa—The Five Auspicious Signs
(track 06)
ya gi dgung sngon mo la skar tshog mang tsam zhig 'dug (2x)
deng sang ngoms su thub pa ya gi nyi zla gnyis ka
deng sang mdangs su gsal ba ya gi nyi zla gnyis ka
dga' ba'i rten 'brel dang po dang po de dang zungs shig
za med rten 'brel dang po dan po de dang zungs shig.
[In yonder blue sky there ever so many constellations (2x)
Now we can be proud of both the sun and moon
Now both yon sun and moon shine.
Let us be mindful of the joyous first auspicious omen.
Let us be mindful of the stainless first, the first auspicious omen.]

ya gi chos grva gru bshi la grva rgyun mang tsam zhig 'dug (2 x)
dengs sang ngoms su thub pa ya gi yar 'dren bla ma
dengs sang mdangs su gsal ba ya gi yar 'dren bla ma
dga' ba'i rten 'brel gnyis pa gnyis pa de dang zungs shig
zag med rteng 'brel gnyis pa gnyis pa de dang zungs shig.
[There are many people in that square Dharma debate court (2x)
We can be proud of those lamas that guide us
Now those lamas that guide us shine.
Let us be mindful of the joyous second, the second auspicious
   omen
Let us be mindful of the stainless second, the second auspicious omen]

ya gi sku mkhar mthon po la drag zhan mang tsam zhig 'dug (2x)
deng sang ngoms su thub pa ya gi mi chen gong ma
deng sang mdangs su gsal ba ya gi mi chen gong ma
dga' ba'i rten 'brel gsum pa gsum pa de dang zungs shig
zag med rten 'brel gsum pa gsum pa de dang zungs shig.
[In that high palace there are many high and low officials (2x)
We can be proud of that great lord
Now that great man shines.

And let us be mindful of the joyous third, the third auspicious
  omen.
Let us be mindful of the stainless third, the third auspicious
  omen.]

ya gi dpal khang gru bzhi la gnyen drung man tsam zhig 'dug (2x)
deng sang ngoms su thub pa ya gi yab yum pa ma
deng sang mdangs su gsal ba ya gi yab yum pa ma
dga' ba'i rten 'brel bzhi pa bzhi pa de dang zungs shig
zag med rten 'brel bzhi pa bzhi pa de dang zungs shig.
[In yon noble house's four corners there are kin nearby (2x)
We can be proud of our fathers and mothers.
Right now, our fathers and mothers shine.
And let us be mindful of the joyous fourth, the fourth auspicious omen.
Let us be mindful of the stainless fourth, the fourth auspicious
  omen.]

ya gi do ra gru bzhi la ya de mang tsam zhig 'dug (2x)
deng sang ngoms su thub pa ge rje dpon chen po
deng sang ngoms gsal ba ya gi rje dpon chen po
dga' ba'i rten 'brel lnga pa de dang zungs shig
zag med rten 'brel lgna pa de dang zungs shig.
[There are many people there in that square courtyard (2x)
Right now, we can be proud of that great lord.
Right now, that great lord shines
Let us be mindful of the joyous fifth, the fifth auspicious omen.
Let us be mindful of the stainless fifth, the fifth auspicious
  omen.]

rten 'brel lnga pa-B—The Five Auspicious Signs-B
(Track 29 first verse) Rhythmic cycle 3
ya gi shed dgung gnam sngon mo dgung gnam bsod nams can
  zhig (2x)
nyi zla ni gnyis ka kun bzhugs pa'i dga' ba la gzigs ang
rgyu skar 'dzoms po kun 'khor ba'i skyid nyams la gzigs
dga' ba'i rten 'brel gyi dang po mar yul gyi gzhung du 'khyil
zag med rten 'brel gyi dang po drug ma nang du 'khyil.

[Behold yon strong blue sky, that blessed sky (2x)
Behold both sun and moon sitting in joy
Happily, behold the many constellations all around,
The blessed perfect first auspicious sign surrounds Ladakh,
The stainless first auspicious sign circles in the the six-columned
    chamber.]

ya gi shed chos grva gru bzhi chos grva bsod nams can zhig (2x)
yar 'dren gyi bla ma kun bzhugs pa'i dga' ba la gzigs ang
bu slob 'dzoms po kun 'khor ba'i skyid nyams la gzigs
dga' ga'i rten 'brel gyi gnyis pa mar yul gyi zhungs du 'khyil
zag med rten 'brel gyi gnyis pa ka drug ma nang du 'khyil.
[Behold that strong, square, blessed Dharma debate court (2x)
Behold the lama guides joyfully seated.
Behold the many disciples surrounding them in happiness.
The blessed perfect second auspicious omen surrounds Ladakh,
The stainless second auspicious omen circles in the six-
    columned chamber.]

ya gi shed sku mkhar mthon po sku mkhar bsod nams can
    zhig (2x)
mi chen gong ma kun bzhugs pa'i dga' ba la gzigs ang
drag zhan dzoms po kun 'khor ba'i skyid nyams la gzigs
dga' ba'i rten 'brel gyi gsum pa mar yul gyi gzhung du 'khyil
zag med rten 'brel gyi gsum pa ka drug ma nang du 'khyil.
[Behold in yon strong high fortress, the blessed fortress (2x)
Behold the great lords joyfully seated there.
Behold all the high and low officials happily surrounding them.
The joyous third auspicious omen circles inside Ladakh.
Let us be mindful of the stainless third auspicious omen circling
    inside the six-columned chamber.]

ya gi shed dpal khang gru bzhi dpal khang bsod nams can zhig
    (2x)
yab yum pa ma kun bzugs pa'i dga' ba la gzigs ang
gnyen drung 'dzoms po kun 'khor ba'i skyid nyams la gzigs
dga' ba'i rten 'brel gyi bzhi pa mar yul gyi gzhung du 'khyil
zag med rten 'brel gyi bzhi pa ka drug nang du 'khyil.

[Behold yon noble square house, that blessed house.
Behold our mothers and fathers joyfully sitting there.
Behold the many kin happily surrounding us.
The joyous fourth auspicious omen circles inside Ladakh
Let us be mindful of the stainless fourth auspicious omen
    circling inside the six-columned chamber.]

ya gi shed do ra gru bzshi do ra bsod nams can zhig (2x)
rje dpon chen po kun bzhugs pa'i dga' ba la gzigs ang
ya do mdza' bo kun 'khor ba'i skyid nyams la gzigs
dga' ba'i rten 'brel gyi lnga pa mar yul gyi gzhung du 'khyil
zag med rten 'brel gyi lgna ka drug ma nang du 'khyil.
[Behold that strong blessed square stage. (2x)
Behold the great lord joyfully sitting there.
Behold the helpers happily surrounding him.
The joyous fifth auspicious omen circles inside Ladakh
Let us be mindful of the stainless fifth auspicious omen circling
    inside the six-columned chamber.] (LYL, 6)

rten 'brel lnga pa C—The Five Auspicious Signs

As sung by Tsering Chorol accompanying herself on daf, July
31, 2012, Rhythmic cycle 4

dgung gnam sngon mo'i g.yas 'phyogs na (2x)
nyi zla gnyis ka khri khar bzhugs (2x)
rgyu skar 'dzom pa'i dga' ba la gzigs
rgyu skar 'dzom pa'i skyid nyams la gzigs
ya sha skyid po'i nyi ma shar ba dan 'dra
ya sha ga' ba'i rten 'brel 'grig pa dan 'dra
[High in the right side of the blues sky (2x)
The sun and moon both sit on a throne (2x)
Behold in joy all the constellations sitting.
Behold in happiness the abundant constellations.
Oh! It resembles the sun of happiness in the east.
Oh! It resembles an auspicious omen of joy.]

chos grva gru bshi g.yas 'phyogs na (2x)
yar 'dren bla ma khri khar bzhugs (2x)

Figure B.2. *rten 'brel lnga pa C* as sung by Tsering Chorol. *Source:* Transcription provided by the author.

bu slob 'dzoms po'i dga' ba la gzigs.
bu slob 'dzoms po'i dkyid nyams la gzigs.
ya sha skyid po'i nyi ma shar ba dang 'dra
ya sha ga' ba'i rten 'brel 'grig pa dang 'dra.

[At the right side of the square Dharma court (2x)
The Lama guide sits on a throne (2x)
Behold in joy his abundant disciples.
Behold in happiness his perfect disciples.
Oh! It resembles the sun of happiness in the east.
Oh! It resembles an auspicious omen of joy.]

sku mkhar mthon po'i g.yas phyogs na (2x)
mi chen gong ma khri khar bzhugs (2x)
drag zhan 'dzoms po'i dga' ba la gzigs
drag zhan 'dzom po'i skyid nyams la gzigs
ya sha skyid po'i nyi ma shar ba dang 'dra
ya sha ga' ba'i rten 'brel 'grig pa dan 'dra
[At the right side of the high palace (2x)
The great lord sits on a throne (2x)
Behold in joy all the high and low officials.
Behold in happiness all the high and low officials.
Oh! It resembles the sun of happiness in the east.
Oh! It resembles an auspicious omen of joy.]

dpal khang gru bzhi'i g.yas phyogs na (2x)
yab yum pha ma khri gar bzhugs (2x)
gnyen drung 'dzoms po'i dga' ba la gzigs
gnyen drung 'dzoms po'i skyid nyams la gzigs
ya sha skyid po'i nyi ma shar ba dang 'dra
ya sha ga' ba'i rten 'brel 'grig pa dang 'dra.
[At the right side of that noble square palace (2x)
Our fathers and mothers are seated on a throne (2x)
Behold in joy our abundant kin.
Behold in happiness our abundant kin.
Oh! It resembles the sun of happiness in the east.
Oh! It resembles an auspicious omen of joy.]

do ra gru bzhi g.yas phyogs na (2x)
rje dpon chen po khri khar bzhugs (2x)
ya do mdza' bo'i dga' ba la gzigs
ya do mdza' bo'i skyid nyams la gzigs
ya sha skyid po'i nyi ma shar ba dang 'dra
ya sha ga' ba'i rten 'brel 'grig pa dang 'dra.

[At the right side of the square stage (2x)
The great lord sits on a throne (2x)
Behold in joy all his attendants.
Behold in happiness all his attendants.
Oh! It resembles the sun of happiness in the east.
Oh! It resembles an auspicious omen of joy.] (LYL:6–8)

rten 'brel bdun pa—The Seven Auspicious Signs
(First verse, track 30) Rhythmic cycle 5
dgung dang nyi zla skar phran 'dzoms dang gsum (2x)
gling bzhi'i mun pa sel ba'i rten 'brel de dang 'grig
phyogs bzhi'i mun pa sel ba'i rten 'brel dang po 'grig.
[The three: abundant sky, sun, moon, the many little stars (2x)
Be mindful of the auspicious omen of the four continents'
    great relief.
Be mindful of the first great auspicious omen that relieves the
    four afflictions.]

gangs dang dar seng g.yu ral 'dzoms dang gsum (2x)
g.yu ral mtha' ru rgyas pa'i rten 'brel de dang 'grig
g.yu ral mtha' ru rgyas pa'i rten 'brel gnyis pa 'grig.
[The three: abundant snow, streams and lakes, and the turquoise-
    maned snow lion (2x)
Be mindful of the great auspicious omen of the turquoise-maned
    lion.
Be mindful of the second great auspicious omen of the
    turquoise-maned snow lion]

ri dang ri dvags rtsa chu 'dzoms dang gsum (2x)
ri dvags skyid nyams chags pa'i rten 'brel de dang 'grig
sha ba la skyid nyams chags pa'i rten 'brel gsum pa 'grig.
[The three: abundant mountains, mountain passes, and springs (2x)
Be mindful of the auspicious omen of happy desire in
    mountain passes.
Be mindful of the third auspicious omen of happy desire for
    hunters.]

spang dang 'brong chung rtsa chu 'dzoms dang gsum (2x)
'brong chung skyid nyams chags pa'i rten 'brel 'grig

'brong chung skyid nyams changs pa'i rten 'brel bzhi pa
  'grig.
[The three: abundant meadows, yak calves, and streams (2x)
Be mindful of the auspicious omen of happy desire in the valley.
Be mindful of the fourth auspicious omen of happy desire in
  the valley.]

ma khang dang ma mdung gral lcam 'dzoms dang gsum (2x)
ka bar ka dar rol ba'i rten 'brel de dang 'grig
ka bar ka dar rol ba'i rten 'brel lnga pa 'grig.
[The three: house nor front sitting row converge (2x)
Be mindful of the auspicious take care enjoying.
Being mindful of the fifth auspicious omen take care enjoying.]

yab dang yum chung bu nor 'dzoms dang gsum (2x)
bu rgyud mtha' ru rgyas pa'i rten 'brel de dang 'grig
bu rgyud mtha' ru rgyas pai' rten 'brel drug pa 'grig
[The three: parents, abundant children, and wealth, (2x)
Be mindful of the auspicious omen of endless children.
Be mindful of the sixth auspicious omen of endless children.]

ma zhing dang g.ya' chu 'bru sna 'dzoms dang gsum (2x)
bsing chang yar dkar rol ba'i rten 'brel de dang 'grig
bsing chang yar dkar rol ba'i rten 'brel bdun pa 'grig
[The three: abundant fields, streams, and grain (2x)
Be mindful of the auspicious omen of the upper, white, last
  strained beer.
Be mindful of the seventh auspicious omen of the upper, white,
  last-strained beer.] (LYL, 8–9)

rten 'brel bdun pa—The Seven Auspicious Signs
sung to the melody of *rten 'brel lnga pa*-B (Track 29)
ya gi shed dgung gnam sngon mo na nyi zla gnyis ka bzhugs (2x)
*rgyu skar 'dzoms pos mtha' zhig bskar song zer na sangs rgyas
  bstan pa de dang dar (2x)*
*sangs rgyas kyi bstan pa dar song zer na rten 'brel dan po de
  dang 'grig. (2x)*
[Both the sun and moon sit in yon strong blue sky. (2x)
The Buddha's teaching reach even the constellations gathered
  round. (2x)

Be mindful of the first auspicious omen when it was said the
Buddha's teachings flourished.] (2x).

ya gi shed chos grva gru bzhi na bzang gsum bla ma bzhugs
grva rgyun 'dzoms pos mtha' zhig bskor song na sangs rgyas
bstan pa de dang dar (2x)
sangs rgyas kyi bstan pa dar song zer na rten 'brel gnyis pa
de dang 'grig.
[The learned, virtuous, and noble[2] lamas sit in yon square
Dharma court. (2x)
The teachings of the Buddha reach even the gathered monks
surrounding him. (2x)
Be mindful of the second auspicious omen when it was said
the Buddha's teachings flourished. (2x)]

ya gi shed sku mkar mthon po na mi chen gon ma bzhugs
(2x)
drag zhan 'dzoms pos mtha' zhig bskor na sangs rgyas bstan
po de dang 'dra (2x)
sangs rgyas kyi bstan pa dar song zer na rten 'brel gsum pa
de dang 'grig (2x)
[In that high castle, great lords and ladies sit prepared. (2x)
The powerful lord dwells in yon high castle.
The teachings of the Buddha reach even the gathered high
and low officials (2x)
Be mindful of the third auspicious omen when it was said
the Buddha's teachings flourished (2x).]

ya gi shed dpal khang gru bzhi na yab yum pha ma bzhugs
(2x)
gnyen drung 'dzoms pos mtha' zhig bskor na sangs rgyas bstan
po de dang dar (2x)
sang rgyas kyi bstan pa dar song zer na rten 'brel bzhi pa de
dan 'grig (2x)
[Our mother and father sit in yon strong, square noble
house (2x)
The Buddha's teachings reach even the kin gathered round
(2x)
Be mindful of the fourth auspicious omen when it was said
the Buddha's teachings flourished (2x).]

ya gi shed gangs stod mtha' po na gans seng dkar po bzugs (2x)

sengge'i g.yu ral mtha' ru rgyas song zer na sangs rgyas bstan pa de dang dar (2x)

sangs rgyas kyi bstan pa dar song zer na rten 'brel lnga pa de dang 'grig (2x)

[The snow lion sits on the high strong snow peak (2x)

The Buddha's teachings reach even the turquoise-maned snow lion (2x)

Be mindful of the fifth auspicious omen when it was said the Buddha teachings flourished (2x)]

ya gi shed brag stod mthon po na bya rgyal rgod po bzhugs (2x)

bya phran 'dzoms pos mtha' nas bskor na sangs rgyas bstan pa de dan dar (2x)

sangs rgyas kyi bstan pa dar song zer na rten 'brel drug pa de dan 'grig (2x)

[The king of birds[3] sits on the strong high rock (2x)

The Buddha's teachings reach even birds gathered in the branches (2x)

Be mindful of the sixth auspicious omen when it was said the Buddha teachings flourished (2x).]

ya gi shed spang stod mthon po na 'brong chen ga ma bzhugs (2x)

sha phran 'dzoms pos mtha' nas bskor song zer na sangs rgyas bstan pa de dang dar (2x)

sangs rgyas kyi bstan pa dar song zer rten 'brel bdun pa de dang 'grig.

[The great wild she-yak sits in the strong high rock meadow (2x)

The Buddha's teachings are said to reach even to the gathered animals (2x)

Be mindful of the seventh auspicious omen when it was said the Buddha teachings flourished (2x).]

(LYL, 10–11)

༼བག་སྟོན་གྱི་གླུ༽

bag ston gyi glu—Marriage Songs

As part of establishing the bride in her new household, a good luck arrow wrapped in a *khatag* (blessing scarf) with a mirror attached is placed in the family shrine room in a vessel of barley. According to Ribbach this arrow is initially carried from the groom's home to the bride's by the Nyatripa (*gnya 'krid pa*) the leader of the groom's party, or witnesses (*gnya' bo pa*). After mock battles between the bride's and groom's parties, songs praising the origins of the arrow were traditionally sung back and forth by the two groups (Ribbach 1985, 64–99) This text is one such example.

mda' dar gyi glu—Ceremonial Arrow Song
bkra shis pa glu sung by Ali Mahmud and Tsering Angchuk Ralam
Note: *bkra shis pa glu* are sung a capella and aren't set in rhythmic cycles

Om bkra shis par gyur cig.
bkra shis bde legs dan ldan par gyur cig. (3x)
[Om. May there be auspiciousness!
May there be congratulations! (3x).]

da ci mtsham gyi rmi lam bzang po mthong.
zhag bzang mtsham gyi rmi lam bzang po mthong.
phu de ya gi ru gangs ri chags pa mthong.
gangs ri de'i thog tu seng chen 'gying ba mthong.

Figure B.3. *bkra shis pa glu* sung by Ali Mahmud and Tsering Angchuk Ralam. *Source:* Transcription provided by the author.

[See how many good dreams there are now.
See how many good dreams of good days there are now.
See boy, yon beloved snow mountain!
See upon that snow mountain a great lion proudly posing.]

seng chen de'i thog tu ru g.yu ral rgyas pa mthong
mdo ma gi ru g.yu mtsho 'khyil ba mthong.
g.yu mtsho de'i thog tu nya mo lding ba mthong.
nya mo de'i thog tu gshog rtsal brkyangs pa mthong.
[See upon that great lion a vast turquoise mane.
See down in the valley the turquoise lake where water flows.
See upon the turquoise lake a female fish floating.
See upon the female fish the agile wing extended.]

gshogs rtsal de'i thog tu 'khyags rom chags pa mthong.
'khyags rom de'i thog tu sa rdo chags pa mthong.
sa rdo de'i thog tu ma zhing chags pa mthong.
ma zhing de'i thog tu 'bru sna smin pa mthong.
[See upon the agile wing the beloved solid ice.
See upon the solid ice the beloved earth and stone.
See upon the earth and stone the beloved mother fields.
See upon the mother fields ripe grain.]

'bru sna de'i thog tu brgya bang 'khyil ba mthong.
brgya bang de'i thog tu bre kha 'dzugs pa mthong.
bre kha de'i thog tu mda' dar bslangs pa mthong.
mda' mo'i ltong yi ltong nas nyams pa.
[See upon the grain the hundred levels whirling.
See upon the hundred levels the measuring pot planted.
See upon the measuring pot the requested ceremonial arrow.]

gshog pa zur bzhi yi zur nas ma nyams pa.
mda' mo tshig gsum gyi tshig nas ma nyams pa.
kha btags dkar po la dri ma sa phog par.
dngul dkar me long la lcags g.ya' ma 'khor bar.
[The arrow was proud of head to notch was very proud of
    its four sides.
The word arrow was very proud of its three words.

The white khatag touched by earth is defiled.
The silver-white mirror is surrounded by the iron handle.]

g.yang dkar mong lo'i g.yang nas ma shor bar.
mde'u thur gsum gyi zur nas ma nyams par.
gzhag dang gzhan gyi lag la gtang dgos med.
pa bzang gi bu gces gcig gi lag la gtad pa yin.
[The sheep from ankle to ankle is very lost.
The triangular arrowhead is proud of its tip.
Rest do not give it into another hand.
It will be given to the hand of the Dear Children of the Good
    Father.]

om bkra shis par gyur cig.
bkra shis bde legs dan ldan par gyur cig. (3x)
[Om. May there be auspiciousness!
May there be congratulations! (3x)] (LYL, 14–15).

thegs glu—Travel Song
bkra shis pa glu sung by Ali Mahmud and Tsering Angchuk
    Ralam
Om bkra shis par gyur cig.
bkra shis bde legs dang ldan par gyur cig.
[OM, may it be auspicious.
may it be auspicious.]

Figure B.4. *thegs glu* sung by Ali Mahmud and Tsering Angchuk Ralam *Source:*
Transcription provided by the author.

mchis su ma zhig dgung gsum ltong na mchis
phug ron gun ma zhig dgung gsum ltong na mchis
khra skya dkar po zhig ma mthong 'dzin du cha'in
'dzin gsum 'dzin pa yi steng nas dkon mchog mchod.
[The three heavens were not seen.
Doves were not seen in the three heavens.
A mottled white light will not be seen.
I supplicate the three recognitions from on top of recognition.]

mchis su ma zhig ri gsum ltong na mchis
g.yang dkar ma mo zhig rig sum ltong mchis
spyang dar ma zhig ma mthong 'dzin du cha'in
'dzin gsum 'dzin pa yi steng nas dkon mchog mchod.
[If three mountains are seen, no one is there.
The sacred white goddess of the three powers is not seen.
The clever adult does not come to be recognized.
I supplicate the three recognitions from on top of recognition.]

mchis su ma zhig dpal khang dkyil na mchis
a drung mna' ma zhig dpal kan dkyil na mchis
gnya' bo mi rta zhig ma mthong 'dzin du cha'in
'dzin gsum 'dzin pa yi steng nas dkon mchog mchod.
[If no one is inside the noble house.
If an oath messenger is not inside the noble house
The groom's attendants[4], man, and horse will not be recognized.
I supplicate the three recognitions from on top of recognition.]

mkhar ram gan du bzhugs pa'i rtse lha mchod
yul lam gang du bzhugs pa'i yul lha mchod
dpal kang 'di la gnas pa'i gshi bdag mchod
gnya' bo mi rta la skyob pa'i rabs lha mchod
[I supplicate the high god dwelling in the high castle.
I supplicate the village god dwelling in whatever village and road.
I supplicate this noble house earth of residence.
I supplicate the protective lineage diety the bride's attendants,
    man and horse.]

Om bkra shis par gyur cig.
bkra shis bde legs dang ldan par gyur cig.

[OM, may it be auspicious.
May it be auspicious.] (LYL, 15–16)

All my informants were unsure about how the generic blessing song (*bra shis pa'i* glu) melody, based on couplets, fits in with the three-line verse scheme of this text. The fact that the text ends with a quatrain adds to the mystery.

dkar 'chol spyir btang gi glu—Universal Libation Song
Om bkra shis par gyur cig.
bkra shis bde legs dang ldan par gyur cig.
[OM, may it be auspicious.
May it be auspicious.]

gser skyems gtsang ma zhig phud na mnyams par
gser skyems gtsang ma zhig steng gi lha la mchod
lha yi dbang po brgya byin zhal du mchod.
[All the golden *chang* is gathered as an offering.
All the golden *chang* is offered to the gods of the earth's surface.
I supplicate the sage of the gods, Indra of the hundred sacrifices.]

gser skyems gtsang ma zhig phud na ma nyams par
gser skyems gtsang ma zhig bar gyi btsan la mchod
btsan gyi a ma skyabs spyin zhal du mchod.
[All the golden *chang* is gathered as an offering.
All the golden *chang* is offered to the subterranean dakinis.
I supplicate the face of the mother of dakinis bestowing refuge.]

gser skyems gtsang ma zhig phud nas ma nyams par
gser skyems gtsang ma zhig 'og gi klu ma mchod
klu yi ma dro gzi can zhal du mchod.
[All the golden *chang* is gathered as an offering.
All the golden *chang* is offered to the dakinis above the earth.
I supplicate the face of the nagas' majestic mother dakini.]

mkhar ram gang du bzhugs pa'i rtse lha mchod
yul lam gang du bzhugs pa'i yul lha mchod
sa cha 'di la gnas pa'i gzhi bdag mchod
gnya' bo mi rta la skyob pa'i rabs lha mchod.

[I supplicate the god living in the high castle or anywhere else.
I supplicate the god living in the village or anywhere else.
I make offering to the protective god inhabiting the earth to this place.
I make offering to the protective god of the bride's attendant kin.] (LYL, 18–19).

This next song would be sung in to welcome the bride and her attendants, as shown by the last line in the fourth verses. As far as I can gather, this song would be performed using the same generic *bkra shis pa glu* melody. However, in the first three verses the second line is spoken, in which case the performance scheme is as follows A (spoken B instead of sung) A B. The fourth verse would be sung in the usual manner.

bsu chang gi glu—Welcome Song
Om bkra shis par gyur cig
bkra shis bde legs dang ldang par gyur cig.
[OM, may it be auspicious.
May it be auspicious.]

dgung dang nyi zla skar phran 'dzoms dang gsum.
(gsung) na ning shed ma mjal bshugs yod sa thag ring.
deng sang da lo shed ma mjal ba'i nyams kyi dga' ba la.
nyams dga' blo bde yi steng nas dkon mchog mchod.
[The three, sun, moon, and little stars, gather in the sky.
(Spoken) last year we didn't meet in a remote place.
Nowadays, this year we didn't meet joyfully.
But I supplicate the precious jewel from the highest happy carefreeness.]

chos grva yar 'dren bu slob 'dzoms dang gsum.
(gsung) na ding shed ma mjal bzhugs yod sa thag ring.
deng sang da lo shed mjal ba'i nyams kyi dga' ba la.
nyams dga' blo bde yi steng nas dkon mchog mchod.
[The three guiding teachers gathered in the Dharma court.
(Spoken) last year we didn't meet in a remote place.
Nowadays, this year we didn't meet joyfully.
But I supplicate the precious jewel from the highest happy carefreeness.]

dpal khang yab yum gnyin drung 'dzoms dang gsum.
(gsung) na ding shed ma mjal bzhugs yod sa thag ring.
deng sang da lo shed mjal ba'i nyams kyi dga' ba la.
nyams dga' blo bde yi steng nas dkon mchog mchod.
[In the noble house, the three, groom, bride, and relatives are
    gathered.
(Spoken) last year we didn't meet in a remote place.
Nowadays, this year we didn't meet joyfully.
But I supplicate the precious jewel from the highest happy
    carefreeness.]

mkhar ram gang du bzhugs pa'i rtse lha mchod.
yul lam gang du bzhugs pa'i yul lha mchod.
sa cha 'di la gnas pa'i gzhi bdag mchod.
gnya' bo mi rta la skyob pa'i rabs lha mchod.
[I supplicate the god living in the castle or anywhere else.
I supplicate the god living in the village or anywhere else.
I supplicate the god in the earth of this place.
I supplicate the god protecting the bride's attendants, man
    and horse.]

om bkra shis par gyur cig.
[OM, may there be auspiciousness.] (LYL, 19–20).

ka dar gyi glu—Pillar Flag Song

This song would be sung when hanging prayer flags from a pillar
to invoke blessings on the newlyweds.

om bkra shis par gyur cig
bkra shis bdel legs dang ldan par gyur cig
[OM, may it be auspicious.
May it be auspicious (3x)]

dgung sngon mthon po la nyi zlas ldem zhig phub
nyi zla'i ldem de la rgyu skar mtha' nas bskor
zhva 'am de 'dra zhig dgung sngon yongs kyi zhva
'thob kyang 'thob byung na 'bul yang mi 'bul lo.

[In the high blue sky, the sun and and moon's image raised
The high bright stars surround the flag of sun and moon.
The crown or what appears to be the crown of the blue sky's coming.
If whatever is attained is attained, whatever accomplished is accomplished.]

chos grva gru bshi la yar 'dren ldem zhig phub
yar 'dren ldem de lbu slob mtha' nas bskor
zhva 'am de 'dra zhig chos grva yongs kyi zhva
'thob kyang 'thob byung na 'bul yang mi 'bul lo.
[In the square Dharma court, the image of a high guide is raised
There the high guide's image is surrounded by disciples.
The crown or what appears to be the crown of the Dharma court's coming.
If whatever is attained is attained, whatever accomplished is accomplished.]

sku mkhar mthon po la mi chen ldem zhig phub
mi chen ldem de la drag zhan mtha' nas bskor
zhva 'am de 'dra zhig sku mkhar yongs kyi zhva
'thob kyang 'thob byung na 'bul yang mi 'bul lo
[In the high castle the lord's image is raised
The lord's image is surrounded by high and low officials.
The crown or what appears to be the crown of the castle's coming.
If whatever is attained is attained, whatever accomplished is accomplished.]

dpal khang gru bzhi la yab yum ldem zhig phub
yab yum ldem de la gnyen drung mtha' nas bskor
zhva 'am de 'dra zhig dpal khang yongs kyi zhva
'thob kyang 'thob byung na 'bul yang mi 'bul lo
[In the noble square house the image of groom and bride is raised
The groom and bride's image is surrounded by attending kin.
The crown or what appears to be the crown of the noble house's coming.
If whatever is attained is attained, whatever accomplished is accomplished.]

Om bkra shis par gyur cig.
[OM, may it be auspicious.] (LYL: 21–22)

Written description provided by Tashi Rabgias:
(bag ma'i mgo la kha bthags kyi rva byed skabs kyang glu snga ma 'di gtong srol yod de. de skabs su gsham gsal gyi sho lo ka de bsnan gyi yod do.)

[(On the bride's head a *khathag* horn is then placed and this fifth song is then performed. Then the following *shloka* is added).]

a drung mna' la phying dkar ldem zhig phub
phying dkar ldem de la rgya sram mtha' nas bskor.
zhva 'am de 'dra zhig a drung yongs kyi zhva
'thob kyang 'thob byung na 'bul yang los kyi 'bul.
[To the messenger a white felt image is raised
The white felt image is surrounded by Chinese otter (fur).
The crown or what appears to be the crown of the messenger's
    coming.
If whatever is attained is attained, whatever accomplished is
    accomplished.]

sgor rdza 'degs skabs—Round Clay Vessel Offering Section

This song follows the standard *bkra shis pa'i glu* format of musical couplets fitting into quatrains after the initial blessing invocation.

OM bkra shis par gyur cig.
bkra shis bde legs dang ldan par gyur cig.
[OM, may it be auspicious.
May it be auspicious.]

dgung gnam sngon po zhig rgya che dpangs su mtho
nyi zla gnyis ka kun rgya che dpangs su mtho
rgyu skar 'dzoms po kun 'dzoms po mi yi mtho
mtho gsum mdzes pa yi steng nas dkon mchog mchod.

[High in the heights of a vast blue sky
High in the heights of both the vast sun and moon
The heights of men, the gathered constellations
From atop the three beautiful high ones I supplicate the three
    jewels.]

chos grva gru bzhi rgya che dpangs su mtho
yar 'dren bla ma kun rgya che dpangs su mtho
bu slob 'dzoms po kun 'dzoms po mi yi mtho
mtho gsum mdzes pa yi steng nas dkon mchog mchod.
[High in the vast heights of the square Dharma court
Heighst of the vast lama guides
The heights of the men, the gathered disciples
From atop the three beautiful high ones I supplicate the three
    jewels.]

sku mthon po zhig rgya che dpangs su mtho
mi chen gong zhig rgya che dpangs su mtho
drag zhan 'dzoms po kun 'dzoms po mi yi mtho
mtho gsum mdzom po yi steng nas dkon mchog mchod.
[High in the heights of a vast, high realm
A high lord in a high place
The heights of the men, gathered high and low officials
From atop the three beautiful high ones I supplicate the three
    jewels.]

dpal khang gru bzhi zhig rgya che dpangs su mtho
yab yum pha ma kun rgya che dpangs su mtho
gnyen drung 'dzoms po kun 'dzoms po mi yi mtho
mtho gsum mdzes po yi steng nas dkon mchog mchod.
[High in the heights of a vast, square noble house
High in the heights, the groom and bride
The height of men, the gathered bride's attendants.
From atop the three beautiful high ones I supplicate the three
    jewels.]

mkhar ram gang su bzhugs pa'i rtse lha mchod
yul lam gang du bzhugs pa'i yul lha mchod
dpal khang 'di la gnas pa'i gzhi bdag mchod
gnya' bo spun dgu la skyob pa'i rabs lha mchod.

[I supplicate the god that lives in the castle and wherever else.
I supplicate the god that lives in the village and wherever else.
I supplicate the earth god of this place.
I supplicate the god that protects the kinfolk.]
OM bkra shis par gyr cig.
OM, may it be auspicious. (LYL, 23–24)

rgya gur gyi glu—Chinese Sable Song

Sung to the *bkra shis pa glu* melody, without the initial invocation
dgung gnam sngon po zhig rgya gur phub pa 'dra

> *nyi zla gnyis ka kun gur shing btsugs pa 'dra*
> *rgyu skar 'dzoms po kun thag brkyangs pa 'dra*
> *rgya gur dkar po yi steng nas dkon mchog mchod.*
> [A blue sky is like a roof of Chinese sable.
> The sun and moon are like a planted tent pole.
> The gathered constellations are like a stretched rope.
> I supplicate the three jewels from the roof of white Chinese
>   sable.]

> *chos grva gru bzhi rgya gur phub pa 'dra*
> *yar 'dren bla ma kun gur shing btsugs pa 'dra*
> *bu slob 'dzoms po kun gur thag brkyangs pa 'dra*
> *rgya gur dkar po yi steng nas dkon mchog mchod.*
> [The square Dharma debate court is like a broad tent.
> All the lama guides are like planted tent poles.
> All the disciples are like stretched tent ropes.
> I supplicate the three jewels from the roof of white Chinese
>   sable.]

> *sku mkhar mthon po zhig rgya gur phub pa 'dra*
> *mi chen gong ma kun gur shing btsugs pa 'dra*
> *drag zhan 'dzoms po kun gur thag brkyangs pa 'dra*
> *rgya gur kdar po yi steng nas dkon mchog mchod.*
> [The high castle is like a broad tent.
> All the high nobles are like planted tent poles.
> All the aristocrats and commoners are like stretched tent ropes.
> I supplicate the three jewels from the roof of white Chinese
>   sable.]

dpal khang gru bzhi rgya gur phub pa 'dra
yab yum pa ma kun gur shing btsugs pa 'dra
gnyen drung 'dzoms po kun gur thag brkyangs pa 'dra
rgya gur dkar po yi steng nas dkon mchog mchod.
[The square noble house is like a broad tent.
All our mothers and fathers are like planted tent poles.
All our kinfolk are like stretched tent ropes
I supplicate the three jewels from the roof of white Chinese
sable.]

khar lam gang du bzhugs pa'i rtse lha mchod
yul lam gang du bzhugs pa'i yul lha mchod
sa cha 'di la gnas pa'i gzhi bdag mchod
gnya' bo spun dgu la skyob pa'i rabs lha mchod.
[I supplicate the god that resides on the palace road I supplicate
the god that resides on the village road.
I supplicate the spirits that reside in this land.
I supplicate the nine gathered groom's attendants.] (LYL, 25–26)

'bras gtsang skabs—Pure Rice Section

Sung to the *bkra shis pa glu* melody, without the initial invocation.
dgung gnam sngon po zhig bkra shis lha yi sras

words
nyi zla gnyis ka kun bkra shis lha yi sras
rgya skar 'dzoms po kun 'dzoms po mi yi sras
lha sras mi sras kyi steng nas dkon mchog mchod.
[The blue sky is a prince of the auspicious gods.
Both the sun and moon are princes of the auspicious gods
All the constellations are princes of men.
I supplicate the Three Jewels for the prince of men to come
from above.]

chos grva gru bzhi zhig bkra shis lha yi sras
yar 'dren bla ma kun bkra shis lha yi sras
bu slob 'dzoms po kun 'dzoms po mi yi sras
lha sras mi sras kyi steng nas dkon mchog mchod.

[The square Dharma debate court is a prince of the auspicious
   gods.
All the lama guides are princes of the auspicious gods.
All the gather disciples are princes of men.
I supplicate the Three Jewels for the prince of men come to
   from above.]

sku mkhar mthon po zhig bkra shis lha yi sras
mi chen gong ma zhig bkra shis lha yi sras
drag zhan 'dzoms po kun 'dzoms po mi yi sras
lha sras mi sras kyi steng nas dkon mchog mchod.
[The high castle is a son of the auspicious gods.
The high lord is a prince of the auspicious gods.
All the gathered aristocrats and commoners are princes of men.
I supplicate the Three Jewels for the prince of men to come
   from above.]

dpal khan gru bzhi zhig bkra shis lha yi sras
yab yum pha ma kun bkra shis lha yi sras
gnyen drung 'dzoms po kun 'dzoms po lha yi sras
lha sras mi sra kyi steng nas kdon mchog mchod.
[The noble square house is a son of the auspicious gods.
All our fathers and mothers are princes of the auspicious
   gods.
All the gathered kinfolk are princes of men.
I supplicate the Three Jewels for the prince of men to come
   from above.]

mkhar ram gang du bzhugs pa'i rtse lha mchod.
yul lam gang du bzhugs pa'i yul lha mchod
dpal khang 'di la gnas pa'i gzhi bdag mchod
gnya' bo spun dgu la skyob pa'i rabs lha mchod.
[The castle road is a son of the auspicious gods.
The village road is a prince of the auspicious gods.
I supplicate the spirits that reside in this noble square house.
I supplicate the nine gathered groom's attendants.]

OM bkra shis par gyur cig.
[OM, may it be auspicious.] (LYL, 26–27)

ya do mdza' bo'i skabs kyi glu—Helper section song

Sung to the *bkra shis pa glu* melody *om bkra shis par gyur cig*
bkra shis bde legs dang ldan par gyur cig.
[OM, may it be auspicious,
May it be auspicious.]

dgung gnam sngon mo zhig rag rkong tha le ma
nyi zla gnyis ka kun ras dkar sdong ras 'dra
rgyu skar 'dzoms po kun 'bri mar ser chung 'dra
ltam gsum ltem pa yi steng nas dkon mchog mchod
[A blue sky is a polished brass lamp.
Both the sun and moon are like the white wick cloth.
The gathered constellations are like golden *dri*[5] butter.
I supplicate the three jewels that fill the three worlds from
on high.]

chos grva gru bzhi zhig rag rkong tha le ma
yar 'dren bla ma kun ras dkar sdong ras 'dra
bu slob 'dzoms po kun 'bri mar ser chung 'dra
ltem gsum ltem pa yi steng nas dkon mchog mchod.
[A square Dharma court is a polished brass lamp.
The guiding lamas are like the white wick cloth.
The gathered disciples are like golden *dri* butter.
I supplicate the three jewels that fill the three worlds from
on high.]

sku mkhar mthon po zhig rag rkong tha le ma
mi chen gong ma kun ras dkar sdong ras 'dra
drag zhan 'dzoms po kun 'bri mar ser chung 'dra
ltems gsum ltem pa ye steng nas dkon mchog mchod
[A high castle is a polished brass lamp.
The great high lords are like the white wick cloth.
The gathered high and low officials are like golden *dri* butter.
I supplicate the three jewels that fill the three worlds from
on high.]

dpal khang gru bzhi zhig rag rkong tha le ma
yab yum pha ma kun ras dkar sdong ras 'dra

ngyen drung 'dzoms po kun 'bri mar ser chung 'dra
ltem gsum ltem pa yi steng nas dkon mchog mchod
[A square, noble house is a polished brass lamp.
The father and mother are like the white wick cloth.
The gathered kin are like golden *dri* butter.
I supplicate the three jewels that fill the three worlds from
on high.]

mkhar ram gna du bzhugs pa'i rtse lha mchod
yul lam gang du bzhugs pa'i yul lha mchod
dpal khang 'di la gnas pa'i gzhi bdag mchod
gnya' bo spun dgu la skyob pa'i rabs lha mchod.
[I supplicate the god that lives in the castle or anywhere else.
I supplicate the god that lives in the village or anywhere else.
I supplicate the god that remains in this noble house.
I supplicate the god that protects the kinfolk.]

OM, bkra shis par gyur cig.
[OM, may it be auspicious.] (LYL, 28–29)

thegs zan skabs—Departure Food Section
Sung to the *bkra shis pa glu* melody
Om bkra shis par gyur cig,
bkra shis bde legs par gyur cig.
[OM, may it be auspicious,
may it be auspicious.]

dgung gnam sngon mo zhig g.yu gdan bting pa 'dra
nyi zla gnyis ka kun g.yu chung rol pa 'dra
rgyu skar 'dzom po kun mu tig tshar la brgyud pa 'dra
rgyan gsum brgyan pa yi nas dkon mchog mchod.
[The blue sky is like a firmly planted turquoise column.
Both the sun and moon are like supreme little turquoise pieces.
The gathered constellations are like shining pearls.
I supplicate the three jewels decorated by the three ornaments.]

chos grva gru bzhi g.yu gdan bting ba 'dra
yar 'dren bla ma kun g.yu chung rol pa 'dra

bu slob 'dzom po kun mu tig tshar la brgyud pa 'dra
rgyan gsum brgyan pa yi nas dkon mchog mchod.
[A square Dharma court is like a firmly planted turquoise
  column.
The lama guides are like supreme, little turquoise pieces.
The gathered disciples are like shining pearls.
I supplicate the three jewels decorated by the three ornaments]

sku mkhar mthon po zhig g.yu gdan bting ba 'dra
mi chen gong ma zhig g.yu chung rol pa 'dra
drag zhan 'dzom po kun mu tig tshar la brgyud pa 'dra
rgyan gsum brgyan pa yi nas dkon mchog mchod.
[A high castle is like a firmly planted turquoise column
A great lord is like supreme, little turquoise pieces.
The gathered high and low officials are like shining pearls.
I supplicate the three jewels decorated by the three ornaments.]

dpal kang gru bzhi zhig g.yu gdan bting ba 'dra
yab yum pha ma kun g.yu chung rol pa 'dra
gnyen drung 'dzom po kun mu tig tshar la brgyud pa 'dra
rgyan gsum brgyan pa yi nas dkon mchog mchod.
[A square noble house is like a firmly rooted turquoise pillar.
The parents are like supreme, little pieces of turquoise.
The gathered kin are like shining pearls.
I supplicate the three jewels decorated by the three ornaments]

om bkra shis par gyur cig.
[OM, may it be auspicious.] (LYL, 30–32)

gdan kha'i glu—Seat Speech Song
This opening section would utilize the standard *bkra shis pa'i glu*
melodic formula.
As sung by Ali Mahmud and Tsering Angchuk Ralam
Om bkra shis par gyur cig
bkra shis bde legs dang ldan par gyur cig.
[OM, may it be auspicious,
may it be auspicious.]

The stanzas are then sung to the following melody (Figure B.5).

Figure B.5. *gdan kha'i glu. Source:* Transcription provided by the author.

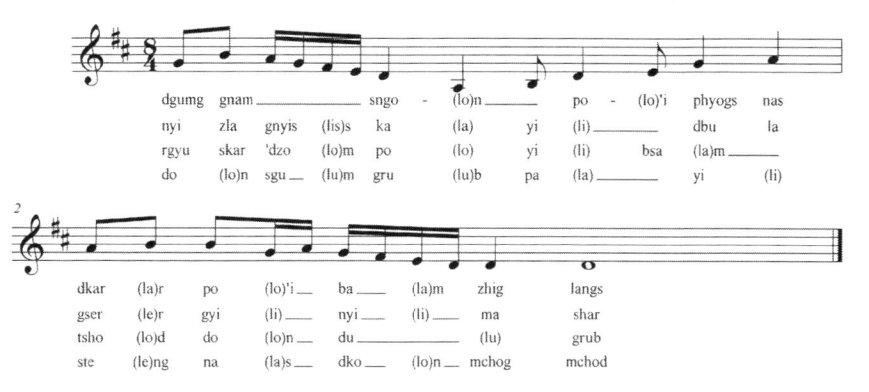

dgung gnam sngon po'i phyogs nas dkar po'i nam zhig langs
nyi zla gnyis ka yi dbu la gser gyi nyi ma shar
rgyu skar 'dzom po yi bsam tshod don du grub
don gsum grub pa yi steng nas dkon mchog mchod.
[From the blue sky comes a dawn of white
The eastern sunlight of gold is on the head of both sun and
  moon.
Contemplate the gathered constellations' contemplative
  intention meaning.
Contemplating the three stages of attainment, I supplicate the
  three jewels.]

chos grva gru bzhi'i phyogs nas dkar po'i nam zhig langs
yar 'dren bla ma yi dbu la gser gyi nyi ma shar
bu slob 'dzom po yi bsam tshod don du grub
don gsum grub pa yi steng nas dkon mchog mchod.
[From the square Dharma court comes a dawn of white.
The eastern sunlight of gold is on the head of the lama guides.
Contemplate the attainment of the gathered disciples.
Contemplating the three stages of attainment, I supplicate the
  three jewels.]

sku mkhar mthon po'i phyog nas dkar po'i nam zhig langs
mi chen gong ma yi dbu la gser gyi nyi ma shar
drag zhan 'dzom po yi bsam tshod don du grub
don gsum grub pa yi steng nas dkon mchog mchod.
[From the high castle comes a dawn of white.
The eastern sunlight of gold is on the head of the great lord.
Contemplate the meaning of the gathered high and low
   officials.
Contemplating the three stages of attainment, I supplicate the
   three jewels.]

dpal khang gru bzhi phyog nas dkar po'i nam zhig langs
yab yum pha ma yi dbu la gser gyi nyi mar shar
gnyen drung 'dzom po yi bsam tshod don du grub
don gsum grub pa yi steng nas dkno mchog mchod.
[From the noble house comes a dawn of white.
The eastern sunlight of gold is on the head of the father and
   mother
Contemplate the meaning of the gathered kin.
Contemplating the three stages of attainment, I supplicate the
   three jewels.]

mkhar ram gang du bzhugs pa'i rtse lha mchod
yul lam gang du bzhugs pa'i yul lha mchod
dpal khang 'di la gnas pa'i gzhi bdag mchod
gnya' bo spun dgu la skyob pa'i ras lha mchod.
[I supplicate the god that lives in the castle or wherever else.
I supplicate the god that lives in the village or wherever else.
I supplicate the god that dwells in the ground of the noble house.
I supplicate the god that protects the family.]

(This section would end with the standard *bkra shis pa'i glu*
   melodic formula).
Om bkra shis par gyur cig.
[OM, may it be auspicious.] (LYL, 32–33)

thod phud skabs—Skull Cup[6] Offering Section
sung to the standard *bkra shis pa glu* melody
om bkra shis par gyur cig.
bkra shis bde legs dang ldan par gyur cig.

[OM, may it be auspicious.
May it be auspicious.]

rgya gar rdo rje gdan gyi shar phyogs na
chu sprin pa tra yi steng nas nyi zla 'khrungs
khyod nor de 'dra zhig lhag bsam dkon mchog mchod
nor bu de 'dra zhig lhag bsam dkon mchog mchod.
[The Diamond Throne of India[7] is in the East,
The sun and moon come from the high swirling clouds.
I supplicate you, the Precious Jewels that are like a jewel of
  highest intentions.
I supplicate the Precious Jewels that are like a jewel of highest
  intentions.]

rgya gar rdo rje gdan gyi lho phyogs na
chu sprin pa tra yi steng nas 'bru sna 'khrungs
khyod nor de 'dra zhig lhag bsam dkon mchog mchod
nor bu de 'dra zhig lhag bsam dkon mchog mchod.
[The Diamond Throne of India is in the South
Grain comes from the high swirling clouds.
I supplicate you, the Precious Jewels that are like a jewel of
  highest intentions.
I supplicate the Precious Jewels that are like a jewel of highest
  intentions.]

rgya gar rdo rje gdan gyi nub phyogs na
chu sprin pa tra yi steng nas sman sna 'khrungs
khyod nor de 'dra zhig lhag bsam dkon mchod mchod
nor bu de 'dra zhig lhag bsam dkon mchog mchod.
[The Diamond Throne of India is in the North,
Grains of medicine come from the high swirling clouds.
I supplicate you, the Precious Jewels that are like a jewel of
  highest intentions.
I supplicate the Precious Jewels that are like a jewel of highest
  intentions.]

rgya gar rdo rje gdan gyi byang phyogs na
chu sprin pa tra yi steng nas shel tshva 'khrungs
khyod nor de 'dra zhig lhag bsam dkon mchog mchod
nor bu de 'dra zhig lhag bsam dkon mchog mchod.

[The Diamond Throne of India is in the West,
Glass crystal comes from the high swirling clouds.
I supplicate you, the Precious Jewels that are like a jewel of
highest intentions.
I supplicate the Precious Jewels that are like a jewel of highest
intentions.]

om bkra shis par gyur cig.
[OM, may it be auspicious.]

[The following couplets are then sung to the main *bkra shis
pa glu* melody]
shva gcig shva gnyis da yang phab tsan
ser pa gser gyi da yang gser gdan 'khyong.
[The relatives once again put on one hat, two hats.
Once again, they bring the gold, the golden throne.
shva gcig shva gnyis da yang phab tsan
dkar po dngul gyi da yang dngul gdan 'khyong.
The relatives once again put on one hat, two hats.
Once again, they bring the silver, the silver throne.]

shva gcig shva gnyis da yang 'phab tsan
sngnon mo 'bru yi da yang 'bru gdan 'khyong.
[The relatives once again bring one hat, two hats.
Once again, they bring grain, the grain throne. *om bkra shis
par gyur cig.*
OM, may it be auspicious.] (LYL, 34–35)

This song would be sung when the bride's dowery is displayed, hung
on a rope (cf. Ribbach 1985). This melody is also used for songs that
describe the bride's leaving her family.[8]

zongs glu—Dowery Song
As sung by Ali Mahmud and Tsering Angchuk Ralam—Rhythmic cycle 4
skya rengs dang po de dgung sngon mthon la shar (2x)
no mo'i a pha bzhengs te no mo la zongs zhig sgrigs
'dzoms pa'i a pha bzhengs te 'dzoms pa la zongs zhig sgrigs
g.ya' chags gyon chas kyi sgo nas no mo la zongs shig sgrigs

Figure B.6. *zongs glu. Source:* Transcription provided by the author.

*g.ya' chags gyon chas kyi sgo nas 'dzoms pa la zongs shig sgrig
no mos mi shes pa 'i yul de shes dgos pa byung
'dzoms pas mi shes pa'i yul de shes dgos pa byung.*
[At the first pre-dawn light in the high, blue eastern sky, (2x)
The girl's father has arisen bringing a dowery to the girl.
The perfect father has arisen to bring a dowery to the perfect one.
He brings a dowery of prosperous clothes from the door to the girl.
He brings a dowery of prosperous clothes from the door to the perfect one.
The people the girl knows from her village want to know.
The gathered people of the village want to know.]

*skya rengs gnyis pa brag stod mthon po la shar (2x)
no mo'i a pha bzhengs te no mo la zongs zhig sgrigs
'dzoms pa'i a pha bzhengs te 'dzoms pa la zongs zhig sgrigs
drug dkar drug dmar gyi sgo nas no mo la zongs shig sgrigs
drug dkar drug dmar gyi sgo nas 'dzoms pa la zongs shig sgrig*

no mos mi shes pa 'i yul de zhes dgos pa byung
'dzoms pas mi shes pa'i yul de zhes dgos pa byung.
[At the second pre-dawn light in the high, blue eastern sky (2x)
The girl's mother has arisen bringing a dowery to the girl.
The perfect mother has arisen to bring a dowery to the
 perfect one.
She brings a dowery of two types of turquoise and coral.
They bring doweries of two types of turquoise and coral.
The people the girl knows from the village want to know.
The gathered people of the village want to know.]

skya rengs gsum pa de spang stod mthon po la shar (2x)
no mo'i ming chung bzhengs te no mo la zongs zhig sgrigs
'dzoms pa'i ming chung bzhengs te 'dzoms pa la zongs zhig sgrigs
'bru sna spun dgu yi sgo nas no mo la zoms shig sgrigs
'bru sna spun dgu yi sgo nas 'dzoms pa la zongs shig sgrig
no mos mi shes pa 'i yul de zhes dgos pa byung
'dzoms pas mi shes pa'i yul de zhes dgos pa byung.
[At the third pre-dawn light in the high, blue eastern sky (2x)
The girl's little brother has arisen bringing a dowery to the girl.
The perfect little brother has arisen to bring a dowery to the
 perfect one.
He brings a dowery of many types of grain from her brother.
He brings a dowery of many types of grain from her brother.
The people the girl knows from the village want to know.
The gathered people of the village want to know.]

skya rengs bzhi pa de mtsho stod mthon po la shar (2x)
no mo'i ya do kun bzhengs te no mo la zongs zhig sgrigs
'dzoms pa'i ya do kun bzhengs te 'dzoms pa la zongs zhig sgrigs
rta g.ya sgo phyugs kyi sgo nas no mo la zongs shig sgrigs
rta g.ya sgo phyugs kyi sgo nas 'dzoms pa la zongs shig sgrig
no mos mi shes pa 'i yul de zhes dgos pa byung
'dzoms pas mi shes pa'i yul de zhes dgos pa byung.
[At the fourth pre-dawn light in the high, blue eastern sky (2x)
The girl's companions have arisen bringing a dowery to the girl.
The gathered companions have arisen to bring doweries to
 the perfect one.
They bring a dowery of pack horses and draught animals to
 the girl.

They bring a dowery of pack horses and draught animals to
   the perfect one.
The people the girl knows from the village want to know.
The gathered people of the village want to know.] (LYL, 36–37)

tho glu—List Song (No melody known to my informants)
(Its question-answer format might indicate a *sgo glu* (door song).)
dri ba: 'dir byon pa'i gnya' bo mi ma 'phrul
khyed yong yong gang dang tsug nas yongs
da 'gro 'gro gang dang tsug nas 'gro.
[Question: Is it not a miracle, this witness that appeared?
You came while whatever comes may come
You go while whatever goes may go.]

lan: nged yong yong shar gyi phyogs nas yongs
da 'gro 'gro nub phyogs o rgyan gling la 'gro.
Answer: I came, came from the East
I go there to the North, to the realm of Orgyan.

dri ba:khyed shar gyi phyogs nas yong tsa na
shar phyogs rgyal po ci 'dri 'dug
bran dang 'khor g.yog ci 'dri 'dug
yid dang cha lugs ci 'dri 'dug.
[Question: Since you come from the East,
What is the Eastern king like?
What are the servants like around him?
What are their manner and dress like?]

lan:nged shar gyi phyogs nas yong tsa na
shar phyogs rgyal po yul 'khor bsrung
bran dang 'khor g.yog chos la dga'
yid dang lugs de 'dra 'dug
skad cha 'dri na khong la dris
nged la skad cha 'chad rgyu med.
[Answer: Since I come from the East,
The Eastern king is "Guards the Country".
The servants around him are dressed in joy of the Dharma.
Their manner is like *tattva*[9]
If they question, they are inner questions.
I have unaffected speech.]

dri ba:khyed lho yi phyogs nas yong tsa na
lho phyogs rgyal po ci 'dri zhig bzhugs
bran dang 'khor g.yog ci la dga'
yid dang cha lugs ci 'dra 'dug.
[Question: Since you come from the South,
What is the Southern king like?
What are the servants like around him?
What are their manner and dress like?]

lan: nged lho yi phyogs nas yong tsa na
lho phyogs rgyal po 'phags skyes po
bran dang 'khor g.yog chos la dga'
yid dang cha lugs de 'dra 'dug
skad cha 'dri na khong la dris
nged la skad cha 'chad rgyu med
[Answer: Since I come from the South,
The Southern king is "High and Low One"
The servants around him are dressed in joy of the Dharma.
Their manner is like *tattva*
If they question, they are inner questions.
I have unaffected speech.]

dri ba:khyed nub kyi phyogs nas yong tsa na
nub phyogs rgyal poci 'dra bzhugs
bran dang 'khor g.yog ci la dga'
yid dang cha lugs ci dang 'dra.
[Question: Since you come from the North,
What is the Northern king like?
What are the servants like around him?
What are their manner and dress like?]

lan: nged nub kyi phyogs nas yong tsa na
nub phyogs rgyal po spyan mi bzang
bran dang 'khor g.yog chos la dga'
yid dang cha lugs de 'dra 'dug
skad cha 'dri na khong la dris
nged la skad cha 'chad rgyu med.
[Answer: Since I come from the North,
The Northern king is "Watching Good People"
The servants around him are dressed in joy of the Dharma.

Their manner is like *tattva*
If they question, they are inner questions.
I have unaffected speech]

dri ba:khyed byang gi phyogs nas yong tsa na
byang phyogs rgyal po ci 'dra bzhugs
bran dang 'khor g.yog ci la dga'
yid dang cha lugs ci 'dra 'dug.
[Question: Since you come from the West,
What is the Western king like?
What are the servants like around him?
What are their manner and dress like?]

lan: nged byang gi phyogs nas yong tsa na
byang phyogs rgyal po rnam thos sras
bran dang 'khor g.yog chos la dga'
yid dang cha lugs de 'dra 'dug
skad cha 'dri khong la dris
nged la skad cha 'chad rgyu med.
[Answer: Since I come from the West,
The Western king is "Son of Perfect Hearing"
The servants around him are dressed in joy of the Dharma.
Their manner is like *tattva*
If they question, they are inner questions.
I have unaffected speech.] (LYL, 38–40)

shing rtse mo lnga—The five wooded hills (Melody not known to my informants)

dri ba: shing rtsab gcig la rtse mo lnga
rtse mo lnga la tshang 'khor lnga
tshang 'khor lnga la sgo nga lnga
sgo nga lnga la bya mo lnga
[Question: In a weedy wood are five hills.
On the five hills are five nests.
In the five nests are five eggs.
In the five eggs are five hens.]

bya gcig kha lo shar la lta.
ka rang ko rong lan gsum zer.
de ci dang gang gi don zhig yin.

[A bird looked to the East.
Thrice it said, "ka rang ko rong."
Whatever for?]

bya gcig kha lo lho la lta.
ka rang ko rong lan gsum zer.
de ci dang gang gi don zhig yin
[A bird looked to the South.
Thrice it said, "ka rang ko rong."
Whatever for?]

gya gcig kha lo nub la lta.
ka rang ko rang lan gsum zer.
de ci dang gang gi don zhig yin
[A bird looked to the North.
Thrice it said, "ka rang ko rong."
Whatever for?]

bya gcig kha lo byang la lta.
ka rang ko rong lan gsum zer.
de ci dang gang gi don zhig yin.
[A bird looked to the West.
Thrice it said, "ka rang ko rong."
Whatever for?]

lan: bya gcig kha lo shar la bsgyur.
ka rang ko rong lan gsum zer.
shar chos la dga' ba'i don zhig yin.
[Answer: A bird flew to the East.
Thrice it said, "ka rang ko rong,"
Because of rejoicing in Eastern Dharma.]

bya gcig kha lo lho la bsgyur.
ka rang ko rong lan gsum zer.
lho 'bru sna 'dzoms po'i don zhig yin
[A bird flew to the South.
Thrice it said, "ka rang ko rong,"
Because of the many kinds of grain in the South.]

bya gcig kha lo nub la bsgyur.
ka rang ko rong lan gsum zer.
nub sman sna 'dzom po'i don zhig yin.
[A bird flew to the North.
Thrice it said, "ka rang ko rong,"
Because of the many kinds of medicine in the North.]

bya gcig kha lo byang la bsgyur.
ka rang ko rong lan gsum zer.
byang shel tshva mang ba'i don zhig yin.
[A bird flew to the West.
Thrice it said, "ka rang ko rong,"
Because of the more plentiful crystal salt in the West.]

bya gcig kha lo steng la bsgyur.
ka rang ko rong lan gsum zer.
dgung rim pa ma mtho ba'i don zhig yin.
[A bird flew up high.
Thrice it said, "ka ran ko rong,"
Because of the high steps in the sky.] (LYL, 41–43)

rgyang bu gcig 'phal ka bcu gsum—One Wood Tablet, Thirteen Notches
(Melody not known to my informants)
dri ba: rgyang bu gcig la 'phal ka bcu gsum yod pa de
ci shig dang gang gi don zhig yin.
[Question: On a wood tablet are thirteen notches.
Whatever for?]

lan: gcig thig le nyag gcig gi don zhig yin
gnyis nyi zla nyis kyi don zhig yin.
gsum rigs gsum mgon po'i don zhig yin.
bzhi phyogs bzhi ru bzhi don zhig yin.
lnga rgyal ba rigs lnga'i don zhig yin.
drug 'gro ba rigs drug gi don zhig yin.
bdun sangs rgyas rabs bdun gyi don zhig yin.
brgyad bkra shis rtags brgyad kyi don zhig yin.
dgu srin po mgo dgu'i don zhig yin.

bcu shar ba ra bcu'i don zhig yin.
bcu gcig sangs rgyas zhal bcu gcig gi don zhig yin.
bcu gnyis lo 'khor bcu gnyis kyi don zhig yin.
bcu gsum rgyu rim pa bcu gsum gyi don zhig yin.
[Answer: It's because of the one sphere.
It's because of the two, sun and moon.
It's because of the three good families.
It's because of the four sides, the four areas.
It's because of the five victorious Buddha families.
It's because of the six classes of sentient beings.
It's because of the seven successive Buddhas.[10]
It's because of the eight auspicious symbols.[11]
It's because of the nine-headed demon.
It's because of the ten manifestations.
It's because of the eleven-faced Buddha.
It's because of the twelve years. (LYL, 43–44)
It's because of the thirteen stages of causation.]

bag ma len du 'gro skabs kyi glu—Song for the Stage of Going to Get the Bride

As sung by Ali Mahmud and Tsering Angchuk Ralam—Rhythmic cycle 1

ya gi shed dgung gnam sngon mo la
nyi zla yi bang mdzod 'khyil

Figure B.7. *bag ma len du 'gro skabs kyi glu. Source:* Transcription provided by the author.

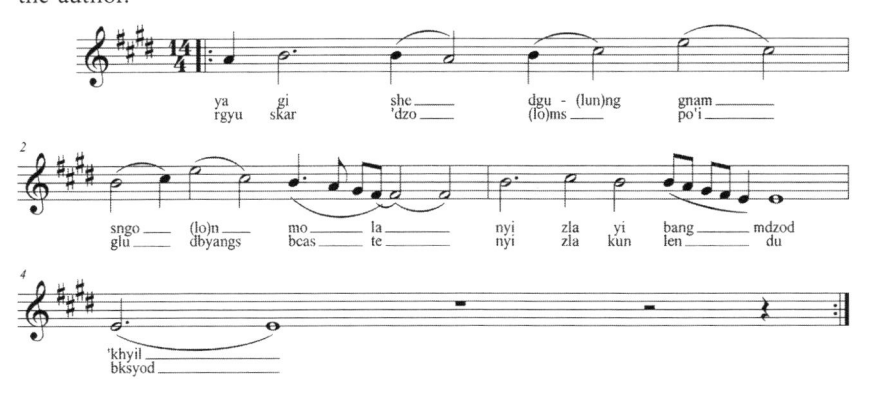

rgyu skar 'dzoms po'i glu dbyangs bcas te
nyi zla kun len du bskyod yin.
[Into yonder blue sky,
Surrounded by a treasury of sun and moon,
With songs of the gathered stars,
We will go join the sun and moon.]

ya gi shed chos grva gru bzhi la
byin rlabs kyi bang mdzod 'khyil
grva rgyun 'dzoms po'i glu dbyangs bcas te
byin rlabs kun len du bskyod yin.
[Into yonder square Dharma courtyard,
Surrounded by a treasury of blessings,
With songs of gathered monks,
We will go join the blessings.]

ya gi shed sku mkhar mthon po la
gser dngul gyi bang mdzod 'khyil
drag zhan 'dzom po'i glu dbyang bcas te
gser dngul kun len du bskyod yin.
[In yonder high castle,
Surrounded by a treasury of gold and silver,
With songs of high and low officials
We will go join the gold and silver.]

ya gi shed dpal khang gru bzhi la
'bru sna lnga'i bang mdzod 'khyil
gnyen drung 'dzom po'i glu dbyang bcas te
'bru sna kun len du bskyod yin.
[In yonder square noble house,
Surrounded by a treasury of five grains,
With songs of gathered attendants,
We will go join the varieties of grain.]

ya gi shed do ra gru bzhi la
g.ya' cag gi bang mdzod 'khyil
ya do mdza bo'i glu dbyang bcas te
g.ya' cag kun len du bskyod yin.
[On yonder square stage,
Surrounded by a treasury of slate mountains

With songs of gathered companions,
We will go join the slate mountains.] (LYL, 45–46)

bag ma thob pa'i rjes kyi glu—Song for Getting the Bride
(LYL, 46–48)
As sung by Ali Mahmud and Tsering Angchuk—sung
unaccompanied, no rhythmic cycle
dkar po yi nam zhig langs
nyi zla gnyis ka'i dbu kun la
gser gyi nyi ma shar.
[From the right side of the blue sky
A white dawn comes.
On the crowns of both sun and moon
Is golden eastern sunlight.]

rgyu skar 'dzoms po'i bsam tshod de
bsam tshod po don du grub
om bkra shis pa'i kha lo de
kha lo po shar la sgyur.
[Contemplate the gathered constellations.
Contemplate the meaning.
OM, that auspicious direction,
Turn to the East.]

chos grva gru bzhi g.yas phyogs nas
dkar po yi nam zhig langs
yar 'dren bla ma'i dbu de la
gser gyi nyi ma shar.

Figure B.8. *bag ma thob pa'i rjes kyi glu dgung gnam sngon po'i g.yas phyogs nas.*
Source: Transcription provided by the author.

[From the right side of the square Dharma court
A white dawn comes.
On the crowns of the lama guides
Is golden eastern sunlight.]

bu slob 'dzoms po'i bsam tshod de
bsam tshod po don du grub
om bkra shis pa'i kha lo de
kha lo po shar la sgyur.
[Contemplate the gathered disciples.
Contemplate the meaning.
OM, that auspicious direction,
Turn to the East.]

sku mkhar mthon po yi g.yas phyogs nas
dkar po yi nam zhig langs
mi chen gong ma'i dbu de la
gser gyi nyi ma shar.
[From the right side of the high castle
A white dawn comes.
On the crown of the great lord
Is golden eastern sunlight.]

drag zhan 'dzom po'i bsam tshod
bsam tshod po don du grub
om bkra shis pa'i kha lo de
kha lo po shar la sgyur.
[Contemplate the gathered officials.
Contemplate the meaning.
OM, that auspicious direction,
Turn to the East.]

dpal khang gru bzhi g.yas phyogs nas
dkar po yi nam zhig langs
yab yum pa ma'i dbu de la
gser byi nyi ma shar.
[From the right side of the square noble house
A white dawn comes.
On the crowns of the parents
Is the golden eastern light.]

gnyen drung 'dzoms po'i bsam tshod de
bsam tshod po don du grub
om bkra shis pa'i kha lo de
kha lo po shar la sgyur.
[Contemplate the gathered kin.
Contemplate the meaning
OM, that auspicious direction,
Turn to the East.]

do ra gru bzhi'i g.yas phyogs nas
dkar po yi nam zhig langs
rje dpon chen po'i dbu de la
gser gyi nyi ma shar.
[From the right side of the square stage
A white dawn comes.
On the crown of the great teacher
Is golden sunlight.]

ya do mdza' bo'i bsam tshod de
bsam tshod po don du 'grub
om bkra shis pa'i kha lo de
kha lo po shar sgyur.
Contemplate the attendants.
Contemplate the meaning.
OM, that auspicious direction,
Turn to the East.]

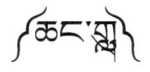

chang glu—Chang Songs

*gser lung lung pa—*The Golden Valley (Sung to the melody
of *bkra shis pa'i glu*)
om bkra shis par gyur cig.
bkra shis bde legs dang ldan par gyur cig.
[OM, may it be auspicious.
May it be auspicious.]

phu de ya gi shed gser lung lung pa na
gser gyi mi chung zhig mgo bo tse le le.
[When yon boy was in the golden valley,
A golden child on the hilltop.]

phyag g.yas g.yas la gser gyi bum pa bsnams.
phyag g.yon g.yon la dngul gyi bum pa bsnams.
[In his right, right hand he took the golden vessel.
In his left, left hand he took the silver vessel.]

gser gyi bum pa tshe chang ltem se ltem.
dngul gyi bum pa tshe chang ltem se ltem.
[Fill the gold vessel to the brim with *chang*.
Fill the silver vessel to the brim with *chang*.]

tshe chang 'don na tshe bsod mtha' ru rgyas
g.yang chang 'don na bu nor mtha' ru rgyas
tshe chang g.yang chang kun spel gyin spel gyin mchod.
[If you drink the *chang* you will have abundant good luck.
If you drink the sacred *changs*, you will have abundant wealth.
I offer the continually propagating *chang*.] (LYL, 50)

bzo thabs—The Skill of Brewing (LYL, 53–54)
Sung to the same melody as "dri wa dri lan" (Question and
    Answer, Track 13).
dri ba: chang 'di la bzo ba'i thabs shig yod
bzo thabs de 'dra zhig bshad na chang yang 'thung
lan: tshogs bzang mtsho mo dang 'dra ba'i zangs shig bkal
g.ya' chu bsil ma dang 'dra ba'i chu zhig blugs.
[Question: There is a skill in brewing this *chang*.
If you explain this type of brewing, we will indeed drink.
Answer: Like the ocean of good offerings, you need a cauldron.
Like a cool brook, pour a bit of water.]

'bru sna spun dgu dang 'dra ba'i 'bru zhig btab
tsan dan me lce dang 'dra ba'i me zhig sbar.
[Like the nine families of grain, cast a bit of grain.
Like the flame of a sandlewood fire, light the fire.]

sa gzhi bro mo dang 'dra ba'i khul 'phyar bting
skar ma gru sog dang 'dra ba'i chang brud.
[Like the folk-dance of the earth, step nimbly
Like the assembly of stars, fill up the chang.]

bzang drug sman sna dan 'dra ba'i phabs drug btab
phad tshe bde po yi nang du mnal zhig gzims.
[Like the medicine of six essential ingredients, sow the six yeasts.
In the sound grain storage basket, put it to bed.]

tho rangs skar chen dan mnyam du mnal zhig sad
rdza ma dmar chung gi nang du sgom zhig brgyab.
[Along with the morning star, wake up.
Put it in a small red pitcher, meditate on it.]

tho rangs skar chen dna mnyam du sgom de bshig
bdud rtsi chu mig dang 'dra ba'i chu zhig btangs.
[Along with the morning star, break your meditation.
Like the spring of nectar, pour a bit of water.]

chang rkyang 'bur dgu ma'i nang du ltems se ltems
o los de 'dra rang ma gsungs skyems gang mchod
gzhon pas de 'dra rang ma gsungs skyems gan mchod.
[Fill to the brim with only the *chang* of nine boiled barleys.
O dear don't talk like that; drink *chang*.
Young one, don't talk like that; drink *chang*.]

lan: tsan dan dmar po'i gsrol cog de.
shing mkhan mkhas pa zhig gi phyag na yod.
'o skol len du chas na sa thag ring.
'o skol nyo ru chas na ring thang che.
o los de 'dra rang ma gsung skyems gang mchod.
gzhon pas de 'dra rang ma gsungs skyems gang mchod.
[Answer: That table of red sandalwood
Is in the hand of a master carpenter's hand,
When we are bringing it in a distant place,
Then we are buying it in a distant town,
Oh surely, don't talk like that; drink *chang*.
Young one, don't talk like that; drink *chang*.]

chang padma'i yul—*Chang* of the Lotus Land (Track 36)—Rhythmic cycle 6

chang padma'i yul la chang a rag bdud rtsi
nye rang sib gcig 'don ang nga rang sib gcig 'tung.
[The *chang* in the lotus country, arak, nectar,
Please take a sip, I myself will take a sip.]

chang zhim po glum gyi mdud pa can yod
bdud rtsi chu mig med na mdud grol mdog med.
[Tasty *chang* has a knotted cloth of boiled grain.
If there isn't a spring of nectar, there isn't a loosened knot.]

sha zhim po tshil gyi mdud pa can yod
sha gri gsha' ma med na mdud brol mdog med.
[Tasty meat has a knot of fat.
If there is no meat knife there isn't a loosened knot.]

sa gzhi bro mo zer ba 'khyags kyis bsdams
nyi zla kun med na mdud brol mdog med.
[The folk dance of the earth is said to be controlled by
    ice.
If there is no sun and moon, there is no loosened
    knot.]

chang padma'i yul la chang a rag bdud rtsi
nye rang sib gcig 'don ang na rang sib gcig 'thung.
[The *chang* in the lotus country, arak, nectar,
You sip, I sip.]

chang 'thung gin 'thung gin da rung zhim du song.
phor ba sa la bzhag pa'i yang phang sa pa la.
[Drinking, drinking, *chang* becomes sweet.
Even putting the cup on the ground is losing [time].]

rta la bzhon gyin bzhon gyin da dung drag tu song
rta po bres la bzhag pa da yang phangs pa la.
Riding, riding the horse becomes better.
Even putting the cup in the manger is losing [time]. (LYL,
    58–59)

ཁ་འཆང་སྒྲ།

gzhung glu—Congregational Songs

dkar po'i nam langs—The White Dawn (LYL, 68–69)
As sung by Ali Mahmud and Tsering Angchuk Ralam

dgung gnam sngon po'i gyas nas dkar po'i nam zhig langs.
nga yi nyi zla gnyis ka thugs g.yeng la skyod.
nga yi rgyu skar 'dzoms po gzigs mo la skyod.
a dang om gsang bkra shis pa'i kha lo shar la gzigs.
[From the right side of the blue sky a white dawn comes.
Both my sun and moon come to distract me.
My gathered stars come to my sight.
Behold the secret "A" and "OM"[12], auspicious rulers in the East.]

chos grva grub bzhi'i gyas nas dkar po'i nam zhig langs.
nga yi bzang gsum bla ma thugs g.yeng la skyod.
nga yi grva rgyun 'dzoms po gzigs mo la skyod.
a dang om gsang bkra shis pa'i kha lo shar la gzigs.
[From the right of the square Dharma court the white dawn
    comes.
My lama of three goods goes on vacation
My continuing monks of auspiciousness go to a show.
Behold the secret "A" and "OM," auspicious rulers in the East.]

Figure B.9. *dkar po'i nam langs. Source:* Transcription provided by the author.

sku mkhar mthon po'i gyas nas dkar po'i nam zhig langs.
nga yi mi chen gong ma thugs g.yeng la skyod.
nga yi drag zhan 'dzoms po gzigs mo la skyod.
a dang om gsang bkra shis pa'i kha lo shar la gzigs.
[From the high castle's right a white dawn comes.
My high lord goes on vacation.
My gathered attendants go to a show.
Behold the secret "A" and "OM," auspicious rulers in the
    East.]

dpal khang grub bzhi'i gyas nas dkar po'i nam zhig langs.
nga yi yab yum pha ma thugs g.yeng la skyod.
nga yi gnyen drung 'dzoms po gzigs mo la skyod.
a dang om gsang bkra shis pa'i kha lo shar la gzigs.
[From the square noble house's right a white dawn comes.
My parents, father and mother, go on vacation
My gathered kin folk go to a show.
Behold the secret "A" and "OM," auspicious rulers in the
    East.]

shel ldan g.yu mtsho—The Crystalline Turquoise Ocean (Track
    28)—Rhythm cycle 1
shel ldan g.yu mtsho bskor pa'i
shel dkar rnam rgyal khang bzang
nang na seng ge'i khri steng
gnya' khri btsan po'i gdung rgyud.
[The crystalline turquoise ocean
The copper, white crystal house of complete victory
Inside on the lion's throne
Nyatri Tsangpo's lineage.]

'jigs med chos kyi rgyal pos
'dzam gling mun pa sel byung
chabs 'bangs sde yi dpal du
zhabs pad bskal brgyar brtan cig.
[The fearless Dharma king
Becomes Jambudvipa's[13] dispeller of darkness
Together with attendants in glory
We beg at his feet that he stay one hundred eons.]

mang yul sprul pa'i mtsho na
mdzes ldan nam mkha'i skar tshogs
mi chen rgyu skar 'dzoms po
skyes chen rin chen mtho gsal.
[In the ocean of incarnations in many lands
The constellations of the beautiful sky
Lord of the perfect constellations
Brilliant ocean of the precious lord.]

gzhon pa'i yid kyi brten sa
yar ngo yid dga' gnas brtan
nam yang 'bral dogs mi 'dug
yid kyi dkyil la zungs shig
[Home of youth's mind,
The waxing moon, the happy hearted elder
Never can be forgotten.
May the mind's circle hold it.] (LYL, 76)

ka ba rin po che—**The Precious Pillar** (LYL, 77) (track
   25)—Rhythmic cycle 2
ka ba la rin po che gser la bzhengs yod
ka stegs gling bzhi ru khyab
ka stegs gling bzhi ru khyab song zer na
sa gzhi po 'od kyis khengs.
[As the golden precious pillar is erected
It spreads over the pedestal of the four continents
When it was said to spread over the pedestal of the four continents
It is filled by the light of the earth.]

khri chen la gong ma yi steng na
nor bu chu shel dang me shel
nor bu me shel po 'bar song zer na
sa gshi po 'od kyis khengs.
[The master on top of the throne
Jeweled water crystal and fire crystal
When it is said that the jeweled fire crystal is blazing,
It is filled by the light of the earth.]

ka gdan po 'og phyogs klu yul na
rtse mo de dgung dang mnyam
da rung 'nga dgung di dang mnyam shig he
stag shar 'dzoms po'i smon lam.
[The *naga's* land is under the pedestal,
That peak, sky and the like,
Even now that sky and the like,
Are the perfect youth's[14] prayer.]

**mkha' spyod dag pa'i zhing kham—The Pure Land of
Heavenly Enjoyment** Rhythmic cycle 6 (track 37)
mkha' spyod dag pa'i zhing khams na
sa gzhi gzil du gnon yod
rgya che phun sum tshogs pa'i
sku mkhar lha yi pho brang
sngar yang srid pa chags pa
shel dkar mtsho mo gyang 'khyil.
[In the Pure Land of Heavenly Enjoyment
The earth is afraid,
Of the abundant prosperity
The castle the god's abode
Before created existence
The sacred crystal ocean was around it.]

lha dang lha mo bzhengs pa yi
lha khang shel dkar dang 'dra
stag shar 'dzom po yis bzhengs pa'i
lha khang shel dkar dang 'dra
bod khams bstan pa'i bstan bsrung
bstan bsrung yul lha gnyan po.
[The birth of gods and goddesses,
Is like a crystal temple,
The birth of the perfect youth,
Is like a crystal temple
Guardian of Tibet's teachings
Sacred guardian deity of the land.]

'dod dgu'i dngos grub stsal mkhan po
lha chen rdo rje chen po.
[Preceptor who bestows the attainment of all desires
The great deity Dorje Chenpo.] (LYL, 80–81)

stod rgya gar—Above, in India

As sung by Ali Mahmud and Tsering Angchuk Ralam—Rhythmic
cycle 6

stod rgya gar gyi yul du
chos kyi bstan pa dar (2x)
chos ma yol ba'i gong du
dung gi bstan pa dar (2x)

Figure B.10. *stod rgya gar. Source:* Transcription provided by the author.

chos dung dkar po zer ba
chos kyi sna 'dren yin (2x)
[Above, in the country of India
Is the silk banner of Buddhist women (2x)
Above the place of Buddhist women
Is the silk banner of the shell (2x)
The white shell trumpet of Dharma is said
To lead all types of Dharma. (2x)]

smad rgya nag gi yul du
khrims kyi bstan pa dar (2x)
khrims ma yol ba'i gong du
dar gyi bstan pa dar (2x)
kha btags dkar po zer ba
khrims ki sna 'dren yin. (2x)
[Below, in the country of China
Is the silk banner of silk[15] (2x)
Above the place of law abiding women
Is the silk banner of silk (2x)
White *khatags*[16] are said
To lead all types of law. (2x)]

bar la dvags kyi yul du
glu yi bstan pa dar (2x)
glu ma yol ba'i gong du
chang gi bstan pa dar (2x)
zhim po a rag gi bdud rtsi
glu yi na 'dren yin.
[In the center, in Ladakh
Is the banner of singing women (2x)
Above the place of singing women
Is the silken banner of *chang.* (2x)
The tasty nectar of *arak*
Will lead all types of songs. (2x)] (LYL, 82–86)

Gar glu—Dance song (LYL, 87–89)
As sung by Ali Mahmud and Tsering Angchuk Ralam, August
    18, 2009
Rhythmic cycle 3

Figure B.11. *gar glu. Source:* Transcription provided by the author.

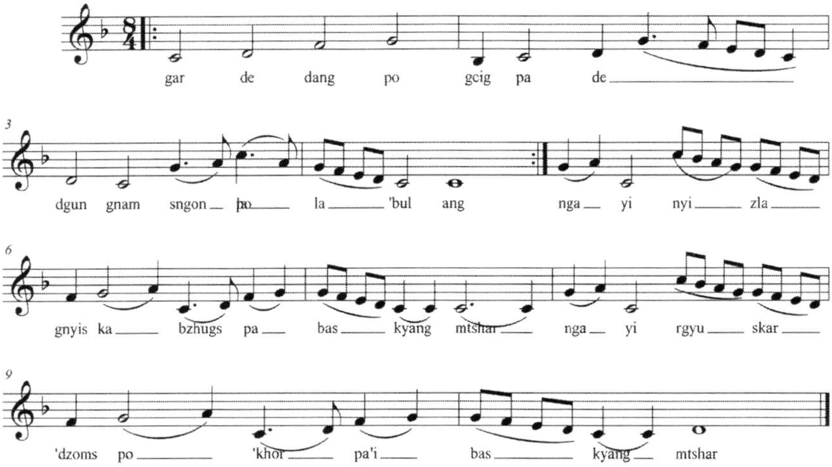

gar de dang po gcig pa de
dgung gnam sngon po la 'bul ang. (2x)
nga yi nyi zla gnyis ka
bzhugs pa bas kyang mtshar. (2x)
nga yi rgyu skar 'dzoms po
'khor pa'i bas kyang mtshar. (2x)
[By that very first dance
Make offerings to the clear blue sky.
Although both my sun and moon
Dwelling there are wonderous
My abundant constellations
Surrounding them are also wonderous.]

gar de dang po'i gnyis pa de
chos grva grub bzhi la 'bul ang.
nga yi yar 'dren bla ma kun
bzhugs pa bas kyang mtshar.
nga yi grva rgyan 'dzoms po
'khor pa bas kyang mtshar.
[By that very second dance
Make offerings to the square Dharma court.

Although my helping lamas
Dwelling there are wonderous
My abundant corner ornaments
Surrounding them are also wonderous.]

gar de dang po'i gsum pa de
sku mkhar mthon po la 'bul ang. (2x)
nga yi mi chen gong ma
bzhugs pa bas kyang mtshar.
nga yi drag zhan 'dzom po
'khor pa'i bas kyang mtshar.
[By that very third dance
Make offerings to the high castle court.
Although my superior great lord
Dwelling there is wondrous.
My abundant high and low attendants
Surrounding him are also wondrous.]

gar de dang po'i bzhi pa de
dpal khang grub bzhi 'bul ang. (2x)
nga yi yab yum pha ma kun
bzhugs pa bas kyang mtshar. (2x)
nga yi gnyen drung 'dzoms po kun
'khor pa'i bas kyang mtshar.
[By that very fourth dance
Make offerings to the square noble house.
Although my parents, mother and father
Dwelling there are wondrous.
My abundant kin folk
Surrounding them are also wondrous.]

gar de dang po'i lnga pa de
do ra grub bzhi 'bul ang. (2x)
nga yi rde dpon chen po
bzhus po bas kyang mtshar. (2x)
nga yi ya do mdza bo kun
'khor pa'i bas kyang mtshar.
[By that very fifth dance
Make offerings to the square dance courtyard.

Although my great lord
Dwelling there is wondrous.
My helpful friends
Surrounding him are also wondrous.]

'di phyi gtso rgyan—The Ornamented Lord of Present and Future[17]

As sung by Ali Mahmud and Tsering Angchuk Ralam August 18, 2009 (LYL, 89–90)

Rhythmic cycle 2

Figure B.12. *'di phyi gtso rgyan. Source:* Transcription provided by the author.

The lyrics shown approximate Ali Mahmud's nonlexical syllables.
It is not clear how the lyrics in the book fit.

di phyi gtso rgyan
skyabs gnas dkon mchog gsum po
bdag cag mos pa'i bu brgyud
ma log par yang mdzod cig
[The ornamented lord of present and future
May we, faith's disciples, again unmistakenly
Take refuge in the Three Jewels.]

yid la 'dod pa'i re skongs
gang bsam 'grub par shog cig
bkra shis phun sum tshogs pa
bzang po'i glu dbyung su sgrogs.
[Fulfilled in the mind of each who wants
May whatever desires be fulfilled,
Perfectly endowed with the auspicious threefold perfection
Who utters songs of goodness.]

bla ma dam pa'i byin rlabs
byin rlabs kyi dngos grub
stag tshang ras par dad pa
ma log par yang mdzod cig.
[Having faith in Stagtshang Raspa
The pure lama's blessing
May we too unmistakenly attain
Those blessings.]

ka ltar zhabs zung—His Two Legs Like Pillars (track 31)—Rhythmic cycle 2

ka ltar zhabs zung brtan cig
bu ram zhing pa yi gdung rgyud
kha ba can gyi 'gro ba yongs la
thugs rje lcags kyu yis zungs shig 2x
[His two legs like pillars,
The Sugar Cane One's[18] lineage
Having transmigrated to the Land of Snows
May he hold the iron hook of compassion.][19] 2x (LYL, 90–92)

rgyab ri shel dkar mchod rten—The Hill of the White Crystal Stupa (Track 32) Rhythm cycle 2

rgyab ri shel dkar mchod rten
mdun de na g.yu mtsho sngon mo
mtha` de na me tog `bar yod
rang yul la skyid nyams chags
mtha` de na gser chen `bar yod
shel dkar la `o ma `khyil.
[The hill of the white crystal stupa
In front of the blue turquoise lake
An arrow there is a blazing flower
Our land is safe from corruption
The edge there is a great golden blaze
On the white crystal wreathed in milk.]

chu mig `gram de ru `khrungs pa
me tog `jam dbyang sgrol ma
chu mig `gram de ru `khrungs pa
ser chen `jam dbyangs sgrol ma
me tog sum gsum `khur te
nga dang bla ma tsho mjal du cha`in.
[Arisen there at the spring's edge,
Tara, gentle like a flower
Arisen there at the spring's edge,
Tara, flower of enlightenment,
That the lama and we shall meet,
Bearing three flowers.]

no mo mos pa yi bla ma dang
lha gang gi lha bris dang `dra
bzang mo mos pa yi bla ma dang
lha khang gi lha bris dang `dra
dam chig gtsang ma`i ngang nas
yar dkon mchog la mchod pa `bul
dam tshig gtsang ma`i gnang nas
mar ngan slong la sbyin pa stsal.
[The girl is devoted to the lama
Like the *thanka* painter to the deity
The good woman is devoted to the lama

Like the *thanka* painter to the temple
From within a sacred vow
Make the higher precious offering
Bestow butter in charity on the destitute.]

yul gyi `go de ru bzhugs pa
yul gyi yul lha gnyan po
shel dkar gyi `go de ru bzhugs pa
a ma rdo rje chen mo
a jo rang gser rkyang gi thod dar
no mo nga dngul rkyang gi pu ri X2
a jo rang gi thugs sems la ma babs song ser na
no mo nga yis lha chos shig byed.
[Residing at the head of the country
Is the sacred god of the country
Residing at the head of the white crystal
Is the great adamantine mother[20]
The lord himself is riding on a golden wild ass's saddle
I, the girl, on the saddle of a silver wild ass. x2
If it is said that the lord himself compassion has not flowed
I, the girl, swear it does.] (LYL, 94–96)

spyi bo`i gtsug tor dgon pa—The Monastery Above the Crown of His Head

(Track 33)—Rhythm cycle 2
spyi bo`i gtsug tor dgon pa
drin can tsa ba`i bla ma 2x
bdag dang `gro drug gi sems can la
thar pa`i lam ston zhig mdzod cig 2x
[The monastery is above the crown of his head,
The compassionate root lama. 2x
To me and the beings in the six realms[21]
May the teacher show the path to deliverance.]

phyi na phyi rkang phra mo
nang na je btsun sgrol ljang X2
je btsun sgrol ljang mkhyen mkhyen
phyi ma`i lam ston mdzod cig
je btsun sgrol ljang mkhyen mkhyen

bar do yi lam ston zhig mdzod cig.
[Outside, among the four subtle planetary motions
Resides revered Green Tara.[22]
Revered Green Tara show compassion
Guide us on the journey to the next life.
Revered Green Tara show compassion
Guide us on the journey through the Bardo.][23]

bu mo nga yi a pha
thugs sems gangs ri dkar po
gyang can `tsho mo`i a pha
thugs sems gangs ri yi ngang nas
dkon mchog la mchod pa zhig `bul
[My, the maiden's, father
Is the compassionate White Ice Mountains.
The blessed, nurturing woman's father
Is from within the compassionate Himalayas.
Let us make offerings to the Three Jewels.]

thugs sems gangs ri yi ngang nas
ngan slong la sbyin re stsal lo
rgya mkhar smug chung gi khyog tong
tshags nang gang gi mda' mo 2x
mda' mo lo tshigs 'khyog med pa
dpon po la zhabs tog 'bul 'ong 2x
[From within the compassionate Himalayas
Let us give alms to beggars.
The vast castle medicinal herb's son
Is the arrow divination shot into the open 2x
The arrow divination is an honest story of former generations.
Give homage to the lord.]

rgya mkhar smug chung gi na chung
'phrul nang gang gi mgron bu 2x
mkron bu la gas 'khrug med pa
dpon po la zhabs tog re 'bul 'ong.
[The vast castle medicinal herb's daughter
Is the cowrie shells inside the magic.

The princess is a tranquil two-year-old sheep
Give homage to the lord.] (LYL, 96–98)

sngar gyi ri bo mchong 'dra—Like the Ancient Carnelian Mountain (track 34) Rhythm cycle 1

sngar gyi ri bo mchong 'dra 2x
sngar gyi ri bo mchong 'dra la 'gyur bya zhing med
a ma'i bu chung gi dga' ba la gzigs ang
dpon bzang khyi bu'i skyid nyams la gzigs
dga' ba la gzigs ang gnyen drung gnam gyi skar ma
skyid nyams la gzigs ang gnyen drung gnam gyi skar ma.
[Like the ancient Carnelian Mountain. 2x
Like the ancient Carnelian Mountain becoming a field of
    non-action[24]
Behold with joy the mother's little son.
Behold with happiness the good lord
Behold with joy the kinfolk's stars in the sky
Behold with happiness the kinfolk's stars in the sky.]

sngar gyi mi kun sngar pa rgyal ba byams pa 2x
sngar rgyal ba byams pa la 'gyur bya zhig med 2x
a ma'i bu chung gi dga' ba la gzigs ang
dpon bzang khyi gu'i skyid nyams la gzigs
dga' ba la gzigs ang gnyen drung gnam gyi skar ma
skyid nyams la gzigs ang gnyen drung gnam gyi skar ma.
[The ancient men ancient times, the ancient king Maitreya[25]
The ancient king Maitreya becomes a field of non-action
Behold with joy the mother's little son.
Behold with happiness the good lord
Behold with joy the kinfolk's stars in the sky
Behold with happiness the kinfolk's stars in the sky.]

sngar gyi shar po sngar la btsan dan sdong po 2x
sngar gyi tsan dan sngon po la 'gyur bya zhing med 2x
a ma'i bu chung gi dga' ba la gzigs ang
dpon bzang khyi gu'i skyid nyams la gzigs ang
dga' ba la gzigs ang gnyen drung gnam gyi skar ma
skyid nyams la gzigs ang gnyen drung gnam gyi skar ma.

[The youth from ancient time, the lord of eternal flowers 2x
The youth from ancient time becomes a field of non-action 2x
Behold with joy the mother's little son.
Behold with happiness the good lord
Behold with joy the kinfolk's stars in the sky
Behold with happiness the kinfolk's stars in the sky.] (LYL,
99–100)

phu ru chags pa gangs ri dkar po—The Valley Formed in the White Mountain Range

As sung by Ali Mahmud and Tsering Angchuk Ralam-Rhythm
cycle 1

phu de ru chags pa gangs ri yi dkar po 2x
gangs ri'i dkar po la gangs rdog gsum chas song 2x
gangs rdog gsum chas song zer na yul chung gi bsod nams
*gangs rdogs gsum chags song zer na rgyal mkhar smug chung
gi bsod nams.*

Figure B.13. *phu ru chags pa gangs ri dkar po. Source:* Transcription provided
by the author.

[The valley formed in the white mountain range 2x
In the white mountain range the single white mountain was
    divided into three parts 2x
When it is said the single white mountain was divided into
    three parts,
the small country is blessed
When it is said the single white mountain was divided into
    three parts,
The royal castle's medicinal herbs are blessed.]

bar de ru bzhengs pa shel dkar gyi mchod rten 2x
shel dkar gyi mchod rten la shel rdog gsum chag song. 2x
shel rdog gsum chags song zer na yul chung gi bsond nams
shel rdog gsum chags song zer na rgyal mkhar smug chung gi
    bsod nams.
[In the midst there is erected a white crystal stupa. 2x
On the white crystal stupa, the crystal was divided into three
    parts 2x
When it is said crystal was divided into three parts, the small
    country is blessed
When it is said crystal was divided into three parts, the royal
    castle's medicinal herbs are blessed.]

mdo de ru 'khyil ba g.yu mtsho yi sngon mo 2x
g.yu mtsho sngon mo la g.yu rdog gsum chags song 2x
g.yu rdog gsum chags song zer na yul chung gi bsod nams
g.yu rdog gsum chags song zer na rgyal mkhar smug chung gi
    bsod nams.
[In that winding valley the blue of the turquoise lake 2x
In the blue turquoise lake, the turquoise is split into three
    parts 2x
When it was said the turquoise is split into three parts, the
    small country is blessed
When it was said the turquoise is split into three parts, the
    royal castle's medicinal herbs are blessed.] (LYL, 100–101)

gangs dang g.ya' yi mtshams su—In the time of snow and dust
Same melody as *rtendel lngapa* B-as sung by Ali Mahmud and
    Tsering Angchuk Ralam

gangs dang g.ya' mtshams su
ba lu sgrug tu song pa'in
gangs dang g.ya' yi mtshams su
g.ya' lu sgrug tu song pa'in.
[In the time of snow and dust
We went to gather dwarf rhododendron
In the time of snow and dust
We went to gather the rusty branches.]

ba lu g.ya' lu dang ma mjal
lha shing shug pa dang mjal
ba lu g.ya' lu dang ma mjal
lha shing shug pa dang mjal
[We did not find the dwarf rhododendron
We did find the juniper
We did not find the dwarf rhododendron
We did find the juniper.]

lha shing shug pa'i du ba po
steng phyogs lha yul la 'bul
lha shing shug pa'i du ba po
'og phyogs klu yul la 'bul
lha shing shug pa'i du ba po
bar phyogs btsan yul la'ng 'bul.
[Offer the smoke of the juniper
Above in the gods' realm
We offer the smoke of the juniper
Below in the *nagas'*[26] realm
We offer the smoke of the juniper
Between in the *tsan* demons' realm.]

gser gzhong gzhong pa'i steng na
mar dkar gyi 'brang rgyas bzhengs 2x
'brang rgyas lag tu 'khur te
bla ma kun mjal du cha'in
'brang rgyas la tu 'khur te
rgyal ba mjal du cha'in.
[Above, on golden and wooden trays
Red and white *drang gyas* cakes were built

Bringing the *drang gyas* in our hands
We will go to meet the lamas
Bringing the *drang gyas* in our hands
We will go to the Victorious One.][27] (LYL, 101–2)

he mis dgon pa—Hemis Monastery

As sung by Ali Mahmud and Tsering Angchuk Ralam—Rhythmic
    cycle 2

lcang ra smug chung gi dkyil na
dgon pa gser gyi bum tshang
lcang ra smug chung gi dkyil na
he mis gser gyi bum tshang.
[In the center of a grove of willows and medicinal herbs
Is the golden monastery, contained as in a vase
In the center of a grove of willows and medicinal herbs
Is Hemis Monastery, contained as in a vase.]

gser khri ser po'i steng na
bzang gsum bla ma bzhugs yod
gser khri ser po'i steng na
skyab mgon stag tshan ras pa.

Figure B.14. *he mis dgon pa. Source:* Transcription provided by the author.

[On the yellow golden throne
Is the lama manifesting the three goods.[28]
On the yellow golden throne
Is the protector, Stagtshang Raspa.]

rtsa ba'i bla ma'i byin rlabs
yul phyogs gzhan la ma stsal
stag tshan ras pa yi byin rlabs
yul phyog gzhan la ma stsal.
[The root lama's blessings
Are not bestowed on other countries
Stagtshang Raspa's blessings
Are not bestowed on other countries.]

rtsa ba'i bla ma'i byin rlabs
rang gi yul stsal cig
stag tshang ras pa'i byin rlabs
la dvags phyogs la stsal cig.
[May the root lama's blessings
Be bestowed on our own country
May Stagtshang Raspa's blessings
Be bestowed on Ladakh.]

dgon sde phan tshun gyi grva pa
ser phreng brgya dan brgya rtsa
he mis lce bde'i dge 'dun
ser phreng brgya dang brgya rtsa.
[The monastery's connecting courtyards
Are a golden rosary of one hundred eternal *tormas*[29]
Hemis Monastery's eloquent, virtuous monks
Are a golden rosary of one hundred eternal *tormas*.]

ser phreng legs mo'i rdo 'dzin
bzang sum rtsa ba'i bla ma
ser 'phreng legs mo'i rdo 'dzin
skyab mgon stag tsang ras pa.
[The essential conciousness of the golden rosary
Is the lama of three goodnesses
The essential conciousness of the golden rosary
Is the protector Stagtshang Raspa.] (LYL, 103–4)

rgyal lung rgyal mo—In the Queen's Royal Valley (track 35)
   Rhythmic cycle 4

rgyal lung rgyal mo yi phu shed na
gangs ri gsum rtsegs zhig chags byung 2x
gangs ri gsum rtsegs ma yin no
rtsa ba'i bla ma yi bzhugs khri yin
gangs ri gsum rtegs ma yin no
mtsho skyes rdo rje yi bzhugs khri yin.
[In the queen's royal valley
Three snowy mountains arose 2x
They are not three snowy mountains
They are the root lama's throne.
They are not three snowy mountains
They are the throne of Guru Rinpoche, Padmasambhava.]

rgyal lung rgyal mo yi phu shed na
gser gyi nyi ma gsum shar byung 2x
gser gyi nyi ma ma yin no
rtsa ba'i bla ma'i dbu zhva yin
gser gyi nyi ma ma yin no
mtsho skyes rdo rje yi dbu zhva yin.
[In the queen's royal valley
Three golden suns rose. 2x
They are not three golden suns
The are the root lama's hat
They are not three golden suns
They are the hat of Guru Rinpoche, Padmasambhava.]

rgyal lung rgyal mo yi phu shed na
dung gi zla ba zhig shar byung 2x
dung gi zla ba ma yin no
rtsa ba'i bla ma'i zhal gdong yin
dung gi zla ba ma yin no
mtsho skyes rdo rje yi zhal gdong yin.
[In the queen's royal valley
A conch-like moon shines.
It is not a conch-like moon
It is the root lama's face
It is not a conch-like moon
It is the face of Guru Rinpoche, Padmasambhava.]

rgyal lung rgyal mo yi phu shed na
rtsa sna dang chu sna kun 'dzoms byung 2x
rtsa sna dang chu sna 'dzoms pa zhig ma yin
lung pa de skyes pa zhig yin.
[In the queen's royal valley
All types of plants and water are gathered 2x
They are not types of plants and water that are gathered
It is the birth of the country.]

rgyal lung rgyal mo yi phu shed na
lug gu la skyid nyams shig chag byung 2x
lug gu la skyid nyam ma yin
ra rji mkha pa yi skyong shes yin 2x
[In the queen's royal valley
In a lamb, happiness has arisen 2x
It is not happiness in a lamb
It is the shepherd sage's nurturing consciousness 2x]

rgyal lung rgyal mo yi phu shed na
mi gsum bka' bgros shig mdzad 'dug 2x
mi gsum bka' bgros ma yin no
rtsa ba'i bla ma yi gsung skad yin
mi gsum bka' bgros ma yin no
mtsho skyes rdo rje yi bka' bgros yin.
[In the queen's royal valley
Three men are conferring
They are not three men conferring
It is the root lama's enlightened speech
They are not three men conferring
It is the enlightened speech of Guru Rinpoche, Padmasambhava.] (LYL, 105–6)

dgon pa bkra shis lhun po—Tashilhunpo Monastery[30]
As sung by Ali Mahmud and Tsering Angchuk Ralam—same
   melody as *rtendel lngapa*
nyi ma shar de nas shar pa de
shar ri dro can gyi nyi ma
ya gi shed gnas chen bzang po'i
pho brang rtse la shar

dgon pa la bkra shis lhun po yi
pho brang rtse la shar.
[The sun rises in the east
The warm eastern sun
It shines at the heights of
The fortress in yon sacred place
It shines at the heights of the fortress
Of Tashilhunpo Monastery.]

rgya yul gzhung de nas thon pa yi
rgya yi rgya ja kham pa
dbus gtsang gzhung de la thon pa yi
rgya yi rgya kham pa
de yang gnas chen bzang po yi
mang ja la 'bul
dgon pa bkra shis lhun po yi
mang ja la 'bul.
[The dark brown Chinese tea
Produced in the center of India
The dark brown Chinese tea
Produced from Central Tibet
Therefore, let us make offerings of tea to monks
Of the sacred pilgrimage place
Make offerings of tea to the monks of Tashilhunpo Monastery.]

rgya yul gzhung nas thon pa yi
bzang po la bkra shis kha btags
dbus gtsang gzhung du thon pa yi
bzang po bkra shis kha btags
de yang gsan chen bzang po yi
snyan dar la 'bul
dgon pa la bkra shis lhun po yi
snyan dar la 'bul.
[The good quality auspicious *khatag*
Produced from the center of India
The good quality auspicious *khatag*
Produced from the center of Central Tibet
A *khatag* will be offered to the holy pilgrimage site.
A *khatag* will be offered to Tashilhunpo Monastery.]

rgya yul gzhung nas thon pa yi
men tse tshon sna 'dzoms po
dbus gtsang gzhun du thon pa yi
men tse tshon sna 'dzoms po
de yang ngas chen bzang po yi
zhal khebs la 'bul
dgon pa bkra shi lhun po yi
zhal khebs la 'bul.
[The multicolored ornament
Produced from the center of India
The multicolored ornament
Produced from the Centre of Central Tibet
The Men-tse[31] will be as a face covering curtain[32] of the holy
    pilgrimage site.
The Men-tse will be offered as a face covering curtain to Tashi
    Lhunpo Gonpa.]

dgon pa yi dkyil de na
dar po che yod
bkra shis lhun po'i dkyil de na
dar po che yod
rtsa ba'i bla ma dar ba yi
darche zhig yin
bzang gsum gyi bla ma dar ba yi
dar chen zhig yin.
[In the centre of the monastery
Put up a large prayer flag
In the centre of Tashi Lhunpo
Put up a large prayer flag
That is a large flag of
The disseminating teachings of the root teacher
That is the large flag of
The disseminating teachings of the Gracious root teacher.]
    (LYL, 107–9)

**dgung nam sngon mo'i dkyil na—In the Center of the Blue
    Sky** (LYL, 111–12)
As sung by Ali Mahmud and Tsering Angchuk Ralam—Rhythmic
    cycle 3

Figure B.15. *dgung nam sngon mo'i dkyil na. Source:* Transcription provided by the author.

dgun na___ (la)m sngon mo'i___ dkyi___ (li)l_____ na___

smin drug gi g.yas___ skor bskor la smin drug gi g.yas___ skor bskor___

(de___ la)_____ smin drug_____ gi___ g.ya (la)s skor_____ ma (la)
(de___ la)_____ smin drug_____ gi___ g.ya (la)s skor_____ ma (la)

yin___ (na)_____ bla___ ma yi___ chos skor_____ yin
yin___ (na)_____ Mi___ 'pham gyi___ chos skor_____ yin

dgun nam sngon mo'i dkyil na
smin drug gi g.yas skor bskor 2x
smin drug gi g.yas skor ma yin
bla ma yi chos skor yin
smin drug gi g.yas skor ma yin
mi 'pham gyi chos skor yin
[In the center of the blue sky
The Pleides turn
The Pleides are not turning
The lama's wheel of Dharma is turning
The Pleides are not turning
Mipham's[33] wheel of Dharma is turning.]

gser zam zam pa'i steng na
bla yi chib sga rol 2x
zam pa'i og gi nya mo de
ngan song la ldung dvogs 'dug 2x
[Above the bridge of the golden road
The lama rides on a horse saddle 2x

Below the bridge is the female fish
Averting bad reincarnations. 2x]

ma Ni man thang ring mo la
skor ba gyas nas bskor 2x
skor ba g.yas na bskor pa
las kyi sgrib pa dag cig
g.yas skor g.yas nas bskor ba
pha ma'i drin lan 'khor cig.
[By the long Mani wall[34]
We circumabulate in a clockwise direction 2x
When we have circumambulated clockwise
May defilements be dispelled.
When we have circumambulated clockwise
May the kindness of our parents be repaid.]

pha ri ri nas shug pa dang
tshur ri ri nas ba lu 2x
bu mo nga gtsang sbra can mo yi
gtsang shug cig ldan cig
kun 'dzom nga gtsang sbra stan mo yi
gtsang shug cig ldan cig.
[The juniper tree from the distant mountain and
The dwarf rhododendron from the nearby moutain 2x
May I, the smart maiden,
Be a wife purified by junniper[35]
May I, smart Kundzom,
Be a wife purified by junniper.]

tshogs bzangs mtsho mo g.yang skyid—The Ocean Cauldron of Wealth and Happiness
As sung by Ali Mahmud and Tsering Angchuk Ralam—Rhythmic cycle 2
dang po srid pa chags pa
tshogs bzang mtsho mo g.yang skyid
sngar yang 'o ma 'khyil ba
tshogs bzang mtsho mo g.yang skyid.
[From the beginning of created existence
The ocean of wealth and happiness

Figure B.16. *tshogs bzangs mtsho mo g.yang skyid. Source:* Transcription provided by the author.

Even in the past the milk was churned
The ocean of wealth and happiness.]

tshogs bzang mtsho mo g.yang skyid
za chu kha ra 'o ma 2x
za chu kha ra 'o ma
gsol la thang rgya za kham pa.
[The ocean of wealth and happiness
Drink its milk at the shore
Drink its milk at the shore
We request the reddish brown drink.]

gsol la thang rgya za kham pa la
gsol la mar 'bri mar ser chung
gsol la mar 'bri mar ser chung la
ljags tshva shel tshva kha ra.
[When we request reddish brown drink
We request the small golden cow's butter
When we request the small golden cow's butter
We taste crystal salt and sugar.]

ljags tshva shel tshva kha ra la
gsol thum gser gyi thum bu

gsol bum gser gyi thum bu la
gsol sgur padma 'dab brgyad.
[When we taste crystal salt and sugar
We request the covered golden ladle
When we request the covered golden ladle
We request to bear the eight petaled lotus[36]]

gsol sgur padma 'dab brgyad la
gsol tib nyi zla kha sbyor
gsol tib nyi zla kha sbyor la
gsol dkar 'brug ris dkar yol.
When we request to bear the eight petaled lotus
We request the teapot of the Union of Sun and Moon[37]
When we request the teapot of the Union of Sun and Moon
We request the China teacup of the dragon [38] lineage.]

gsol dkar 'brug ris nang nas
rtsa ba'i bla ma mchod do
gsol dkar 'brug ris nang nas
stag tshang ras pa mchod do.
[When we request the China teacup of the dragon lineage
We make offerings to our root lama
By requesting from the white dragon lineage[39]
We make offerings to Lama Stagtsang Raspa.[40]] (LYL, 114–15)

steng phyogs lha yul nas—From the World of Gods Above
as sung by Ali Mahmud and Tsering Angchuk Ralam—Rhythmic
   cycle 1
steng phyogs lha yul nas
g.yu 'brug sngon mo zhig ldir byung 2x
g.yu 'brug sngon mo ma yin te
bla ma'i gsung skad cig yin no
g.yu 'brug sngon mo ma yin no
bde ba bsam 'grub kyi gsung skad.
[From the world of gods above
The blue turquoise dragon/thunder sprang
It was not the blue turquoise dragon/thunder
It was the exalted speech of the lama

Figure B.17. *steng phyogs lha yul nas. Source:* Transcription provided by the author.

It was not the blue turquoise dragon/thunder
It was the exalted speech of Dewa Samdup[41]]

gur de rgya gur ni dkar mo'i
steng shong gi nang na
mi chen nye rang bzhugs pa yi
dga' ba la gzigs ang
bde ba bsam 'grub bzhug pa yi
skyid nyams la gzigs ang
[In the upper space of
The broad white pavillion
Behold how happily your highness resides
Behold how comfortably Dewa Samdup resides.]

rtsig pa ma brtsigs pa'i
gser gyi cha 'grig pa'i nang na 2x
dri ma ma phog pa yi
she dkar gyi mchod rten

[Inside the pair of golden walls
Not built (by human hands)
Stands a stainless, flawless,
White crystal stupa.]

dben 'dum shel dkar mchod rten la
srog shing tsan dan gyi sdong po
srog shing tsn dan gyi sdong po la
snyan dar bkra shis kha btags
[The re-unification cystal white stupa
Has got a central pole of sandal wood
On the central pole of sandal wood
Has an auspicious white scarf.]

snyan dar brka shis kha btags la
ri mo bkra shis btags brgyad
kha btags 'jol song zer na'ng
ri mo 'jol mdo go mi 'dug
[The auspicious white scarf is designed with
Eight auspicious symbols
Even if the white scarf gets loose
The lucky signs will not degrade.] (LYL, 116–17)

rgya nag nor bu gling—China, the Country of Gems (LYL: 117–19)

As sung by Ali Mahmud and Tsering Angchuk Ralam—Rhythmic cycle 3

Figure B.18. *rgya nag nor bu gling. Source:* Transcription provided by the author.

rgya nag nor bu gling du, nor bu 'tshal du ma song 2x
nor bu pha ma 'dra ba, nyi ma shar la bskyod
phun tshogs rnam rgyal 'dra ba, rtsab rang gi rtse la bskyod
[Don't go in search of wish fulfilling gems, In China the
  country of gems

Parents are like wish fulfilling gems, went to the east.
Like Phuntsog Namgyal, [42] went from the bottom to the top.]

'brug chen hang sgra che byung, 'brug chung stong sgra chung
  byung
'ja' de kha dog legs po, nyi ma'i shar la bskyod song
phun tshog rnam rgyal 'dra ba. rtsab rang gi rtse la bskyod
  song.
[The thundering of the large dragon[43] is high,
The thundering of the small dragon is less
The rainbow, having beautiful color, went towards the east,
  where the sun rises.
Similarly, Phuntsog Namgyal, went from the bottom to the
  top.]

bkra shis gtams pa'i nang la, ser mo nas kyi bang mdzod
bkra shis gtams pa'i nang na, sngon mo nas kyi bang mdzod
[The house filled with auspiciousness, has the treasure of a
  warehouse
The house filled with auspiciousness, has the treasure of a
  warehouse from the sky]

zin pa med pa'i nor la, bkra shi gsum gsum mchod
zin pa med pa'i nor la, g.yas chang gsum gsum mchod ang
[To the unceasing wealth, offer blessings thrice for
  prosperity
To the unceasing wealth, offer auspicious wine thrice.]

da ci mtsham gyi rmi lam, rmi lam bzang po zhig mthong
zhag bzang mtshan gyi rmi lam, rmi lam bzang po zhig
  mthong
[The dream seen last night, was a dream of good omen
The dream of an auspicious day was a dream of an
  auspicious sign.]

dpon po bzang mjal ba'i, mjal ba'i mjal dar mthong
zhag bzang mtshan gyi rmi lam, rmi lam bzang po zhig
    mthong
[(In the dream) the noble lord was seen, offering a *khatag*
In the dream of a dream with good signs, some good
    dreams were seen.]

dpon po bzang po'i sku gdung, sku gdung shel dkar mchod rten
phun tshog rnam gyal gyi sku gddung, sku gdung shel dkar
    mchod rten
[The remains of the noble lord, are in the crystal white stupa
The remains of Phuntsog Namgyal, are in the crystal white stupa]

sku gdung shel dkar gyi mchod rten la
srog shing tsan dan gyi sngon po
[In the reliquary stupa
Is a sandal wood pole of sapphire.]

srog shing tsan dam gyi sngon po la
snyan dar bkra shis kha btags
[On the sandal wood pole of sapphire
With an auspicious *khatag*]

snyan bkra shis kha btags la
ri mo bkra shi btags brgyad.
[On the auspicious *khatag*
Eight auspicious symbols are drawn.]

**dpal ldan bal ma'i g.yas zur na—On the Right Side of the
    Glorious Teacher**
As sung to the tune of *rten 'brel lnga pa* D by Ali Mahmud
    and Tsering Angchuk Ralam
dpal ldan bla ma'i g.yas zur na
kha btags tshon can dum spung zhig x2
[A heap of colored scarves is piled up
On the right side of the glorious teacher.]

bla chen mkhyen mtshams pa mkhyen x2
de kun la pho mdud gsum gsum zhig rol

de la yan mdud gsum gsum rol
[Oh! Glorious Lama, meditator
Knot them thrice
Knot them thrice for prosperity.]

dpyid gsum dpyid kar chu sna 'dzoms x2
dpon po dang nya chung gser mig dang 'dra
dpon bzang gsod nams nya chung gser mig dang 'dra
dpon bzang bsod nams nya chung gser mig 'dra
ya sha skyid po'i nyi ma shar pa dang 'dra
ya sha dga' rten 'bral 'grig pa dang 'dra
[During the three months of spring
Water of three different origins meet
The lord is like a small golden-eyed fish
The noble lord Sonam is like a small golden-eyed fish
It is as if an esteemed sun of pleasure has risen
It is as if auspicious things have occurred.]

dbyar gsum dbyar khar rtsa sna ru 'dzoms x2
dpon po dang ser chen me tog dang 'dra
dpon bzang bsod nams ser chen me tog 'dra
ya sha skyid po'i nyi ma shar pa dang 'dra
ya sha dga' ba'i rten 'brel 'grig pa dang 'dra
[Various kinds of grass have come together
During the three months of summer
The lord is like a yellow flower
The noble lord Sonam is like a yellow flower
It is as if the esteemed sun of pleasure has risen
It is as if the esteemed sun of auspicious things has
     occurred.]

dgun gsum dgun kha gangs sna ru 'dzoms 2x
dpon po dang gangs ri dkar po dang 'dra
dpon bzang bsod nams gangs ri dkar po 'dra
ya sha skyid nyi ma shar pa dang 'dra
ya sha dga' ba'i rten 'brel 'grig pa dang 'dra
[Various types of grains come together.
During these three months of autumn
The lord is like a store house of grains
The noble lord Sonam is like a store house of grains

It is as if the esteemed sun of pleasure has risen
It is as if the esteemed sun of auspicious things has occurred.]
  (LYL, 120–21)

bkra shis phun sum tshogs pa—*The Auspicious Marvels* (LYL,
  122)
by Ali Mahmud and Tsering Angchuk Ralam—Rhythmic cycle 1
bkra shis phun sum tshogs pa
bde ldan dkar bzo'i skyid tshal
ma bzhengs lhun du grub yod
tshang sras nyi ma'i pho brang
[In the heaven-like white orchard
Endowed with auspiciousness
The castle of the sun-like goddess Saraswati
Is miraculously formed without being built.]

dgung gsal nam mkha'i klong na
nyi zla'i gdugs dang land byung
ngo mtshar dga'i ba'i ltad mo

Figure B.19. *bkra shis phun sum tshogs pa. Source:* Transcription provided by the
author.

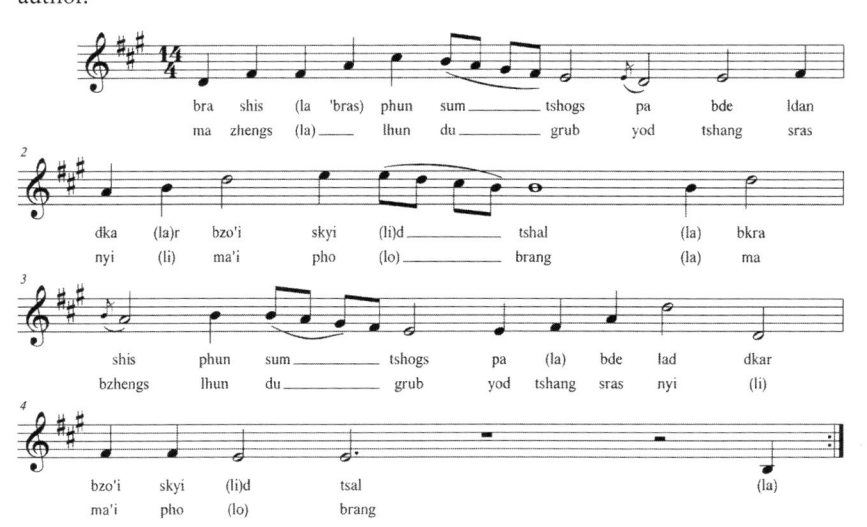

zab khang ka ba zung ldan
[In the depth of the clear sky
The wonderful and pleasurable looking
Building of twin pillars
Stand as if parasols of sun and moon.]

nang na seng ge'i khri steng
gnya' btsan po'i gdung rgyud
chos rgyal tse dpal yum sras
sku tshe bskal brgyar brtan cig
[On the lion throne inside
Sits the lineage of Nyatri Tsanpo
The Dharma king Tsepal,[44] his wife and son
May live for hundreds of eons.]

ljon shing star ga'i steng na
'dab chags pho mo'i gsung skad
'og ga stag shar gzhon pa
bde skyid dga' ba'i glu dbyungs
[From the walnut tree above
Voices of birds, both male and female, come
Below it are the gathered youth
Singing melodious songs out of pleasure.]

Notes

Introduction

1. Modern Balti cultural activists have been making efforts to revive the use of the Tibetan *bod yig* script as part of asserting cultural solidarity with the larger Tibetan cultural sphere. A Balti acquaintance of mine named Mohammed Hasnan has even adopted the Tibetan name Senge Tsering as a political gesture.

Chapter 1

1. According to the official website of the Ladakh Autonomous Hill Development Council, Leh District (http://leh.nic.in/), accessed September 29, 2012.

2. According to the official website of the Ladakh Autonomous Hill Development Council, Kargil District (http://kargil.nic.in/profile/profile.htm), accessed September 29, 2012.

3. This *lobchak* (literally, "yearly homage"—actually every three years) caravan also included a two-way exchange of goods. It continued up until Indian Independence in 1947.

4. One of several brother deities consulted at the oracle at Matho.

5. Zhabdrung Ngawang Namgyal (1594–1651) one of the two incarnations of the fourth Drukchen (head of the Drukpa sect), contributed to unite Bhutan as a state—(Rangjung Yeshe)

6. Saskyong Namgyal.

7. The term Bon (the practitioners are called Bonpo) has several meanings. Archeologist and Bon scholar John Belleza (2005) describes Bon in upper Tibet as having various dimensions:

- Indigenous folk culture related to the physical and numinous environment of Upper Tibet.

- Doctrinal material derived from Vajrayana.

- gCod cult practices.

- Gling ge-sar bardic content.

- Phya-gshen elements specifically pertaining to dpyad (diagnosis), gto (beneficial rites) and the cult of dgra-lha (sgra-bla).

8. Francke notes that these may be the fulfillment of four prophecies in what he calls the "Springtime Myth."

9. "Division" or "regions" (Monier-Williams 1899, 36)

10. The chief demon of Bonpo, somewhat analogous to Satan (Tucci 1980).

11. Francke further notes that instead of "Yārkandis," the word *Hor* may well be translated as "Mongolians."

Chapter 2

1. According to Tashi Rabgias the word refers to the twelve stages of cognition (*Rten-'brel-yan-lag-bcu-gnyis*) as relating to dependent origination (Skt. *Pratītyasamutpāda,* Tib. *rten cing 'brel bar 'byung* ba), the causal relations between the psychophysical phenomena that sustain *dukkha* (dissatisfaction) in worldly experience (personal comm., July 25, 2009).

2. The descendants of the legendary first Tibetan King are compared to buddhas or bodhisattvas.

3. This is a derivative of one of the meditation practices by which one generates *bodhicitta,* the mind of enlightenment where one resolves to seek enlightenment for the benefit of all sentient beings. This practice, known as the Seven-Point Cause and Effect Instruction, teaches you to generate *bodhicitta* based on developing affectionate love towards all sentient beings. As for the seven points of the cause and effect instruction, one begins by meditating on equanimity and then proceeds through the following steps:

> Recognizing all sentient beings as one's mother
> Recognizing the kindness of mother sentient beings
> Repaying their kindness
> Affectionate love
> Great compassion
> The extraordinary intention
> Bodhicitta (Ribur Rinpoche 1997)

4. The mantra of Chenrezig, *Om Mani Padme Hum.*

5. This is a metaphysical reference, with the jewel or precious one being the Buddha, and/or the Dharma.

6. A possible double meaning of the Buddha or King Sengge Namgyal, protector of the faith.

7. An interesting borrowing from Islam, Alam means "world" in Arabic, and could be a reference to Sengge's Muslim Mother, Gyal Khatun. In addition, with the preceding word, king, it could be equal to Shah Alam, King of the World, or emperor, and could be a signal to visiting Muslim dignitaries.

8. This is a clear reference to Sengge Namgyal, who built the palace in Leh.

9. The peacock is a bird associated with royalty, as well as being a symbol of spiritual purity and strength. This discussed in the Buddhist treatise, *The Wheel of Sharp Weapons,* verses 1–2:

1) In jungles of poisonous plants strut the peacocks,
Though medicine gardens of beauty lie near.
The masses of peacocks do not find gardens pleasant,
But thrive on the essence of poisonous plants.
2) In similar fashion the brave Bodhisattvas
Remain in the jungle of worldly concern.
No matter how joyful this world's pleasure gardens,
These Brave Ones are never attracted to pleasures,
But thrive in the jungle of suffering and pain (Dharmaraksita).

10. Gyal Khatun is compared to the musical nightingale, probably because of her bringing *khar mon* or palace musicians as part of her retinue from Baltistan. Was she also a singer? It would have been unusual, although there was the practice of noble women singing for the kings.

11. The swan is a symbol of spiritual purity, gliding along the surface of the muddy waters. This is possibly a reference to the king's lama Stag Tsang Ras Pa.

12. Buddhist philosophy speaks of "generating the mind of X," where X is either a mental state one focuses on, such as wisdom, compassion, loving kindness, etc., or a given meditational figure with which one identifies, such as a buddha or bodhisattva.

13. Garuda are mythical, enormous predatory birds with intelligence and social organization, having characteristics of both birds and gods. They are depicted with unicorn-like horns.

14. Offering cake either in the shape of a young girl's breast or a stupa.

15. Apricot seed oil is a prestige oil, native to Ladakh. Oil lamps are an offering analogous to candles in Christianity.

16. http://www.khandro.net/deity_Chakrasamvara.htm

17. Gods, demi-gods, human beings, animals, hungry ghosts, hell beings.

18. The Indian analogy of an elephant driver's hook (Hindi, *ankush*) that steers the animal, or the crook of a shepherd's staff.

19. Heavenly realm where Guru Padmasambhava, one of the prominent founders of Tibetan Buddhism, resides.

20. The jeweled ornament on top of a person's head shown in religious iconography that indicates royalty.

21. Central Tibet, where Lhasa is located.

22. Many of the notable male singers I know are hired as *nyer pon*-s for weddings, and are often brought from outside the village, especially for their prowess in song battles.

23. OM, may everything be auspicious. May everything bear auspiciousness.

24. Published in the 1930s in German, translated into English in 1985.

25. "*rgyal chen sde bzhi*—four orders of the great kings, class of the four great kings. syn {*phyogs skyong*} guardian of the four directions. syn {*rgyal chen sde bzhi*} Four Great / Guardian [directional) Kings, the Four Mighty Rulers. 1) {*yul 'khor bsrungs*} king Dhritarastra of the east. 2) {*'phags skyes po*} king Virudhaka of the south. 3) {*spyan mi bzang*} king Virupaksha of the west. 4) {*rnam thos sras*} king Vaishravana of the north" (Ranjung Yeshe Dictionary).

26. Oḍḍiyāna-kingdom in NW India from whence came Guru Padmasambhava, also a blessed realm presided over by him.

27. "Thusness"—the ultimate nature of reality

28. As a monk in Likir Gompa described, the only things people could traditionally do in winter were to have monastic festivals, drink, and make babies (personal comm., August 2001).

29. This and all the subsequent feats are reputedly gained by yogic austerities (like abstaining from alcohol).

30. *phur ba*—Sacred dagger used in tantric rituals. Piercing the boulder symbolizes penetrating ignorance with meditative insight.

Chapter 3

1. Mani walls are long, earth-filled walls covered with stones with the inscription "Om mani padme hum" carved on them and placed on the wall as an act of devotion.

2. Kora is an Uzbek word for "black tea," which was popular in Tashkent as well as in China.

3. *Begar* means "forced labor."

4. The Kashmiri capital was viewed by the region's Muslims as the center of culture, religion, and economics.

5. Perhaps Masjid (Abu Bakr) in Gund Jahangir, J&K /Abu Bakar Masjid in Jawahar Nagar or Masjid Baba Dawood Khank in Anantnag.

Chapter 4

1. I mentioned this incident to Dawa Tsering, who was the Hill Councilor for the area, and he said the matter was subsequently worked out in a local *panchayat* (five-man village council) court. However, Dawa felt that the main

issue was the Mon kid's having trespassed on some inviolate space. He noted that there are areas that even he is prohibited from, and that this was a matter-of-fact arrangement within any village (personal comm., August 12, 2012). This complex of affinities, prohibitions, and social classes is beyond the scope of the current study but bears further investigation.

2. According to the Ethnologue website (http://www.ethnologue.com/language/bkk), the total number of *Brokskad* speakers in the area is less than ten thousand

3. The women's dance traditionally performed at the Losar New Year in the royal palace.

4. A week later I went to the village of Baima, near Hanu, and noted differences in musical practice, such as different dances and songs, mixed with mainline Ladakhi styles. One important difference is the use of a large barrel drum, the *gring jang*, which is also part of ensembles in Baltistan (cf. Sakata 1989).

Chapter 5

1. His name is variously spelled "Murup" or "Morup." On his Facebook page it is spelled "Morup."

2. Tashi Rabgias is his uncle, and Lama Jamspal is an older cousin or "uncle"—so many Ladakhis I meet are related to each other.

3. Jangsem Sherab Zangpo (1395–1457). Rinpoche is a title indicating a reincarnated lama, usually occupying a monastic and sometimes political position, for example, the Dalai Lamas as political heads of Tibet.

4. Thiksey Rinpoche Ngawang Jamyang Chamba Stanzin, b. 1943, is the ninth incarnation of Jansem Sherab Zangpo. Besides his scholarly and religious accomplishments, he served as a member of the Rajya Sabha (upper house of parliament) from 1989 to 2002, addressing grassroots problems in Ladakh.

Chapter 6

1. The Buddha is often referred to as the Victorious One. The servant in this case might refer to Je Tsongkhapa, founder of the Gelugpa sect, who was active at Chuzang Monastery in eastern Tibet.

Chapter 7

1. Lake Manasarovar near Mount Kailash—a pilgrimage place said to cleanse all sins

2. Bowls of water are put daily on Buddhist altars as an offering—the lake is being likened to a mammoth water offering.

3. This is said to refer to the woman's husband as she seeks to become a nun.

Appendixes

1. King Jamyang Namgyal invited the famous Tibetan lama *Stagtsang Raspa* (Tib. *Stag* = tiger, *tsang*=nest) to come to Ladakh, but it was not until the reign of his son, Sengge (Lion) Namgyal (ruled 1616–1642), that he actually came. Under the tutelage of the tiger lama, the lion king founded a number of important monasteries devoted to the Drukpa Kargyu sect, including Hanle, and Hemis.

2. Literally *bzang gsum*—the three goods.

3. The vulture or eagle

4. The costumed male attendants who go to fetch the bride (Hamid, 97).

5. A *dri* is a female yak

6. A cup made from the top of a human skull is a power ritual object in tantric practice.

7. Diamond Throne of India, the present Bodhgaya in Bihar, where Buddha Shakyamuni attained enlightenment.

8. An example was recorded as a video by Kunzes Dolma (http://www.youtube.com/watch?v=8q2mJe3e7VA accessed August 1, 2013).

9. "Thusness": the ultimate nature of reality

10. *sangs rgyas rabs bdun*—the Seven Successive Buddhas: {*rnam par gzigs, gtsug tor can, thams cad skyob, 'khor ba 'jig, gser thub, 'od srungs, sha kya thub pa*}; the Seven Generations of Buddhas (Ranjung Yeshe Dictionary).

11. *bkra shis rtags brgyad*—eight happy emblems. {*gser nya, bum pa, pad ma, dung dkar, dpal be'u, rgyal mtshan, 'khor lo*}, eight auspicious emblems; eight auspicious symbols; eight good luck symbols. eight happy emblems (Rangjung Yeshe Dictionary).

12. Important mantra syllables in Vajrayana Buddhist meditation practice

13. The mythical continent on which the known world is located in ancient Hindu/Buddhist cosmology.

14. The Buddha

15. This means a silken banner representing silk.

16. *khatags* (blessing scarves) are made of silk

17. Buddhas and bodhisattvas are said to be able to function in the past, present and future, as in the phrase "The buddhas who reside in the three times (Tib. *dus gsum sangs rgyas*).

18. The Buddha

19. iron hook (used to train or steer elephants) as a metaphor for the Buddha's teachings

20. Tara is often refered to as "Mother."

21. Gods, demi-gods, human beings, animals, hungry ghosts, hell beings.

22. Tara (Tib. *sgrol ma*) is a female bodhisattva of compassion and action. She is viewed as the female aspect of Avalokitesvara (*Chenrezig*). Her aspect of Green Tara is a mother-like saviouress and protector of children.

23. The intermediate state between death and rebirth.

24. Non-action would be free from negative karma

25. The future buddha of loving kindness

26. Subterranean water and earth spirits.

27. Epithet for the Buddha.

28. Buddha, Dharma, Sangha

29. Symbolic offering cakes made of barley flour, butter, milk, curd, sugar, brown sugar, and honey, decorated with colored butter shapes.

30. Tashilhunpo Monastery in Western Tibet was the seat of the Panchen Lamas, the second most important lamas in the hierarchy of the Gelugpa sect.

31. Ornament

32. Religious paintings (*thangka*) or relics are traditionally covered with a curtain, except when on ritual display.

33. Probably refers to one of the heads of the Drukpa sect, maybe Gyalwang Mipham Wangpo (1654–1717), Fourth Gyalwang Drukchen, who helped negotiate the Treaty of Tingmosgang which ended the Tibet-Mongolian-Ladakh War of 1679–1684. The Ladakhi kings considered this line of lamas to be their gurus.

34. Broad, roadside walls that are topped with stones carved with the mantra "*Om mani padme hum*" (Hail the jewel in the lotus). Devout travelers will always pass them on their right and may circumambulate them as an act of devotion, as well as adding their own carved stones to the pile.

35. Juniper is a main constituent in Tibetan and Ladakhi incense.

36. This symbolizes the Eightfold Path of Buddhism.

37. One of the seventeen tantras (esoteric treatises) of Dzogchen meditation practices—somewhat akin to the meditative practices of Zen Buddhism (Rangjung Yeshe Dictionary)

38. The word '*brug* (pronounced "druk"—dragon, thunder, or Bhutan) refers to the Drukpa Kargyu sect, of which the Ladakhi Kings were adherents.

39. This refers to the *padma dkar po* (white lotus) lineage, named after the Fourth Gyalwa Drukpa Rinpoche, *padma dkar po* (1527–1592), guru of Lama Stagtsang Raspa.

40. Drukpa Kargyu lama (1573–1651) who was guru to King Sengge Namgyal

41. I have not been able to identify this lama, but he is clearly connected to the Drukpa lineage.

42. King from about 1740 to 1760 (Francke 1907: 120)

43. The dragon ('*brug*) no doubt refers to the Drukpa ('*brug pa*) sect of Buddhism, which the Ladakhi kings followed.

44. Tsepal Namgyal, 1790–1841, was the last king of independent Ladakh (Francke 1907, 128).

Bibliography

Aabedi, Zain-ul-Aabedin. 2009. *Emergence of Islam in Ladakh.* New Delhi: Atlantic.

Aggarwal, Ravina. 2001. "At the Margins of Death: Ritual Space and the Politics of Location in an Indo-Himalayan Border Village." *American Ethnologist* 28, no. 3 (August): 549–73.

al Faruqi, Lois Ibsen. 1985. "Music, Musicians and Muslim Law," in *Asian Music* 17, no. 1: 3–36.

Baily, John. 2001. "Learning to Perform as a Research Technique in Ethnomusicology." *British Journal of Ethnomusicology* 10, no. 2 (2001): 85–98

Bakhle, Janaki. 2005. *Two Men and Music: Nationalism in the Making of an Indian Classical Tradition.* Cary, NC: Oxford University Press.

Balfour, Edward. 1885. *The Cyclopædia of India and of Eastern and Southern Asia: Commercial, Industrial and Scientific, Products of the Mineral, Vegetable, and Animal Kingdoms, Useful Arts and Manufactures.* London: Berrnard Quadritch.

Bauman, Richard, ed. 1992. *Folklore, Cultural Performances, and Popular Entertainment: A Communications-Centered Handbook.* New York: Oxford University Press.

Beer, Robert. 1999. *The Encyclopedia of Tibetan Symbols and Motifs.* Boston: Shambhala Publications.

Bellezza, John Vincent. 2005. *Spirit-Mediums, Sacred Mountains and Related Bon Textual Traditions in Upper Tibet: Calling Down the Gods.* Leiden and Boston: Koninklijke Brill NV.

Bertelsen, Kristoffer Brix. 1997. "Protestant Buddhism and Social Identification in Ladakh." *Archives de sciences sociales des religions*, 42e Année (99): 129–51.

Berzin, Alexander. 2003. "The Meaning and Use of a Mandala." Accessed October 4, 2011, http://www.berzinarchives.com/web/en/archives/advanced/tantra/level1_getting_started/meaning_use_mandala.html.

Blum, Stephen. "Central Asia." In *Grove Music Online.* Oxford University Press. Accessed March 6, 2013, http://www.oxfordmusiconline.com/subscriber/article/grove/music/05284.

Bray, John, ed. 2005a. *Ladakhi Histories: Local and Regional Perspects.* Leiden and Boston: Brill Academic Publishers.

———. 2005b. "Introduction: Locating Ladakhi History." In *Ladakhi Histories: Local and Regional Perspectives,* edited by John Bray. Leiden and Boston: Brill Academic Publishers.

———. 2008. "Corvee Transport Labour in 19th and Early 20th Century Ladakh: A Study in Continuity and Change," in *Modern Ladakh. Anthropological Perspectives on Continuity and Change,* edited by Martijn van Beek and Fernanda Pirie: 43–66. Leiden: Brill.

Butler Schofield (formerly Brown), Katherine. 2010. "Reviving the Golden Age Again: 'Classicization,' Hindustani Music, and the Mughals." *Ethnomusicology* 54, no. 3: 484–517.

Collinge, Ian. 1996. "Developments in Musicology in Tibet: Emergence of a New Tibetan Musical Lexicon." *Asian Music* 28, no. 1: 87–114.

Crossley-Holland, Peter. 1967a. "The State of Research in Tibetan Folk Music." *Ethnomusicology* 11, no. 2: 170–87.

———. 1967b. "Form and Style in Tibetan Folksong Melody." *Jahrbuch für musikalische Volks- und Völker-Kunde* 3: 9–69.

———. 1982. *Musical Instruments in Tibetan Legend and Folklore,* Monograph Series in Ethnomusicology Vol. 3. Los Angeles: University of California at Los Angeles.

Das, Sarat Chandra. 1902. *A Tibetan-English Dictionary.* Calcutta, reprinted. Delhi, India: Sri Satguru Publications, 1979.

Flynn, Dennis O., and Arturo Giráldez. 2002. "Cycles of Silver: Global Economic Unity through the Mid-Eighteenth Century," *Journal of World History* 13, no. 2: 391–427.

Dharmaraksita. 2007. *The Wheel of Sharp Weapons.* Translated by Geshe Ngawang Dhargyey, Sharpa Tulku, Khamlung Tulku, Alexander Berzin, and Jonathan Landaw. Dharamsala. Library of Tibetan Works and Archives.

Diehl, Keila. 2002. *Echoes from Dharamsala: Music in the Life of Tibetan Refugee Community.* Berkeley: University of California Press.

Dollfus, Pascale. 2006. "The Seven Rongtsan Brothers in Ladakh: Myth, Territory and Possession." *Études mongoles etsibériennes, centrasiatiques et tibétaines* [En ligne]: 36–37. Accessed February 17, 2013, http://emscat.revues.org/index 1036.html.

Dolma, Rinchen. 2009. "Ladakh: Nothing to read." *Hard News.* Accessed March 22, 2011, http://www.hardnewsmedia.com/2009/04/2863.

Dundes, Alan. 1980. *Interpreting Folklore.* Bloomington: Indiana University Press.

Ellingson-Waugh, Ter. 1974. "Musical Flight in Tibet." *Asian Music* 5, no. 2: 3–44.

———. 1979. "Don rta dbyangs gsum: Tibetan Chant and Melodic Categories." *Asian Music* 10, no. 2: 112–56.

English-Tibetan Dictionary of Modern Tibetan. Dharamsala, India: Library of Tibetan Works and Archives.

Eriksen, Thomas Hylland. 1991. "Ethnicity versus Nationalism." *Journal of Peace Research* 28, no. 3:263–78.

Fewkes, Jacqueline H. 2012. *Modern Asian Studies* 46, no. 2 (2012): 259–81. Cambridge: Cambridge University Press 2012. http://doi.org/10.1017/S0026 749X11000904.

Fiol, Stefan. 2010a. "Dual Framing: Locating Authenticities in the Music Videos of Himalayan Possession Rituals." *Ethnomusicology* 54, no. 1: 28.

———. 2010b. "Sacred, Polluted and Anachronous: Deconstructing Liminality among the *Baddī* of the Central Himalayas." *Ethnomusicology Forum* 19, no. 2: 135–63.

———. 2011. "Recordings and Festival Dance-Songs in Uttarakhand, North India." *Asian Music* 42, no. 1: 24–53.

Fishman, Joshua. 1970. *Sociolinguistics: A Brief Introduction.* Rowley, MA: Newbury House.

Flynn, Dennis O., and Arturo Giráldez. 2002. "Cycles of Silver: Global Economic Unity through the Mid-Eighteenth Century," *Journal of World History* 13, no. 2: 391–427.

Francke, A. H. 1901. "The Ladakhi Pre-Buddhist Marriage Ritual." *Indian Antiquary* 30: 131–49.

———. 1901a. "A Ladakhi Bon-pa Hymnal." *Indian Antiquary* 30:359–64.

———. 1902. "Ladakhi Songs." *Indian Antiquary* 31: 304–11.

———. 1904. "A Language Map of West Tibet with Notes." *Journal of the Asiatic Society of Bengal* 73, part 4: 362–67.

———. 1905. *Ladakh: The Mysterious Land.* Reprinted New Delhi: Ess Ess, 1980.

———. 1905–41. *A Lower Ladakhi Version of the Kesar Saga.* Calcutta: Royal Asiatic Society of Bengal.

———. 1907. *A History of Western Tibet.* Reprint. Delhi: Pilgrims Book Pvt. Ltd, 1999.

———. 1910. "Ladvags rGyalrabs, Chronicles of Ladakh according to the Schlagintweit MSS." *Journal of the Asiatic Society of Bengal* 6, no. 8: 393–423.

———. 1923. *Tibetische Hochzeitslieder.* Darmstadt: Folkwang-Verlag.

———. 1926. "Ladakh Chronicles." *Antiquities of Ancient Tibet,* Vol. 2, Calcutta: 83.

Francke. A. H., and Ana Paalzow. 1931. "Tibetische Lieder aus dem Gebiet des chemaligen westtibetischen Königreiches." *Mitteilungen des Seminars für orientalische Sprachen an der Friedrich Wilhelm Universitat zu Berlin Abteilung 2, Westasiatische Studien* 34: 93–136.

Geertz, Clifford. 1973. *The Interpretation of Cultures: Selected Essays.* New York: Basic Books.

Gulistan News Today. 2023. "Jashn-E-Nawroz Celebrated at Hardass Kargil, orgd. Ladakh Academy of Art Culture & Language Kargil."

Goldstein, Melvyn C., and Ngawangthondup Narkyid. 1986. *English-Tibetan Dictionary of Modern Tibetan.* Berkeley: University of California Press.

Greene, Paul D. 2003. "Nepal's *Lok Pop* Music: Representations of the Folk, Tropes of Memory, and Studio Techniques." *Asian Music* 34, no. 1: 43–65.

Hakeem, Abdul. 1998. "Tsik-Lu: Teasing Songs of Ladakh." *Ladakhs Melong,* April: 26–27.

Hamid, Abdul. 1998. *Ladakhi-English-Urdu Dictionary: with an English-Ladakhi Index.* Leh, Ladakh: Melong Publications.

Haskett, Christian P. B. 2007. Review of *Identity, Ritual and State in Tibetan Buddhism: The Foundations of Authority in Gelukpa Monasticism* by Martin A. Mills. Buddhist-Christian Studies 27: 187–92.

Hayagriva Buddhist Centre. 2012. http://hayagriva.org.au. Accessed June 10, 2012.

Helffer, Mereille. 1994. *mChod-rol: les instruments de la musique tibétaine.* Paris: CNRS Editions.

———. 1999: "Tibet." In *Die Musik in Geschichte und Gegenwart* (MGG). Kassel: Bärenreiter-Verlag.

———. 2000. "Tibetan Culture in South Asia." In *The Garland Encyclopedia of World Music*, Vol. 5, South Asia: The Indian Subcontinent, edited by Alison Arnold. New York and London: Routledge.

Henderson, David. 2003. "Who Needs 'The Folk'?" A Nepali Remodeling Project." *Asian Music* 34, no. 1: 19–42.

Henrion-Dourcy, Isabelle, and Tsering Dhondup. "Tibetan music, III, 1." In *Grove Music Online,* edited by L. Macy. Accessed December 8, 2005. http://www.grovemusic.com.

Hermanns, P. Matthias. 1965. *Das National-Epos der Tibeter Gling König Ge Sar.* Regensburg, Verlag Josef Habbel.

Joldan, Eliezar. [1985] 2018. "Adventures of Baba Kalam." In *Central Asian Trade and other Essays on Ladakh*, 1–29. Srinagar: Gulshan Books Kashmir.

Kaufmann, Walter. 1975. *Tibetan Buddhist Chant:* Musical Notations and Interpretations of a Song Book by the Bkah Brgyud Pa and Sa Skya Pa sect. Bloomington: Indiana University Press.

Kaul. H. N. 1998. *Rediscovery of Ladakh.* New Delhi: Indus.

Keil, Charles. 1978. "Who Needs 'The Folk'?" *Journal of the Folklore Institute* 15, no. 3:263–65.

Khan, K. Asfandyar. 1998. *Ancient Wisdom (Sayings and Proverbs of Ladakh).* Kargil, Ladakh: Kachio.

Khandro.net. 2001. "Heruka Chakrasamvara." Accessed October 15, 2011, http://www.khandro.net/deity_Chakrasamvara.htm.

Koshal, Sanyukta. 1981. *Conversational Ladakhi.* Delhi: Motilal Banarsi Das.

Ladakh Cultural Academy, Leh. 2014. A Collection of Ladakhi Folk Songs. Leh, Ladakh. J & K Academy of Art, Culture, and Language.

Lorraine Sakata. 1989. "Skardu and Khapalu: Baltistan, Northern Area." In *Musical Survey of Pakistan: Three Pilot Studies*, by Farhana Faruqi, Ashok Kumar, Anwar Mohyuddin, and Hiromi Lorraine Sakata. Islamabad: Lok Virsa Research Centre.

Macdonald, Kenneth Iain. 2006. "Memories of Tibet: Transnationalism, Transculturation and the Production of Cultural Identity in Northern Pakistan." *India Review* 5, no. 2: 190–219.

Manuel, Peter. 1993. *Cassette Culture: Popular Music and Technology in North India (Chicago Studies in Ethnomusicology)*. Chicago: University of Chicago Press.

———. 2015. "The Intermediate Sphere in North Indian Music Culture: Between and Beyond "Folk"and "Classical." *Ethnomusicology* 59, no. 1: 82–115.

Maqam World. 2007. http://maqamworld.com/index.html. Accessed June 9, 2013.

Marcus, Scott. 2002. "Rhythmic Modes in Middle Eastern Music." In *The Garland Encyclopedia of World Music, Volume 6 (The Middle East)*, edited by Virginia Danielson, Scott Marcus, and Dwight Reynolds, 89–92. New York: Garland.

Mills. Martin A. 2000. "Vajra Brother, Vajra Sister: Renunciation, Individualism and the Household in Tibetan Buddhist Monasticism." *Journal of the Royal Anthropological Institute* 6, no. 1: 17–34.

———. 2003. *Identity, Ritual and State in Tibetan Buddhism: The Foundations of Authority in Gelukpa Monasticism*. London: Routledge Curzon.

Monier-Williams, Monier. 1899. *Sanskrit-English Dictionary*. Oxford: Clarendon.

Naim, C. M. 2004. *Urdu Texts and Contexts: The Selected Essays of C.M. Naim*. Orient Blackswan.

Nathani, Sultan. 2018. *Urdu for Pleasure fo Ghazal Lovers: Intekhab-o-Lughat*. New Delhi: Nathani Trust.

Norman, Rebecca. 2001. *Getting Started in Ladakhi: A Phrasebook for Learning Ladakhi*. Ladakh: Melong Publications.

———. 2011. *A Dictionary of the Language Spoken by Ladakhis*. Unpublished draft, edited by Örgyen Dorje et al. 1997. *Lho kha'i dmangs gzhas phyogs btus* [Collection of Folk Songs of the South]. Tibet: Bod ljongs mi dmangs dpe skrun khang [Tibet People's Press].

Paske, Edward. 1879. "Buddhism in the British Provinces of Little Tibet." *The Journal of the Anthropological Institute of Great Britain and Ireland* 8: 195–210.

Picken, Laurence E. R. 1957. "Tibet." In *New Oxford History of Music, 1: Ancient and Oriental Music*, edited by E. Wellesz, 137–42. London: Oxford University Press.

Powers, Harold S. 1980. "Classical Music, Cultural Roots, and Colonial Rule: An Indic Musicologist Looks at the Muslim World." *Asian Music* 12, no. 1: 5–39

Rabgias [Rabgyas], Tashi, ed. 1970–2003. *Ladvags gyi yul glu*. [Ladakhi Folk Songs]. Ladakh: Jammu and Kashmir Academy of Art, Culture and Languages.

———. 2000. *La dvags kyi yul glu: snyan pa'i pi wang*. [Ladakhi Folk Songs: The Sweet Fiddle]. Leh, Ladakh: Ladakh Ecological Development Group.

———. 2006. *Mar yul la dvags kyi sngon rabs kun gsal me long zhes bya ba bzhugs so: History of Ladakh called the Mirror Which Illuminates All*. Leh, Ladakh: Tashi Rabgias.

———. 2007. *'jig rten jun sun dga' ba'i glu: Poems and Songs*. Leh, Ladakh: Tashi.

Rather, Ali Mohmad. 1993. "Discrimination in Ladakhi Society: A Study of Mons & Bedas of Ladakh." In *Recent Research on Ladakh 6: Proceedings of the Sixth International Colloquium on Ladakh, Leh 1993*, edited by Henry Osmaston and Nawang Tsering. Bristol: University of Bristol.

Ribbach, Samuel H. 1985. *Culture and Society in Ladakh*. Translated by John Bray. New Delhi: Ess Ess Publications.

Ribur, Rinpoche. 1997. "How to Generate Bodhicitta," Lama Yeshe Archive. Accessed January 8, 2011, http://www.lamayeshne.com/index.php?sect=article&id=433&chid=767.

Rizvi, Janet. 1998. *Ladakh: Crossroads of High Asia,* 2nd ed. Delhi: Oxford University Press.

———. 1999. *Trans-Himalayan Caravans: Merchant Princes and Peasant Traders in Ladakh*. Delhi: Oxford University Press.

Richardson, Hugh E. 1984. *Tibet and its History*. Boulder, CO: Shambhala.

Salvatori, Marta. 2006. "The Ladakhi Lute and Related Folk Songs." *Tibet Journal*: 65–81.

Samuel, Geoffrey. 1976. "Songs of Lhasa." *Ethnomusicology* 20, no. 3: 407–49.

———. 1986. "Music of the Lhasa Minstrels." In *Zlos-gar: Performing Traditions of Tibet,* edited by Jamyang Norbu. Dharamsala, India: Library of Tibetan Works & Archives.

SECMOL. 2006. SECMOL (website) www.secmol.org. Accessed March 22, 2011.

Seitel, Peter. 2002. "Defining the Scope of the Term Intangible Cultural Heritage." Paper presented at the International Meeting of Experts on Intangible Cultural Heritage: Establishment of a Glossary, UNESCO Headquarters, Paris, June 10–12, 2002.*www.unesco.org/culture/ich/doc/src/00270-EN.doc, accessed April 15, 2012.*

Shakspo, Ngawang Tsering. 1985. *Songs of the Himalayas, Ladakhi folk songs*. Leh, Ladakh, India: n.p.

———. 1988. *A History of Buddhism in Ladakh*. Delhi: Ladakh Buddhist Vihara.

———. 1999. "The Foremost Teachers of the Kings of Ladakh." In *Recent Research on Ladakh,* edited by Martijn van Beek, Kristoffer Brix Bertelsen, and Poul Pedersen. Aarhus: Aarhus University: 284–89.

———. 2006. "Tibetan (Bhoti)—An Endangered Script in Trans-Himalaya." *Tibet Journal*.

———. 2008. *The Culture of Ladakh Through Song and Dance*. Leh: The Solitudinarian.

———. 2010. *A Cultural History of Ladakh*. Leh, Ladakh: Center for Research on Ladakh, Aya-Changchung, Saboo, Leh.

Sharma, Manorma. 2004. *Folk India: A Comprehensive Study of Indian Folk Music and Culture, 1, Jammu & Kashmir and Himachal Pradesh*. New Delhi: Sundeep Prakashan.

Sikand, Yoginder. 2006. "Muslim-Buddhist Clashes in Ladakh: Politics Behind the 'Religious' Conflict." Accessed September 15, 2011, http://www.countercurrents.org/comm-sikand130206.htm.

Singh, Rohit. 2016. *Buddhists and Muslims in Ladakh: Negotiating Tradition and Modernity.* PhD diss., University of California at Santa Barbara.

Stirr, Anna M. 2018. "Making a Living as a Musician in Nepal: Multiple Regimes of Value in a Changing Popular Folk Music Industry. *Himalaya* 38, no. 1: 160–76.

Warikoo, K. 1996. "Trade Relations between Central Asia and Kashmir Himalayas during the Dogra Period (1846–1947)." *Cahiers d'Asie centrale*, no. 12: 113–24.

Slobin, Mark. 1976. *Music in the Culture of Northern Afghanistan.* Tucson: University of Arizona Press.

Snellgrove, David L., and Hugh Richardson. 1968. *A Cultural History of Tibet.* New York and Washington, DC: Frederick Prager.

Snellgrove, David L., and Tadeusz Skorupski. 1977. *The Cultural Heritage of Ladakh, Vol. 1: Central Ladakh.* Warminster, UK: Amis and Philips.

Srinivasan, Amrit Reform and Revival. 1985. "The Devadasi and Her Dance." *Economic and Political Weekly* 20, no. 44: 1869–76.

Stein, Rolf Alfred. 1972. *Tibetan Civilization,* translated by J. E. Driver. Stanford, CA: Stanford University Press.

Tethong, Rakra. 1979. "Conversations on Tibetan Musical Traditions" (interview by Ter Ellingson). *Asian Music* 10, no. 2: 5–22.

Thiksey Monastery. 2012. http://thikseymonastery.org. Accessed October 6, 2012.

Tibetan Institute of Performing Arts. 1993. *Bod kyi Nang-ma Stod-szhas* [Tibetan Nangma and Toeshay]. Dharamsala, H.P., India: Tibetan Institute of Performing Arts.

Tibetan and Himalayan Library. 2011. THL Tibetan to English Translation Tool. http://www.thlib.org/reference/dictionaries/tibetan-dictionary/translate.php.

Tibet Information Network (TIN). 2004. *Unity and Discord. Music and Politics in Contemporary Tibet.* London: Tibet Information Network.

Tibet People's Press. 1997. *Bod-ljong srol rgyun rol dbyangs gces bsdus: dmangs khrod rig -pa chung-bu-khrid kyis btang-ba'i glu yangs.* [Anthology of Traditional Tibetan Music: Songs to be Sung in Groups by Children]. Tibet: Xizang ren min chu ban she [Tibet People's Press].

Tremblay, Reeta Chowdhari. 1996. "Nation, Identity and the Intervening Role of the State: A Study of the Secessionist Movement in Kashmir." *Pacific Affairs* 69, no. 4: 471–97.

Trewin, Mark, and Susan M. Stephens. 1987. *The Music Culture of Ladakh: Report of the City University Ladakh Expedition 1986.* London: The City University.

Trewin, Arthur Mark. 1995. *Rhythms of the Gods: The Musical Symbolics of Power and Authority in the Tibetan Buddhist Kingdom of Ladakh.* PhD diss., City University of London.

———. 1990a. "Rhythmic Style in Ladakhi Music and Dance." In *Wissenschaftsgeschichte und gegenwärtige Forschungen in Nordwest-Indien*, edited by L. Icke-Schwalbe and G. Meier. Dresden: Dresden Museum of Ethnology.

———. 1990b. "Musical Studies in Western Tibet (Ladakh): Some Historical and Comparative Aspects of the Pioneering Work of August Hermann Francke." *European Studies in Ethnomusicology: Historical Developments and Recent Trends: Selected Papers Presented at the VIIth European Seminar in Ethnomusicology, Berlin, October 1–6, 1990*, edited by Max Peter Baumann, Artur Simon, and Ulrich Wegner. Wilhelmhaven: Florian Noetzel Verlag: 69–86.

———. 1999. "Tibetan and Ladakhi Popular Music in India." *Intercultural Music 2*, edited by Cynthia Tse Kimberlin and Akin Euba. Point Richard, CA: MRI Press.

Trivedi, Madhu, 2010. *The Making of the Awadh Culture*. New Delhi: Primus Books.

Tsukamoto, Atsuko. 1983. "The Music of Tibetan Buddhism in Ladakh: The Musical Structure of Tibetan Buddhist Chant in the Ritual Bskaṅ-gso of the Dge-Lugs-pa Sect." *Yearbook for Traditional Music* 15: 126–40.

Tucci, G. 1966. *Tibetan Folk Songs from Gyantse and Western Tibet*. Vancouver: UBC Press.

———. 1980. *The Religions of Tibet*. Translated by Geoffrey Samuel. Berkeley, CA, and Los Angeles: University of California Press.

UNESCO. 2003. "Language Vitality and Endangerment." Accessed April 4, 2010. http://www.unesco.org/culture/ich/doc/src/00120-EN.pdf.

UNESCO. 2009. "UNESCO Culture Sector—Intangible Heritage—2003 Convention: A methodology for assessing language vitality and endangerment." Accessed April 4, 2010, http://www.unesco.org/culture/ich/index.php?pg=00142.

van Beek, Martijn. 2000. "Beyond Identity Fetishism: "Communal" Conflict in Ladakh and the Limits of Autonomy." *Cultural Anthropology* 15, no. 4: 525–69.

van Beek, Martijn, Kristoffer Brix Bertelsen, and Poul Pedersen, eds. 1999. *Ladakh: Culture, History, and Development between Himalaya and Karakoram, Recent Research on Ladakh: Proceedings of the Eighth Colloquium of the International Association for Ladakh Studies held at Moesgaard, Aarhus University, 5–8 June 1997*. Aarhus, Denmark: Aarhus University Press.

Warikoo, K. 1996. "Trade relations between Central Asia and Kashmir Himalayas during the Dogra period (1846–1947)," *Cahiers d'Asie centrale*, nos. 1–2: 113–24.

Witzleben, J. Lawrence. 1997. "Whose Ethnomusicology? Western Ethnomusicology and the Study of Asian Music." *Ethnomusicology* 41, no. 2: 220–42.

———. 2010. Performing in the Shadows: Learning and Making Music as Ethnomusicological Practice and Theory. *Yearbook for Traditional Music* 42:135–66.

Wu, Ben. 1998. "Music Scholarship, West and East: Tibetan Music as a Case Study." *Asian Music* 29, no. 2: 31–56.

Zeisler, Bettina. 2004. *Relative Tense and Aspectual Values in Tibetan Languages: A Comparative Study*. Berlin: Walter de Gruyter.

———. 2005. "On the Position of Ladakhi and Balti in the Tibetan Language Family." In *Ladakhi Histories: Local and Regional Perspective,* edited by John Bray. Leiden and Boston: Brill Academic.

Sound Recordings

David Lewiston (recorder). 1971. *Ladakh: Songs and Dances from the Highlands of Western Tibet.* Nonesuch LP H-72075.

Dinnerstein, Noé, and Stephen Dydo. 2013. "Basgo Castle: Songs and Dances of Ladakh." Pan Records CD PAN 2118.

Dolma, Tsewang, and Padma Dorjay (singers). 2004. *Jaabro: Folk Songs of Nomads.* Leh, Ladakh, India: Zee Music Centre cassette.

Dolma, Kunzes (singer). *Ladakhi Marriage Ballad Folk Song Chang Dey Ga Ru Gang Part 1.* http://www.youtube.com/watch?v=Y9ueEZYAJVY. Accessed June 16, 2013.

———. *Ladakhi Marriage Ballad Folk Song Chang Dey Ga Ru Gang Part 1.* http://www.youtube.com/watch?v=8q2mJe3e7VA. Accessed June 16, 2013.

Fida Hussain Shamim Baltistani. https://www.youtube.com/watch?v=zsfY0jwpViw. Accessed July 7, 2023.

Hussain Silmo, Haji Master. March 9, 2020. "Part 01 | Lchangra | Master Hussain Silmo | Folk Song | Historian | Kargil Today." https://www.youtube.com/watch?v=Mh-6bqNAgUo. Accessed July 16, 2023.

———. 2020a. "Part 02 | Lchangra | Master Hussain Silmo | Folk Song-Historian | Kargil Today." https://www.youtube.com/watch?v=m4dLOx0SZN0. Accessed July 16, 2023.

———. 2020b. "Losar Special| Master Hussain Silmo| Father of Ladakhi Folk Song| Kargil Today." https://www.youtube.com/watch?v=z—ZIMg1Yos&t=1173s. Accessed July 15, 2023.

Kargil Today. 2023. "Jashn E Navroz Celebration, 2023 Hardass Kargil, Report Hosain Khalo." https://www.youtube.com/watch?v=zBrRq-jjeR4&t=284s. Accessed July 16, 2023.

Stakmo, Dorjay. 2005. *Junglu: Folk Song of Ladakh, Vol. I.* Leh, Ladakh, India: Chagzot Music World VCD.

———. n.d. *gzhung glu : Junglu : Folk Song of Ladakh.* Leh, Ladakh, India: Chagzot Music World CD CMW-05.

———. n.d. *gzhung glu : The Folk Songs of Ladakh.* Leh, Ladakh, India: Vajra Vision CD.

———. n.d. *gzhung glu : First Folk Video Album of Ladakh.* Video Sources.

Index